This book is dedicated to the memory of
'Sir' Bill Nicholson, 'Mr Tottenham' 1919-2004

EXCLUSIVE SIGNED EDITION

JIMMY GREAVES who scored more goals for Spurs than any other player

STEVE PERRYMAN who played more games for Spurs than any other player

NORMAN GILLER Author/Publisher who verifies the autographs are authentic

NMG

A NormanMichaelGillerEnterprises publication
© Norman Giller/Michael Giller 2009

First published in 2009 by NMG Enterprises
PO Box 3386, Ferndown, BH22 8XT

A CIP catalogue for this title is available from the British Library
ISBN 978-0-9543243-4-6

Typeset and designed by NMG Enterprises, Dorset, UK
Printed and bound in the United Kingdom by Antony Rowe Limited
Bumper's Farm, Chippenham, Wiltshire SN14 6LH

*The majority of photographs in this book have been provided by the premier
picture agency Press Association (www.paphotos.com), with special thanks to
Kezia Storr and Sam Stewart. There are also photos from the private collections
of Jimmy Greaves, Steve Perryman, Terry Baker, NMG Publishing and various
Tottenham supporters. Best efforts have been made to clear all copyrights.*

THE LANE
OF DREAMS

A complete history of White Hart Lane

NORMAN GILLER

Statistical sections compiled by Michael Giller

Introduced by
JIMMY GREAVES and STEVE PERRYMAN

NMG

AUTHOR'S ACKNOWLEDGEMENTS

Author/Publisher Norman Giller thanks, first and foremost, the scores of Tottenham supporters who have contacted him with their memories and encouragement for this book on White Hart Lane before the grand old ground is bulldozed into history.

He bows to Lane Legends Jimmy Greaves and Steve Perryman for their fee-free introductions. They have done it as a favour. What an example they are to the modern, money grabbing players with their big wage packets and small sense of loyalty. Just before we went to press, we heard the sad news of the passing of Jimmy Neighbour, and both Jimmy and Steve requested that we should pay our respects. He was not only pleasing to watch on the pitch but a pleasure to know off it. Rest easy, old friend.

This is a fairly unique book in that much of it has been written on the Internet, with fans queuing to give their views. Several webmasters have kindly given their time and support to the project, including in particular Harry Hotspur (www.oleole.com/blogs/harryhotspur), Paul Smith (www.spursodyssey.com), Jim Duggan (www.topspurs.com), Paul Elmes (www.planetspurs.com), Trevor Kramer and Neil (www.tottenhamhotspur.rivals.net), Adam H. (www.tottenhamhotspurs.tv.com), and the all-knowing Wyart Lane (www.mehstg.com). Thanks, also, to the informative *Tottenham Weekly Herald*.

I forced myself into the modern world and joined the Facebook internet social network, purely with mercenary motives. But I quickly turned from book salesman into an avid follower of Facebook gossip, comments and laughter, and found myself being made welcome with what I can only describe as the spirit of The Shelf. To all my Facebook friends, thank you. Naming names is a dangerous game because I am bound to forget somebody, so I will not go down that road apart from saying that James 'Yid' Carolan, Dave Eaves, 'Spurs Boy' William Smith, and 'Spurs Girl' Loretta Fontaine were a huge source of inspiration in my early forays into the Facebook world. And I apologise to the two Maureens (Carpenter and Turner) for continually getting them mixed up.

Steven Downes, Secretary of the Sports Journalists' Association, was a constant motivator, Alec East an expert guide, Vic Power a willing adviser, Terry Baker a patient go-between, and Chris Jones, Dave Biggs, Libby Rodger, Mark Radley, Geoff Fisher and the entire team at Antony Rowe thoroughly professional in helping to get this book published. You have made an old man very happy. And I could not have written the book without the safety-net work of my son and business partner Michael Giller, and the loving support of my soul partner Jackie Jones, daughter Lisa and daughter-in-law Sarah, whose Grandpa Ray Beadman followed Spurs for 90 years!

Thank you if you have bought this book. If you have borrowed it, don't forget to give it back. If you have stolen it, be warned that I have worked a special incriminating, finger-staining Arsenal-red substance into the cover. You will be caught red handed, and sentenced to watching the Gooners. Enjoy the read. Come On You Spurs!

It's Saturday, 24 August 1957 and seventeen-year-old Jimmy Greaves scores his first goal at White Hart Lane ... uh, for Chelsea! Here he is on his way to the first of a record 357 First Division goals. It earned Chelsea a point. Four years later, on the same ground but wearing a Tottenham shirt, he scored a hat-trick against Blackpool in his first game for Spurs after his £99,999 transfer from AC Milan.

I WAS thirteen years old when I first trod on the sacred White Hart Lane turf, side-stepping a strolling policeman who told me to get off the grass. I had one target in mind – to get the autograph of one of my heroes, England captain Billy Wright. He was skippering Wolves, who had just been beaten 3-2 by the Push and Run Spurs a couple of years after they won the League championship.

It was my mate Lennie Sugarman who had persuaded me to go with him to The Lane from our Hainault, Essex, homes on what was a rare Saturday off for me. I usually played for my school team. In fact the previous Saturday I got my first big newspaper headlines when I scored 11 goals in a 13-0 victory over the school where Martin Peters was a young pupil. Please don't think I am being big headed when I mention this. It was just that Martin reminded me of it when we appeared together in a recent road show in which I regularly feature, usually talking to Spurs fans.

Anyway, there I was on the White Hart Lane pitch in my first pair of long trousers aiming for Billy Wright with a piece of paper and a pencil in hand. Lennie Sugarman had bet I wouldn't get Billy's signature, but the great man ruffled my hair and signed his name even though he must have been feeling choked over the defeat. Imagine that happening today? And I could not have envisioned then that one day Billy would be my first England captain, and later my boss in the world of television. It's a funny old game.

While I was almost kneeling in front of my hero, Tottenham right-back Peter Baker, just starting out on his Spurs career, came and shook Billy's hand, and I got his autograph too before the Old Bill ushered me off the pitch.

Who would have thought that just four years later I would play my very first League game at White Hart Lane, wearing the blue of Chelsea and scoring in my debut in a First Division match that ended 1-1. As we came off at the end Spurs skipper Danny Blanchflower, one of four players I had managed to dribble past on my way to the equaliser, said: "Well done, son. You have a big future in the game. Keep your feet on the ground, except when you're heading the ball." Typical Danny blarney.

Move the calendar forward just over four years and I was back at White Hart Lane, this time as a Spurs player. In my debut against Blackpool, I got lucky and managed to score a hat-trick. One of my team-mates was the same Peter Baker who had given me his autograph when I was a wide-eyed kid.

My happiest days in football were those I spent at Tottenham, and playing at White Hart Lane was always worth a goal start. The roar of the crowd at your back was like a gale force wind, and it made you raise your game and go that extra mile; okay, yard.

Ask anybody who was there in the 'Glory-Glory' days and they will confirm there have not been football nights to match them for atmosphere. It was not just electric; it was nuclear!

I am not going to do a Victor Meldrew and say things are not as good now as in the old days. It is a completely different game, and any modern player landing on planet football in the 1960s would think they had arrived in a foreign land.

We did things differently then, and it was a game of strong physical contact. The likes of Norman 'Bites Yer Legs' Hunter, Chopper Harris and Tommy 'Iron' Smith would not last five minutes in today's game. I am not saying it is better, and I am not saying it is worse. I am saying it is different, and in my view less exciting.

I thought White Hart Lane lost a lot of its soul and spirit when The Shelf went and fans were ordered to sit down. I can understand the safety aspect, but it has robbed the game of a lot of the passion. I hope they go out of their way with the new ground to build it in such a way that the crowd noise stays locked in rather than disappearing to the heavens.

This book is a wonderful memento of the good, occasionally the bad and just sometimes the ugly side of the history of White Hart Lane.

If anybody can bring back the Glory Glory days and some of the 1960s atmosphere it's my old mate Harry Redknapp, Mr Motivator. But he has got to go some to match the management skills of Bill Nicholson, who was The Master of White Hart Lane.

The history is in good hands with Norman Giller, a walking record book on all sport, and my partner in eighteen previous books. He and his sports statistician son, Michael, have left no turf unturned to get every fact that matters about White Hart Lane, the ground I was proud to call home for nine years. Enjoy.

Jimmy Greaves

THERE are three main reasons I am happy to put my name to this book. One, because it involves the memories of the people who matter most at Tottenham – the supporters; two, because it gets me reacquainted with my old mate Norman Giller, who was there right at the start of my career at White Hart Lane and nicknamed me the Babyfaced Assassin; and, three, the book is dedicated to the memory of my favourite of all Tottenham people, Bill Nicholson.

Back in the days when I was a schoolboy footballer in West London, the odds were on me joining Queen's Park Rangers. But from the moment I met Bill Nicholson I knew that he was the manager and Tottenham were the club for me. Bill Nick was the most honest man to cross my path, either in or out of football. He did not offer me any illegal inducements to sign for Spurs, just his word that he would treat me fairly and that he would make sure I got the best possible coaching support.

Tell a lie ... I suppose the tickets he offered to me and my parents to watch the 1967 FA Cup final between Tottenham and Chelsea could be called an inducement. From the moment I saw the great Dave Mackay lift the Cup for Spurs I knew I was going to join them. I never dreamed then that I would go on to play the little matter of a record 854 first-team games for Tottenham. In those days it was very much a family club, with Bill Nick surrounding himself with a staff of likeable, friendly people who were Spurs through and through. There was no talk of public companies and stocks and shares. The only thing that mattered was the football, and serving up the best we could for the fantastic fans.

There are no better or more loyal supporters in the world of football, and I still think of myself as part of their family – even though the club has changed out of sight from when I was playing, and I was so proud to lift the FA Cup two years in a row. I still get a glow when I think of the days of Alan Mullery, Martin Peters, Big Chiv and Gilly, and then Ossie Ardiles, Ricky Villa and the golden skills of Glenn Hoddle.

And I will never forget the support I used to get, particularly from the fanatics on The Shelf. Norman has produced a book that captures the spirit of The Shelf, which is also the spirit of Spurs. You had better have tissues ready to wipe away the tears when you read the memories of the Tottenham fans, many of which are MY memories. COYS!

Steve Perryman, pointing the way as Spurs skipper from the age of just twenty

I STARTED writing this book with just Jimmy Greaves and Steve Perryman as company, but by the end had an army of Tottenham supporters joining in the anthems of acclaim for White Hart Lane. It is not just a football ground. For thousands of people it is their spiritual place of worship, their Valhalla, their second home.

In an effort to make this a shared experience I set up a website (www.thelaneofdreams. co.uk) inviting fans to provide me with their outstanding memories of matches and moments at The Lane. I also gathered a legion of Tottenham-tinged supporters on Facebook, turning this into a book of two halves. The first features my FACTS, the second the FEELINGS of the fans as I tap into their passion and pulse.

So that this is as much their book as mine, I squeezed as many of their memories as possible into what I hope is a suitable memento of White Hart Lane before the bulldozers and wrecking balls move in to knock the wonderful old ground into history.

Lucky old me, I have reported from football grounds around the world, from Moscow to Madrid, Barnsley to Buenos Aires, Turkey to Torquay. I can honestly say that White Hart Lane equals and even surpasses many of the major grounds for atmosphere and a passion that is almost tangible. As Greavsie said in his introduction, the Glory-Glory nights of the 1960s were just about unbeatable for frenzy and feeling. Those were occasions when the crowd stoked up so much heat that your mouth dried, and the hairs on the back of your neck stood on end. My fingers used to tremble on the typewriter keys in those pre-computer days. It was something very special to be there at The Lane.

What are my qualifications for being the author (and publisher) of this book? Well let me start by confessing that I am not a blue and white blooded Tottenham fan. As a football journalist since the years BC (Before Clough) I have trained myself to remain neutral. But I think this is a help rather than a hindrance in telling the story of one of my favourite grounds. There is no bias or blinded loyalty, so when I say that Ricky Villa's goal in the 1981 FA Cup final replay was the best I ever witnessed at Wembley then you can believe me. I am not looking at things through blue-and-white tinted glasses.

I pride myself on being a well-informed, well-read and well-seasoned sports historian, and I hope you will find a lot of facts in the book that will be new to you. This is my 82nd book, and while that sounds impressive I should add that I specialise in writing only first editions. I was clever enough to rear my son, heir and best friend, Michael, as a clone, and his facts and figures help to give the book a bedrock of information that will, I hope, satisfy the most discerning and dedicated Tottenham disciples. Michael used to sleep in Steve Perryman's shirt, so we know where his loyalties lie.

I was proud to call Bill Nicholson and his side-kick Eddie Baily personal friends, was able to 'phone any of the 60s/70s Tottenham players at their homes in the days before agents took over as footballers' mouthpieces, have known Terry Venables for nearing half a century, and have a relationship with Greavsie that is as close as any between a journalist and a sports icon, without consenting adults coming into the equation. I was there for all the major moments in Steve Perryman's glorious Tottenham career.

And I come up to date with present Tottenham manager Harry Redknapp. I was in the Bobby Moore drinking school with Harry, Frank Lampard Snr, Budgie Byrne and Greavsie, when after matches we used to drink and tell football tales into the late hours at the Black Lion pub in West Ham.

When Harry made his debut at Upton Park in the mid-1960s he was so fast on the wing that in the *Daily Express* I described him as the Boleyn Greyhound. A pity that sometimes he forgot to take the ball with him (joke, Aitch). And at the White Hart I used to kneel at the throne of Dave Mackay when he ruled a drinking school that included Cliffie Jones, Bobby Smith, Alan Gilzean, young Joe Kinnear. Phil Beal and, of course, Greavsie. The only rule was that you kept your mouth shut and got a round in.

The point is, I have always been close to Tottenham football folk, and I hope my inside knowledge comes across in the following pages as I take you through the history (and sometimes the hysteria) of White Hart Lane. This is not so much about the politics of Tottenham as the pride and the passion.

I am grateful to have had Tottenham Head of Retail Victoria Howarth and Press Officer John Fennelly steering me through this project, and I am indebted to a weave of Spurs webmasters who gave me the benefit of their growing influence. My old and much respected Fleet Street colleague, Harry Harris, motivated me with his excellent book, *Down Memory Lane*, but most of all I want to thank those scores of supporters who gave me their memories and their encouragement. My thanks, too (this is sounding like a Kate Winslet acceptance speech) to Graham Rowe, son of Tottenham legend Arthur Rowe, the unsung architect of Push and Run. Graham now lives in America, but dug into his memory for wonderful recollections of the team his Dad built. Finally, a thank you to the procession of Tottenham teams who have put the style, the smile and the guile into the Spurs.

That's enough waffle from me. Quick, the bulldozers are coming. Let's get on with the tale of The Lane of Dreams ...

THIS is the story of a plot of land that started out as a nursery and was destined for housing development until it became a football ground that has fed and fired the dreams of generations of Tottenham Hotspur fans. This is the story of White Hart Lane.

We need to start at the beginning, when Tottenham Hotspur was first founded back in the reign of Queen Victoria and at a time when football was just developing as the national sport. Come back with me to the late nineteenth century, and a season-by-season account of the journey that led to the birth of the Lane of Dreams.

1882-83: A legendary meeting took place under the yellow glare of a gas-lit lamppost in Tottenham High Road, a corner-kick's distance from what would one day become the White Hart Lane ground. It was a late summer's evening and the gathering consisted of members of the Hotspur Cricket Club and pupils from the local St John's Presbyterian and Tottenham Grammar Schools. These well-educated youths, most of them from middle-class backgrounds, wanted something to do in the winter months, and there under the lamplight they decided unanimously to start a football team to be called Hotspur Football Club.

The name 'Hotspur' was inspired by Shakespeare's Henry IV character Harry Hotspur (Sir Henry Percy), who was the son of the Duke of Northumberland and a brave and spirited warrior. There were local connections because the Duke owned large swathes of North London. Perhaps we should gloss over the fact that Hotspur finished with his head being exhibited on the spikes of the gates of York following a defeat in battle in 1403 when he was just 39. It gives a whole new meaning to calls from the dug-out to Spurs players: "Keep your heads!"

Their first match on September 30 1882 was a defeat by two goals on Tottenham Marshes against a team called the Radicals, this at a time when football, particularly in the south, was almost exclusively amateur and six years ahead of the launch of the Football League. The London-based Football Association was the governing body and jumped on anything that hinted of commercialism or anybody earning from playing the game. What they would make of today's £100,000-a-week footballers defies imagination.

Most of the boys who played against the Radicals were still at school, and club accounts showed that they bought the leather-pannelled ball with which they played on the day of the match for one shilling.

As a matter of record, the eleven founder members of the Hotspur Football Club following the meeting under the lamp-post were Edward Beaven, Robert Buckle, Frederick Dexter, Stuart Leaman, Edward Wall, John and Thomas Anderson, Lindsay and Hamilton Casey, John and Philip Thompson. They were the original Hotspurs.

To encourage them, the father of the Casey brothers presented the team with a set of home-made wooden goalposts painted in blue and white, which the boys carried to and from the Marshes (it would be another eight years before nets were introduced to the game).

The Hotspur club's official formation day is generally accepted as September 5 1882, when the boys paid their first annual subscriptions of sixpence (2.5p) each.

It was quickly obvious that the club was rudderless and in need of discipline and a sense of direction. Yellowing club records show they lost heavily 8-1 to Edmonton-based side Latymer on January 6 1883.

1883-84: Enter John Ripsher, a Bible class teacher at historic All Hallows Church, the oldest surviving building in the borough of Tottenham dating back to Norman times. He was a force behind the scenes in the Hotspur Cricket Club and accepted an invitation to take over the running of the football club as President and honorary Treasurer.

If anybody could claim to be the Founding Father of Tottenham Hotspur, it is John Ripsher. The young team was in danger of breaking up when he took over because they were being bullied off their patch of grass on the Marshes by teams with older, bigger players. Ripsher, a clerk in a North London iron foundry, brought order and organization and introduced navy blue as the official club colours. He also established regular team talks at the Tottenham YMCA, and arranged for the players to use a back room of the Northumberland Arms as a dressing-room. YMCA to Yiddos! Some journey.

Ripsher was not only a pioneer but also a peacemaker. When the players were turfed out of the YMCA for being too noisy and high spirited he restored order and got them a new meeting place at, first, nearby Dorset Villas and then in The Red House in Tottenham High Road, little realizing that this would one day become the administrative offices of Tottenham Hotspur.

A scholarly man, it was Ripsher who agreed to the club motto that survives to this day: *Audere est Facere* (To Dare Is To Do). Hotspur won their first match in the Ripsher era 9-0 against Brownlow Rovers on October 6 1883.

Ripsher remained President of the club for eleven years and then became Patron. But as Hotspur Football Club went from strength to strength he hit hard times. He lost his sight and had severe heart problems, finally dying in the Union Workhouse in Dover at the age of 67 in 1907. He was penniless and forgotten and buried in an unmarked pauper's grave.

Fast forward one hundred years to the setting of Dover cemetery. Here, the Tottenham Tribute Trust raised a headstone on his grave that had been rediscovered by author Peter Lupson. His enlightening book, *Thank God for Football* (Azure Books), spotlights the plight of Ripsher and reveals how twelve of our major clubs owe their origins to Christianity. How ironic would Ripsher find it that Tottenham have since earned the nickname 'Yiddos,' referring to their large following among the North London Jewish fraternity. The nickname started out as abusive and anti-Semitic, but has now been largely accepted as an affectionate reference to the club.

Ripsher's legacy was that he always demanded that any player wearing the Hotspur shirt should compete with sportsmanship and a spirit of fair play. That, on the whole, has always been the Spurs way, through good times and bad.

But there was one time when they struggled to show the face of fairness. Their old rivals Latymer turned up with just five players for the start of their December 27 match at Tottenham Marshes. They were up to seven men by the final whistle, with Spurs recording – so they thought – a 2-0 victory. It was the responsibility of the captains to contact the local *Tottenham Weekly Herald*. They gave contradictory reports, each claiming victory, and the Herald refused to publish a result. It was March the following year before the dispute was settled, with Tottenham winning 2-0 at Latymer's Edmonton ground.

1884-85: Secretary Sam Casey reported that he had been receiving correspondence meant for a club called London Hotspur. To avoid future confusion, it was decided to officially register as Tottenham Hotspur Football and Athletic Club.

The team started to create local heroes. Ripsher recognized that the club needed more experience, and he brought in John Randall from near neighbours Radicals. He took over as captain from Bobby Buckle, who for ten years formed a left-wing partnership with Billy Hartson.

Billy became one of the club's most loyal servants, working as a member of the backroom team on his retirement and he was still active as a press box steward sixty years after his debut as a player.

Jack Jull was a young player making a name for himself, even though he could only play when allowed time off from his boarding school. Listed as a full-back, Jack was often on the score sheet and netted a hat-trick in a 3-0 victory over North London Albion. He continued playing for Spurs after leaving school, and was made Club President in 1895 and an honorary life member on his retirement as club captain in 1896.

1885-86: On a club outing to The Oval in Kennington, the Hotspur players watched Blackburn Rovers winning the FA Cup for the second successive time on the way to a hat-trick of victories in the oldest of all domestic competitions. They were so impressed that they decided to change colours to the Rovers' distinctive light blue and white halves shirts (we got an up-to-date taste of what it was like with the 125th anniversary reissue of the colours in 2007 … very nice, but it didn't look like Spurs).

To date, the Spurs had taken part in only friendly matches but they got their first taste of competitive play in the London Association Cup. They were drawn against St Albans – not the Hertfordshire one, but a team from the City of London – and won decisively 5-2. Six of the club founder members, grown into young men, played in the game.

They were crushed 8-0 in the second round on a visit to London Casuals, one of the great amateur sides of the Victorian Age.

For the first time, Spurs ended the season in credit … with a surplus of nine shillings (about 45p).

1886-87: Spurs entered two cup competitions, and reached their first final as their popularity started to catch hold. They were playing on common ground at the Marshes, and so spectators watched them for free, and the crowds were growing with every match.

Upton Park hammered them 6-0 in the first round of the London Association Cup, but in the East End Cup they managed to power through to the final with victories over Phoenix (6-0), Park (2-0) and St Luke's (2-1). In the final against London Caledonians – some historians insist it was a semi-final – Spurs went down 1-0 after a bizarre episode. On the given date for the final, Spurs turned up but there was no sign of the Caledonians. They kicked off with no opposition, scored and then claimed the tie. Caledonians complained that they had been given the wrong date, and when the match was finally played won with a scrambled goal that was described as "a comedy of errors."

1887-88: November 19 1887 is carved into Tottenham history – the date of their first match with Arsenal, who were then Royal Arsenal and based in Woolwich, south-east London. The game kicked off late because of Arsenal's traffic-delayed arrival. Spurs were leading 2-1 after 75 minutes when the Arsenal captain suddenly decided the light was too bad to continue and led his team off. Spurs claimed a victory and that's how it went into their record books. The bad blood between the two teams was already running thick, and this was long before the Gunners became near neighbours.

In the return match on Plumstead Common three months later, Spurs turned up two players short and were soundly beaten 6-2. You have to remember that these were true-blue amateur days, and players combined football with their nine-to-five jobs.

Tom Morris played in Tottenham's first match at White Hart Lane in 1899, and went on to set what was then a club record 523 appearances before joining the backroom staff. In all he served Spurs for more than 45 years

1888-89: Bobby Buckle, captain Jack Jull and Secretary Sam Casey were instructed to look for a new closed-in ground because Spurs had quickly outgrown the Marshes, where they had no control over the huge and often ill disciplined crowds who were gathering to watch them. Opponents complained that they were being pelted with rotten fruit whenever decisions went in their favour.

Spurs knew they needed to move, and they found a private pitch for rent for £17 a year just off Northumberland Park on a hedged-in, slightly sloping field known as Asplins Farm. Mobile stands were brought in to house the spectators. Now they could charge an admission fee and it was set at three old pennies – a threepenny bit – a head. The 'B' team played the first match there in September and they beat Stratford St John's in front of just 80 supporters, who provided gate money of 17 shillings (85 pence).

A previous tenant had left behind a large old wagon, and this was converted into a changing room for the players.

The next home game featured a match against the giants of the game, Old Etonians. At this distance it seems laughable to describe the Old Etonians as giants, but they were the top amateur team of the time and had eight FA Cup final appearances to their name. Spurs could not live with them in their first round London Challenge Cup tie and were slaughtered 8-2.

At the end of the season the club could boast a profit of £6!

The Midlands and the North had embraced professional football, and Proud Preston had won the inaugural League championship without a single defeat and the FA Cup without conceding a goal in the tournament. No wonder they were known as 'The Invincibles'.

1889-90: Now that they had a settled home, Spurs were admitted to the all-powerful Football Association as full members, but they had the worst possible start to their new season with (if you're of a nervous disposition look away) a 10-1 humiliation against Royal Arsenal at the Sportsman Ground, Plumstead Marshes, on a heavy pitch that used to be a pig field. The Gunners were then masquerading as *Royal* Arsenal because of their links with the Royal munitions factory in Woolwich.

Spurs made Westminster pay for it the following week on their new home ground when they stormed to a 13-0 victory.

1890-91: Perhaps it was because they saw red when being hammered by Arsenal that made Spurs switch the colour of their shirts to – wait for it – red. They wore the red up until 1896 before having two seasons in a chocolate and gold striped number that was an assault on the eyes. It was 1898 before they settled on white shirt and blue shorts, inspired by the Invincibles of Preston. Come on you Lilywhites!

1891-92: Familiar names were beginning to pop up on the Spurs fixture list, including Clapton Orient (later Leyton Orient, 4-1 winners at Northumberland Park but beaten 2-0 on their home ground), Queen's Park Rangers (a 2-1 home defeat), and Luton Town (a 3-1 defeat at Luton). They were all friendlies.

There was a mumbling among the Southern clubs because they were not being allowed to join the professional circuit under the threat from the FA that they would be drummed out of the game. Spurs officials took part in secret meetings to try to find a way around the impasse.

It got to the point where twelve teams were elected for a Southern League, with Spurs scraping in with just one vote! But it was all swept back under the carpet when the FA repeated their threats of widespread suspensions.

1892-93: The risk of a revolt eased when Tottenham joined the Southern Alliance, losing only three times in their first season. But playing the likes of the Scots Guards, the Coldstream Guards and Windsor and Eton did little to excite major interest among fans frustrated at seeing the best players going North to join the gravy train. They finished third in the Alliance behind Old St Stephens and Erith.

1893-94: Back to a heavy diet of friendlies after just a single season of Southern Alliance football, Spurs were showing no hint that they would eventually be considered one of the great cup-fighting sides. They went out in the first rounds of four competitions – the FA Amateur Cup, London Senior Cup, Middlesex Senior Cup and London Charity Cup. The good news is that they reached the semi-final of the Wolverton & District Charity Cup, the bad news that only eight teams competed.

There was an air of frustration and depression hanging over Northumberland Park, and the growing rift between Spurs and the FA widened following the infamous Ernie Payne Affair.

Fulham reported Spurs for poaching when a player listed as 'Burton' appeared on their left wing in a London Senior Cup tie against Old St Marks. It transpired that Mr. Burton was in fact Ernie Payne, who had been on Fulham's books but unable to get a regular first-team place.

An inquiry by the fuss pots of the London Football Association cleared Tottenham of poaching, because Payne was not a current member of the Fulham team. In fact it had been so long since he played that he did not even have a pair of decent boots. This was the root of the real anger at the Football Association. Spurs had provided Burton, alias Payne with a pair of new boots at a cost of ten shillings (50p). This was seen as a financial inducement, and Tottenham were suspended for two weeks and Payne for one week.

1894-95: Still smarting over their harsh treatment following the Ernie Payne 'scandal', Spurs reached the fourth qualifying round of the FA Cup, going down 4-0 in a replay at Luton after a 2-2 draw at Northumberland Park. Their first ever FA Cup tie was on October 13 1894 when they beat West Herts (later Watford F.C.) 2-1 in a first round qualifying home tie in front of 2,000 spectators. For the record, Tottenham's first FA Cup goal was scored by Peter Hunter.

They also battled through four qualifying rounds of the FA Amateur Cup before being walloped 5-0 in the second round proper by Old Carthusians at home.

It was the final season of amateur football for the Spurs. The Football Association were under heavy fire and realised they could no longer hold back the tide of professionalism. The Corinthian-spirited FA knew that cash-in-the-boots payments were rife in the southern game to stop players emigrating to the Promised Land of the North.

1895-96: It was agreed that Tottenham players would each receive 15 shillings (75p) a game as negotiations began to join the infant Southern League. They got into the swing for the full seasons ahead by playing 42 friendlies, winning 24, drawing eight and banging in 107 goals while conceding 71. Again they fought through the qualifying rounds of the FA Cup before being eliminated in the first round proper with a 5-0 thumping at Stoke City.

Professionalism cost Spurs one of their finest players. Captain Stanley Briggs was against it on principle, and resigned as club skipper and went hunting for strictly amateur clubs with which to play.

1896-97: The new professionals of Spurs made a satisfactory rather than stunning start to life in the Southern League, finishing fourth while scoring 45 goals in their 20 matches and conceding 30. They finished eighth in the United League that ran on alternate weeks to the Southern League matches, and were runners-up in the Wellingborough Charity Cup.

A friendly match against Aston Villa drew a record crowd of 6,000 spectators to Northumberland Park to give Spurs the confidence to look for a bigger, better permanent home. They held mighty Villa to a 2-2 draw.

1897-98: With the move to White Hart Lane on the horizon, Spurs had a fine season, finishing third in the Southern League and runners-up to Millwall in the United League. Everything was being put on a professional footing. Under the driving chairmanship of local entrepreneur Charles Roberts and with generous support from benefactor John Oliver, the club became a limited company with a share capital of £8,000, and in February 1898 Frank Brettell was appointed the first secretary-manager of the club.

This is John Cameron, player-manager for Tottenham as the 19th Century gave way to the 20th Century. He was considered a troublemaker because of his union activities.

Brettell had been a player with St Domingo (later Everton), became Everton secretary in between reporting for the *Liverpool Mercury*, and he joined Spurs from Bolton. He hardly had time to get his seat warm before he moved on to Portsmouth in May 1899.

An astonishing crowd of more than 14,000 watched Tottenham and Arsenal in a goalless draw at Northumberland Park in a United League match on April 8 1898 (It is not recorded whether there were any shouts of 'boring, boring Arsenal'). Some spectators were hurt in the crush in an overcrowded stand, and it convinced the club they were right to be seeking a more accommodating ground.

A former Baseball pitcher with the Brooklyn Dodgers and a rugby player, Roberts was a larger-than-life character who specialised in organising fund raising events and military tattoos. He wore eye-catching fedoras that he had collected while living in the States, and was astute enough to bring in high-powered businessman John Oliver in what could be described as a cash-cow capacity. Roberts and Oliver were the twin forces on the first board of directors, with former players Bobby Buckle, Jack Thompson and Ralph Bullock given back-seat roles in the boardroom.

1898-99: Preparing for the ambitious switch to White Hart Lane, Spurs appointed John Cameron as successor to the now-you-see-me-now-you-don't Frank Brettell. The 27-year-old Glaswegian had been a hugely talented forward with Queen's Park, Everton and Scotland, and was brought to the club as a player by the man he was about to replace.

He had the ambition and the energy necessary to carry out his triple job as inside-forward, secretary and manager, and in his spare time he was the first secretary of the controversial Association Footballers' Union, the forerunner of the PFA.

At Everton, Cameron was seen as a troublemaker because of his union activities and was virtually black listed by the professional clubs "oop north" because of his campaign for fair pay for the players. He led and lost a fight to stop the wages of League footballers from being capped at £4 a week.

In his first game in charge as player-manager, Cameron scored the goal that lifted Tottenham to a stunning second round FA Cup victory over the high-ranking Sunderland side.

Following a 4-1 defeat at Stoke in the third round, Cameron strengthened the side by recruiting several fellow-Scots, starting a Tottenham tradition that carried on throughout the next hundred years.

There was a Scottish burr about the place as Spurs got ready for their move to The Lane of Dreams.

FOR more than a quarter of a century, veteran publican George Beckwith had been using the vast field behind his White Hart Inn for growing flowers, plants and home produce. It was part nursery and part vegetable patch, and in a hostelry census back in 1874 he classified himself as 'landlord of the White Hart Inn and nursery'. More than twenty years on it was to be the roots of The Lane of Dreams.

Beckwith rented the ground from the long-established brewers Charrington, whose headquarters were in Mile End in East London where they had started in the beer business in 1738. They decided they could make greater profit from the White Hart land by selling it for the development of a row of houses.

Spurs, desperately hunting for a new home, heard about the housing plan and put forward a counter proposal for developing the land as a football ground. The brewers at first could not see how that would be more profitable than selling to property developers. It was then pointed out that they could almost guarantee as many as one thousand customers descending on the White Hart pub every match day. So, with their eyes on the profits from pints, Charrington gave Spurs the go-ahead to rent the ground behind the White Hart. It can be said to have been launched on a sea of beer.

The area, just a Ted Ditchburn punt from Northumberland Park, was originally known as Gilpin Park. This was after the character featured in an eighteenth century William Cowper ballad called The Diverting History of John Gilpin, involving a comical journey on a runaway horse that leads to the Bell at Edmonton. There was also a move to call the new headquarters the High Road ground or Percy Park (after Harry Hotspur), but supporters gradually popularized the ground as simply White Hart Lane, referring to the lane that ran off the High Road leading to the stadium. This was to become the Lane of Dreams for generations of Spurs fans.

The market garden acres that Spurs took over had been let go by the aging George Beckwith. There were rusting greenhouses and wooden sheds to be cleared, and the overgrown flowerbeds and vegetable patch had to be smoothed into a playable football pitch; certainly without the slope that was an aggravating feature of the Northumberland Park ground.

In a masterstroke, the club invited John Over to take on the task. He was arguably the best groundsman in the country, and had been the man trusted with laying the pitch for the first England-Australia Test at The Oval in the year of Grace, 1880. Truly a green-fingered man.

Over, who agreed to join Spurs from Edmonton Cricket Club, became infamous for his temper tantrums if anybody dared set foot on his beloved pitch between matches. He laid what was one of the finest pitches in the world of football, and jealously guarded it for forty years before handing responsibility to his son, Will.

The mobile stands that had been used at Northumberland Park just 200 yards away were transferred to White Hart Lane, giving cover to 2,500 spectators. Player-Manager-Secretary John Cameron and his small staff moved into club offices at the new ground. They were cramped but an improvement on the previous offices at 808 Tottenham High Road.

Cameron worked hard at providing football to match the splendid surface of John Over's pitch, encouraging the Scottish method of along-the-ground football with precise passes rather than the hoof-and-hope of so many English teams. It set a style and a standard that has always been the mark of the greatest Tottenham sides.

A crowd of 5,000 gathered for the first game at White Hart Lane on Monday, September 4 1899. The visitors for a friendly were the oldest club in the Football League, Notts County, who were then in the First Division. After a ceremonial kick-off by club chairman Charles Roberts, Southern League Spurs went behind to a Tommy McCairns shot that was deflected into the net past wrong-footed goalkeeper George Clawley. Ex-Preston marksman Tom Pratt quickly equalised before Scottish forward Dave Copeland helped himself to a hat-trick to lift Tottenham to a flattering 4-1 victory. The second and third of his goals were scored after the County goalkeeper Ernie Suter had gone off injured. The gate money was £115.

Five days later 11,000 spectators turned out to see Tottenham's first competitive match at their new headquarters, a 1-0 victory over Queen's Park Rangers in a Southern League fixture. Tom Smith, another import from Preston, scored the goal.

Spurs came into the new century full of fire and ambition and marked their first year at White Hart Lane by winning the Southern League championship.

The following season – 1900-01 – they pulled off one of the most remarkable of all their triumphs when they captured the FA Cup, remaining the only non-League side to achieve it since the Football League's launch in 1888-89.

It was never easy. They played eight matches against five teams, four of them from the League's First Division. Spurs were behind in four of the games, but showed tremendous fighting spirit to eventually come out top in each of them.

They met roasting-hot favourites Sheffield United in the final, an all-star team that included England legends Bill 'Fatty' Foulke in goal and left-half Ernest 'Nudger' Needham. Just two seasons earlier they had won the League championship.

United and Spurs met in the final at Crystal Palace in a pulsating duel that attracted 110,820 spectators, a world record for a football match at that time (some records put the gate at 114,815). The game ended in a 2-2 draw, with United's second goal the subject of considerable heated debate. Jerky film of the match – one of the first major sporting events to be filmed – showed that the ball did not cross the Tottenham goal-line. Goalkeeper George Clawley is clearly seen scrambling the ball away for a corner, which is what the linesman signalled. But autocratic referee Arthur Kingscott astonished everybody by awarding a goal, and – in the spirit of the time – the Tottenham players accepted without protests. Today, he would have no doubt been hung from the crossbar! Kingscott was the leading official of the day, and later became FA treasurer.

The replay was set for Everton's ground at Goodison Park, but following protests from Liverpool – who had a League match scheduled for the same day – the match was switched to Bolton's Burnden Park. Just 22,000 fans watched Spurs come from a goal down to win 3-1, again with Kingscott in charge. The goal scorers were player-manager Cameron, right winger Tom Smith and centre-forward Sandy Brown. This was to prove a rarity – a Tottenham victory at Bolton! It completed a remarkable contribution by Scottish international Brown, who created a record by scoring in every round and netting an incredible 15 of Tottenham's 20 goals during the Cup run. His haul included all four goals against West Bromwich Albion in the semi-final.

White Hart Lane was jam-packed when the team returned to London to show off the trophy, and the club started a new trend by tying ribbons in the club colours to the handles of the Cup. It had been the idea of the wife of Tottenham director Morton Cadman, and has been carried on as a tradition for winning finalists ever since. The beribboned Cup was back in the 'soft' South for the first time in eighteen years.

For the record, the triumphant Tottenham team (starting the happy habit of winning a major trophy when there is an 01 in the year) was:

George Clawley, Harry Erentz, Sandy Tait, Tom Morris, Ted Hughes, Jack Jones (captain), Tom Smith, John Cameron, Sandy Brown, David Copeland, Jack Kirwan.

Just three years later the FA Cup that had brought Tottenham glory brought them shame. After beating Everton in the first round, they were drawn at home against one of the most powerful teams in the land in Aston Villa. White Hart Lane was filled to overflowing and after Villa had taken the lead the crowd spilled over on to the pitch and the referee abandoned the game after thirty-eight minutes.

The Football Association were determined to make an example of Tottenham. They fined them a whopping (for the time) £350, and ordered the game to be replayed at

A rare and understandably grainy shot from the 1901 FA Cup final at Crystal Palace. Sheffield United's legendary goalkeeper Bill 'Fatty' Foulke is about to retrieve the ball from the net after Sandy Brown had headed an equaliser for Tottenham. Brown scored in every round, including the replay at Bolton that Spurs won 3-1 to bring the Cup back to the South for the first time in 18 years.

Villa Park. Spurs beat the mighty Midlanders 1-0 before falling in the third round to Sheffield Wednesday.

To avoid any future over-crowding, club chairman Charles Roberts and his directors concentrated on making continual improvements and enlargements, truly a work in progress. Within five years, the ground had main stand seating for five hundred, and 12,000 could now watch under cover. The capacity had gone up to 32,000.

There was growing frustration because the terms of the lease with Charrington prevented wholesale changes to the ground. This eventually led to a buy-the-ground plan, and in 1905 an offer of 5,000 £1 shares was issued to help raise the £8,900 needed to purchase the freehold, plus the additional £2,600 for land at the Edmonton end that would allow for an extra stand. A total of 2,000 shares were snapped up and a large, tiered bank was built at the Paxton Road end as a twin to the one developed a year earlier at the Park Lane end. The capacity was now up to 40,000.

AN INTERLUDE

I interrupt my ramblings to bring to you something fairly unique, the assessment of Tottenham in the early 20th Century by a man who was there: C.B. (Charles Burgess) Fry, arguably the greatest sporting all-rounder Britain has ever produced. He played cricket and football for England, held the long jump world record, and was an international-class rugby player. Fry was also an outstanding gymnast, and his party piece – hard to believe, this – was to somersault backwards and land on a mantelpiece. CBF, as he signed his articles, became a prominent sportswriter, who owned and edited *C. B. Fry's Sports Magazine*. In my early Fleet Street days as a sportsroom assistant on the London *Evening News* I helped esteemed journalist/author Julian Holland with research on his acclaimed 1950s-published history of Tottenham. I uncovered the following article that had first appeared in Fry's magazine in 1907. Julian could not find space for it, but I am now delighted to have this opportunity to give it the airing it deserves. It captures the spirit of Spurs in those early days when they were on the brink of joining the Football League. The article is written in the respectful and erudite style of the time (perhaps you much prefer it to my sledgehammer touch):

❛Than the famous Spurs there is probably no more popular club in England. The reasons are not far to seek. Did the Spurs not recover the Association Cup for the South? Do they not play pretty and effective football? Are they not scrupulously fair? Are they not perfectly managed? No wonder that, whatever their fortune, their "gates" seldom suffer. Their supporters often travel long distances to see them play, and it is doubtful if any team attracts a bigger crowd, This popularity was not achieved in a day.

As from the acorn springs the mighty oak tree, so from the smallest of beginnings have sprung some of the greatest institutions. This generalisation is particularly applicable to the rise of the great football clubs of the country, and the history of Tottenham Hotspur is no exception to the rule. It was founded by a band of enthusiastic young men who used to play on Tottenham Marsh and hold their committee meetings under a convenient lamp-post in Northumberland Park.

Mr. Robert Buckle (familiarly known as Bob) was one of the leading spirits in those early days; and many a time he took 'the chair' at the *al fresco* committee meetings in the park to hear the minutes read by Mr. John Thompson (who, when not so engaged, was simply Jack), a no less enthusiastic member, and to listen to the comments of another founder member, Mr. Samuel Casey, who in more casual times away from the business of football is known as Sam.

To these three lovers of the game the great club that bears the name of Tottenham Hotspur today must look with affectionate respect at the originators of its being. And that they are so regarded I have reason to know. This leads me to chronicling of another fact, that the good fellowship which characterised the early stages of the club's history still exists, despite change of circumstances and rise to fame.

I have no hesitation in saying that there is no club in the country in which there is better feeling between the players and the directors and more widespread patriotism than at Tottenham.

Hotspur started out as a most unpretentious little club. It is on record that they made their own goal-posts and touch-line sticks – and it is said that if they could have done they would have willingly made their own footballs to save expense. Everything that energy and enthusiasm could achieve for the welfare of the club was done by its members. And it is largely owing to the fact that the same spirit prevails today that Tottenham Hotspur has climbed to the pinnacle from which its supporters can view the events of the past with satisfaction, for whatever temporary spells of misfortune attend the club, it must not be forgotten that to Tottenham belongs the honour of having brought the English Cup to the South, and it had been in the North for nineteen years.

Tottenham's great season was that of 1900-01, when all other achievements were thrown into the shade by the winning of the Football Association Cup, the most prestigious of all the trophies. It will be remembered that a record crowd assembled at the Crystal Palace to witness the match, which ended in a draw. The Spurs were opposed by Sheffield United; and according to the official returns 110,820 spectators watched the exciting struggle. On that day's form there was absolutely nothing to choose between the two teams, and when at length the whistle was blown at the end of the game each had scored two goals.

Would you mess with him? This is Alex 'Sandy' Tait, who was the Dave Mackay of his day in the Tottenham midfield – a driving captain and feared tackler.

The replay took place at Burnden Park in Bolton, and then 22,000 people saw the Tottenham Hotspur win an occasionally excellent game by three goals to one.

An interesting fact in connection with the replayed match is that Alexander Brown – better known to lovers of football as Sandy Brown – scored two of the three goals. Now at Luton, Brown performed the quite magnificent feat of scoring in every round.

It has to be recorded, although controversy should never be allowed to spoil the spirit of the game, that the second United goal at Crystal Palace did not appear to cross the goal-line. But true to their sporting attitude, Tottenham accepted the referee's rather dubious and debatable decision.

When the first match was in progress at the Palace, two men of mark were seated next to one another, each ignorant of the identity of his neighbour, They were Mr. C. D. (Charles) Roberts, chairman of the Spurs, and Mr. C.F. (Charles) Stokes, chairman of the United. The comedy of the situation was enhanced by the fact that Mr. Stokes did not hesitate to predict victory for his own team, though he was ever ready to applaud the good play of the Spurs – and there was much of it.

Towards the end of the game, Mr. F.J. Wall, illustrious Secretary of the Football Association, came up and spoke to both men. Still they were not enlightened as to each other's identity, until just as he was going away Mr. Wall said to Mr. Roberts, "If the Spurs win you will be expected to make a speech, you know!"

Mr. Stokes turned to his unknown neighbour and said, "What's that he says? You make a speech? Who the dickens are you?"

Mr. Roberts revealed himself as chairman of Tottenham Hotspur. Both men had a hearty laugh and shook hands warmly when Mr. Stokes identified himself as chairman of Sheffield United.

This I know to be true, when the Spurs won the Cup a week later, one of the first people to offer them his sincerest congratulations was Mr. Stokes.

Though Tottenham's progress along the thorny road to fame was not very rapid, it was steady and in 1887 the old pitch on the Marsh was abandoned for a much better ground at Northumberland Park. It was with their arrival at the new premises that they embarked on their rise towards becoming a highly respected football institution.

They had an excellent captain in Jack Jull, and set out to play the type of football that requires brains as well as brawn. This was much appreciated by their followers, increasing a thousandfold every week in their first season at their new ground as word spread that Tottenham were a team worth watching.

They were particularly lucky to find a generous patron in the person of Mr. John Oliver, who had the stands at Northumberland Park erected at his own expense. Mr. Oliver was ever ready to further the aims of the ambitious youngsters by every means in his power. His financial aid in those formative years was always to be relied upon, and his personal interest in the venture was ever awake – indeed, to him more than to any one else, it can be said that the Tottenham club owes its existence today.

Fortunate in having Mr. Roberts for a visionary chairman, the club is no less happy in its secretary and former Tottenham player, Mr. John Cameron. He is one of the best judges of players in the country, and he has his finger on the pulse of the team, so that there is nothing that concerns the welfare of the club of which he is ignorant. He was a fine player in the inside-right position, and was a member of the famous Cup team. Tottenham were fortunate to have him available to take over as secretary-manager on the departure of Mr. Frank Brettell to Portsmouth in 1900.

The two events which have most influenced the fortunes of the club were its transformation into a limited liability company, which took place in 1898, and its removal from Northumberland Park to its present Tottenham High Road locality, which many refer to as White Hart Lane. The ground is an excellent one, with an atmosphere that is worth the wind at the back of the home players. The directors have been well advised to secure the permanence of tenure. This is a football ground that will be a popular destination long into this young century.

Of the famous players who have worn the Spurs colours a few must be mentioned. G. Clawley, an excellent goalkeeper now of Southampton, and C. Williams of Norwich City is another fine custodian. They have a worthy successor in J. H. Eggett; he has a fine pair of hands.

H. Erentz, who partnered A. Tait when the Cup was won, is now in retirement. Prolific goal marksman Sandy Brown is now playing for Luton, and J. Jones fell a victim to typhoid.

Kirwan and Copeland, the renowned left wing partners, are dazzling for Chelsea as the Tottenham team gradually changes its personnel, preparing for what is rumoured to be a long-awaited place in the Football League, where I am certain they will equip themselves proudly, with passion and with an emphasis on fine football, because that is the way they do things at Tottenham.*

I hope you agree with me that it was worth that journey back into the past to get a taste of Tottenham's standing in those early years. Eyewitness accounts are much better and more accurate than hearsay and borrowed facts dug up from more than 100 years ago.

Once Spurs had established themselves as one of the outstanding clubs in the South, they became increasingly conscious of the limitations of such a parochial competition as the Southern League. But it was seven long years before they were finally elected to the Football League's Second Division just a few weeks before the kick-off to the

A wonderful photograph of the Tottenham squad, circa 1905. Some key characters worth pin-pointing – first left, back row is legendary groundsman John Over ... third row extreme right, with the fedora, chairman Charles Roberts ... second left, third row secretary-manager John Cameron ... centre third row with the huge moustache, Tom Morris .. holding the ball, skipper Alex 'Sandy' Tait ... and the unathletic looking player second from right in the first row is the colourfully named Jabez Darnell, a left-half who played 150 games for the Lilywhites.

1908-09 season. It was a change of status loaded with stress and suspense.

Spurs had been given the impression they were guaranteed a League place, and surrendered their membership of the Southern League. Imagine their shock when they went to the League annual meeting for what they expected to be a rubber-stamp acceptance of their nomination, only to find they did not have sufficient votes.

Just as they were calculating the cost – and hurting from the humiliation – Stoke City announced they were having to resign from the League because of a financial crisis.

Their place went to Spurs, but not without nail-biting drama. Lincoln, Rotherham and Southport were also up for election. Laughable as it seems at this distance, Tottenham tied with Lincoln on seventeen votes each. It was left to the eight-man Management Committee to decide, and Spurs got the nod by five votes to three.

The sigh of relief could have been heard all the way across North London.

While the transformation was being planned there were the beginnings of what were to become familiar managerial changes at Tottenham. John Cameron resigned in 1907, later becoming a respected journalist and publisher after spending the First World War in prison in Germany, where he had been coaching when war was declared. In the same prison camp were Cameron's former Tottenham team-mate John Brearley and the great Steve Bloomer, both of whom had also been coaching in Germany. On May 2 1915 an 'England X1' of prisoners of war – including Brearley and Bloomer – played a 'World X1' captained by Cameron, a game watched by a crowd of 5,000 other POWs.

When Cameron left Tottenham in 1907, the directors made an appointment that astonished the football world and dismayed their players. The man put in charge was former referee Fred Kirkham, who had officiated at two FA Cup finals and was noted for his curt manner. He had refereed the Spurs-West Herts (later Watford) Southern League game on April 13 1907, and five days later was given the manager's job. The players had no respect for his football knowledge, and there was a bad dressing-room spirit throughout his brief 15-month reign.

The club directors were content to let secretary Arthur Turner – who gave 43 years service to Spurs – hold the managerial reins in a caretaker capacity at the start of Tottenham's greatest challenge to date. Turner's quiet influence on those formative years at White Hart Lane were every bit as strong as that of Charles Roberts, who reigned as club chairman from 1898 until 1943.

It was September 1 1908 when Tottenham made their long-awaited debut in the League, and a crowd of 20,000 gathered at White Hart Lane to see them play FA Cup holders Wolves. Within six minutes they were celebrating a goal by amateur Vivian Woodward, one of the golden giants of his generation who the following month scored the victory-clinching goal for Great Britain against Denmark in the Olympic football final at the White City. He was rewarded with an honorary place on the Tottenham board.

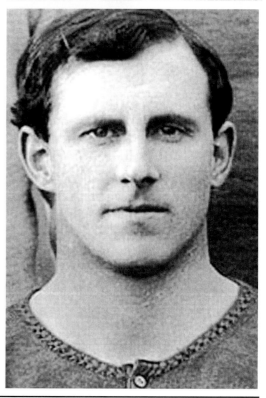

A TRIO OF EARLY
WHITE HART LANE HEROES

Top left, Joe Walton, who featured as a flying right winger in Tottenham's first Football League game at White Hart Lane on September 1, 1908.

Top right: John Brearley, who scored 24 goals in 133 games for Spurs, and met up with his old manager John Cameron in a German Prisoner of War camp..

Right, the great Vivian Woodward, an Olympic gold medal winner who was a director of Tottenham while still playing.

Woodward, all gliding style and skill, added a second goal against Wolves soon after half-time and Tom Morris wrapped it up with a 30-yard drive to give Tottenham an impressive 3-0 send-off to their new life in the League. It was fitting that Morris scored in this history-making match because he was the lone survivor from the FA Cup winning team, and one of the longest-serving of all players. He went on to make 523 appearances for the Lilywhites, and continued to serve the club in a backroom capacity right up until his death in 1942.

For the record, the Tottenham line-up for their first match in the Football League:

Hewitson; Coquet, Burton; Morris, Danny Steel, Darnell; Walton, Woodward, Macfarlane, Bobby Steel, Middlemiss.

Danny and Bobby Steel were brothers from Newmilns in Scotland.

Spurs won promotion to the First Division at the first time of asking, but it was a desperately close run thing. They drew their last match at Derby, and then had to wait two days for West Bromwich – level on points – to go to the Baseball Ground. Derby beat the Baggies 2-1, which meant that Tottenham went up in second place with a 2.93 goal average to Albion's 2.74. Spurs did not concede a goal in sixteen of their 38 matches; just one more goal against them would have meant they stayed down.

A year later they suffered another tense finale, this time to their debut season in the First Division and at the wrong end of the table. They struggled throughout the season, and needed to beat Chelsea in their final match to avoid relegation. Spurs won 2-1, the winner coming from Percy Humphreys who had arrived at White Hart Lane from Chelsea a few months earlier. His goal meant that it was Chelsea who went down, and Tottenham who stayed up.

Now owners of the ground, Spurs set about building a home fit for footballing kings. As with the appointment of John Over as their groundsman, they went for the very best and appointed renowned architect Archibald Leitch as the man to design the new White Hart Lane. He had literally built a reputation for himself as the master builder of football stadiums, kicking off with the Rangers headquarters at Ibrox in his native Glasgow. In all he designed stands for more than twenty major football stadiums in the Scottish and English Leagues.

His first job at White Hart Lane was to plan for a new stand, which seated 3,500 and with a paddock area for more than 6,000 in front. It was constructed and ready in time for the visit of Manchester United on September 11 1909, the first home game as a First Division club. The game ended in a 2-2 draw, with all four goals coming in the second-half.

Before the season was over, a huge, nine-foot tall cockerel perched on a giant old-style leather football had been mounted at the apex of the mock-Tudor gable above the main stand. It was made of bronze and sculpted by former Spurs player William

James Scott. The cockerel was adopted as the Tottenham emblem because of the link with Harry Hotspur and the fact that he wore spurs going into battle, hence a fighting cockerel suitably fitted with spurs. It was to become one of the most famous and unique emblems in world football, appearing on Spurs shirts from 1921.

The entire East Stand was also covered during 1909 and enlarged two years later, with concrete terracing replacing the old wooden tiers. It brought the ground capacity up to 50,000.

In 1908 Spurs signed a young player – Walter Tull – from Clapton who was to make history as the first black footballer to appear in the League in the 20th century, following in the footsteps of Ghana-born Arthur Wharton who had played with distinction for among other clubs Preston and Sheffield United late in the 19th Century.

The grandson of a slave, Walter was born in Folkestone in 1888. His father was a West Indian who had arrived in Britain from Barbados in 1876 and married a Kent girl.

His parents both died before he was ten, and Walter was brought up along with his brother in a Methodist-run orphanage in Bethnal Green in London's East End. A Tottenham scout spotted him playing amateur football for Clapton (not to be confused with the professional club Clapton Orient), and he started on an adventure that could have come out of the imagination of a Hollywood screenwriter.

A quick and powerful inside-forward or wing-half, he spent two seasons with Tottenham during which he was involved in an unpleasant and unsettling racial incident while playing at Bristol City. He was verbally abused by ignorant City fans, who according to one report used "language lower than Billingsgate."

It led to a loss of confidence, and in 1910 Tull was sold to Northampton where he played 110 games. He was good enough to attract the interest of Rangers, a move that appealed to him because his brother, Edward, was working in Glasgow as a qualified dentist. Just as a deal was being discussed, war was declared. He enlisted with the 1st Football Battalion of the Middlesex Regiment, and was quickly promoted to sergeant.

Tull served on the Somme until being invalided back to England in December 1916 suffering from trench fever. On his recovery, he was sent to officer's training school at Gailes in Scotland and received his commission in May 1917. This was an astonishing achievement at a time when the British Manual of Military Law specifically excluded "Negroes from exercising actual command" as officers. It was Tull's superiors who recommended him for officer training, a remarkable testimony to his charisma and leadership qualities.

Second Lieutenant Tull was sent to the Italian front, and he was mentioned in dispatches for his "gallantry and coolness" following the bloody Battle of Piave. The obscenely named 'Great War' was into its last months when he was transferred to France,

Walter Tull, a hero on the football field and the battlefield.

where a push was on to break through the German Western Front defence.

He was ordered to make an attack on a heavily fortified German trench at Favreuil on March 25 1918. Soon after entering No Man's Land, leading from the front, Tull was hit by a German bullet and fell mortally wounded. His men risked their own lives against heavy machine gun fire in a bid to retrieve his body. It was an indication of how highly he was thought of by those to whom he had to give orders. Walter was 29.

His commanding officer personally broke the news to Walter's brother, Edward. "He was so brave and conscientious and popular throughout the battalion," he told him in extraordinarily emotional terms. "The battalion and company have lost a faithful officer, and personally I have lost a good friend."

It was 1999 before Tull, a hero on the pitch and in the trenches, got long overdue recognition with the opening of a Walter Tull Memorial Garden next to Northampton Town's Sixfields Community Stadium.

Many White Hart Lane fans have put their names to a petition to get Tull the posthumous Military Cross that he so bravely earned.

> *There was a brave sporting man called Tull*
> *Who on the battlefield soared free as a gull*
> *It mattered not the colour of his skin*
> *To comrades who were as close as kin*
> *A hero whose memory will never ever dull*
> – Norman Giller 2009

Back to our journey through the history of White Hart Lane: Tottenham's first six seasons in the First Division were mainly about surviving, and three times they narrowly escaped relegation before finishing bottom in the final season before the First World War that put a finish to the football programme for five years.

Waiting for them immediately after the war was a sickening defeat by Arsenal, without a ball being kicked; more like Tottenham being kicked in the balls.

THE Football League roared back into action nine months after the November 11 1918 Armistice, boasting of being "bigger and better" than ever. They expanded from 40 clubs to 44, with the First and Second Divisions now made up of 22 clubs each. The shock, particularly for Spurs, was that the restructured First Division included their new-to-North-London neighbours Arsenal – but *not* Tottenham.

It was naturally assumed – with the extra places available – that the teams that finished in the last two places in the 1914-15 season, Chelsea and Tottenham, would automatically retain their First Division status, with Derby and Preston promoted as the top two teams in the Second Division to make up the 22 clubs.

But nobody took into account the Machiavellian manoeuvres of Arsenal chairman Sir Henry Norris. He secretly negotiated behind the scenes and behind the backs, and had powerful Liverpool chairman and League president John McKenna – nicknamed 'Honest John' – giving him surprisingly strong support.

Despite finishing only fifth in the Second Division in 1914-15, it was Arsenal who were promoted along with Chelsea, Derby and Preston. The team that lost out was Tottenham, and all these years later it still rankles.

Chairman Charles Roberts, who always played by the book, was speechless. Privately, the Spurs directors and – more vociferously, the supporters – were wondering just how 'Honest' John McKenna was.

It was not only Tottenham who felt left out in the cold. The stench carried all the way up through Wolverhampton and to the coalfields of Yorkshire. Wolves and Barnsley had finished third and fourth in the old Second Division, and they could not fathom how Arsenal had managed to leapfrog them without a ball being kicked.

Norris, the man who stubbornly transferred Arsenal to Highbury from Woolwich against the wishes of most people in 1913, got the comeuppance wished on him by Tottenham. In 1927 the Football Association suspended him and a fellow director, and the club was censured for illegally inducing players, including the great Charles Buchan, to join Arsenal.

Sir Henry became embroiled in a huge libel case against the FA and the *Daily Mail*, who alleged he had been using Arsenal funds to pay his personal expenses and the

Charles Roberts (left) was the driving-force chairman of Tottenham for 45 years from 1898. His first love was baseball. Here he is front row right opposite secretary/manager John Cameron as they pose with their 1901 FA Cup prize, captured while they were still in the Southern League. The four directors standing at the back in this newspaper cutting photo are J. Hawley, T. Deacock, Morton Cadman and Ralph Bullock. It was Morton Cadman's wife who came up with the idea of hanging the club-colour ribbons from the handles of the Cup, a tradition that carries on to this day. The trophy is the second FA Cup. The original was stolen from a shop window while on display following Aston Villa's victory in 1895.

wages of his chauffeur. The newspaper produced evidence that he had pocketed £125 from the sale of the club team bus, endorsing the cheque with Herbert Chapman's forged signature and paying the money into his wife's account.

The cheers in Tottenham when he lost the case could no doubt be heard all the way to the Law Courts.

Norris, whose ancestor had been beheaded for – euphemistically – flirting with Anne Bolyen, fitted the image of a Victorian villain, complete with a huge twirling moustache and a monocle that distorted his features. One of his first managers at Highbury, Leslie Knighton, revealed in his autobiography: "I have never met his equal for logic, invective and ruthlessness against all who opposed him. When I disagreed with him at board meetings and had to stand up for what I knew was best for the club, he used to flay me with words until I was reduced to fuming, helpless silence … he made me abandon the Arsenal scouting system, and ordered me never to sign a player under 5 foot 8 inches or weighing less than 11 stone."

A former Conservative MP, Mayor of Fulham and chairman at Craven Cottage when he tried to merge the club with Woolwich Arsenal, Norris was drummed out of football for the rest of his life.

Arsenal, the team he talked into the First Division, has been at the top table ever since – without ever earning the right to a place on the field of play.

These shenanigans gave Spurs the motivation to win a First Division place through playing rather than politicking. The on-fire Lilywhites ran away with the Second Division title in 1919-20 with an avalanche of 102 goals and a six-point advantage over runners-up Huddersfield (this, of course, in the days of two points for a win). Their collection of 70 points from a possible 84 was a Second Division record and the best in the League for twenty-seven years.

One anecdote worth repeating before we leave the Arsenal Affair: In 1908 Spurs went on a goodwill tour to South America, spreading the gospel of the game in Argentina and Uruguay, where the fervour for football was in its infancy. They played seven games including two exhibition matches against fellow tourists Everton. On the long haul home Charles Roberts became friendly with the ship's captain, who as a mark of respect presented the Spurs chairman with a parrot as a souvenir of the trip. Legend has it that the parrot – who took up residence at White Hart Lane – was found dead on its perch the very day that Arsenal were voted into the First Division ahead of Tottenham. Some clever wag invented the story that this is how the "sick as a parrot" football cliché originated, but I will not spoil a good story by pointing out that it was more than 40 years before the saying entered the limited vocabulary of interviewed footballers. The parrot story by then had been lost in the mists and the myth of time. 'Sick as a parrot' came into regular use in the early 1960s when a comedian called Freddie 'Parrot Face'

A photograph of wee wing wizard Fred 'Fanny' Walden in 1913, the old-style ball being a giveaway that it is a pre-war picture. A tiny tot standing just 5ft 2in tall, he was famous for his wriggling right wing runs for Spurs and England. In later life, the Northants cricketer became a leading umpire.

Davies used it as a catchphrase (actually, "Thick, thick, thick as a parrot", said with a pronounced lisp).

I was there when it was first uttered by a footballer, and I diligently reported what were to become immortal words following a match at Fulham. Step forward to a roll of drums Tosh Chamberlain, Fulham's long-serving and swerving winger who was one of the great characters of Craven Cottage in the days when pass master Johnny Haynes was king of the castle.

Tosh, as Cockney as a jellied eels stall, was sent off for allegedly calling the referee a Berkshire hunt, only he did not use the rhyming slang.

Pleading his innocence, Tosh told the referee: "But I wasn't talking to you, ref. I was calling 'Aynsie a c***, and I'm allowed to 'cos he's on my side."

As we interviewed Tosh in the Craven Cottage forecourt after the game, he reached for a description of how he felt and said (with the Freddie Davies lisp): "I'm thick as a parrot."

By the time it got into Monday's newspaper reports that had become "as sick as a parrot" ... a cliché was born, and it has been tumbling from the lips of footballers ever since. Sorry, but it had nothing to do with the Spurs parrot.

Back to football facts: The man masterminding the post-war Tottenham revival was Peter McWilliam, who had been an exceptional wing-half with Newcastle and Scotland. The Geordies nicknamed him 'Peter the Great'. He joined Spurs in 1912 after injury had ended his career at the age of thirty-three, but the War interrupted before he could make any impact. As war clouds were gathering, he uncovered in Arthur Grimsdell an even better wing-half than he himself had been, while Jimmy Seed shone at inside-right, and Bert Bliss and Jimmy Dimmock formed a potent left wing partnership. The squad was further strengthened by the arrival from Northampton of wee wizard winger 'Fanny' Walden, along with assured right-back Tommy Clay, and the two Jimmys – Cantrell and Banks. After the War was over, McWilliam completed the jigsaw by bringing in goalkeeper Alex Hunter, centre-half Charlie Walters, hard-as-nails right-half Bert Smith and specialist left-back Bob McDonald.

McWilliam resumed control at White Hart Lane as the unspeakable horrors of the First World War were laid to rest beneath a riot of celebration that turned the 1920s into what F. Scott Fitzgerald concisely and colourfully summed up as The Jazz Age. A sense of hopelessness and doom had been replaced by one of euphoria as the young people of the world got up and danced the Charleston, discovered the pleasure of leisure, and played and watched sport like never before. Goodness, they even gave women the vote – provided they were over 30, and of sound mind.

The terraces of football grounds heaved with huge crowds as the game in England rivalled cricket as the national sport. The only time the crowds would ever be bigger was immediately after the next little World War dust-up, but the Roaring Twenties promised peace and progress … except with the blind and bland rulers of the Football Association. They obstinately reigned over a shameful age of soccer slavery. As well as contracts that bound them hand and foot to their clubs, the players were told at the start of the 1922-23 season that the maximum wage was going to be cut from £9 to £8 in the season, and £6 to £5 in the summer. Strike action was threatened, but it proved an empty threat. The wages chop was forced on the players because of the entertainment tax, introduced to help pay off war debts as the Government cashed in on the game drawing record attendances.

There were a spate of injuries and even deaths caused by over-crowding at grounds, and in a bid to keep spectator numbers down and lessen the chances of mass injuries, the FA increased prices for the 1921 FA Cup final between Tottenham and Wolves at Stamford Bridge. It cost a guinea (21 shillings, £1.5p) for the best seat in the house, and two shillings to stand. The match still drew a capacity crowd of 72,805 and record receipts of £15,400.

It was the wettest final on record, with everybody getting soaked by a non-stop downpour. Newly promoted Tottenham, with skipper Arthur Grimsdell, Jimmy Seed and left wing partners Bert Bliss and Jimmy Dimmock in dominating form, kept their feet better on the quagmire of a pitch. "Dodger" Dimmock scored the only goal eight minutes into the second-half to make Tottenham the first southern winners of the Cup since they first won it twenty years earlier as a Southern League outfit. Manager McWilliam, a winner with Newcastle in 1910, became the first man to play in and then manage an FA Cup winning team. The winning team:

Hunter; Clay, McDonald; Smith, Walters, Grimsdell; Banks, Seed, Cantrell, Bliss, Dimmock.

Spurs finished sixth in the League that season. A year later they were second to Liverpool, and went out of the FA Cup at the semi-final stage against Preston after having a perfectly good looking goal disallowed.

The profits from the 1921 FA Cup run were ploughed into ground improvements. Archie the Architect Leitch designed split-level covered terraces at the Paxton Road end, and then two years later at the Park Lane end. This increased the capacity to 58,000, with room for 40,000 under cover. They also invested in buying the Red House restaurant at the front of the ground, which was converted into the club offices.

But in a way White Hart Lane had become dressed up with nowhere to go. After those heady immediate post-war years the ageing team started to break up, and following six seasons of mainly struggling the club was relegated in what can only be described as astonishing circumstances. After 35 games they were a comfortable seventh in the 1927-28 First Division with 35 points. But they ran out of steam and in the last seven games gathered only three points, sliding down the table at alarming speed. They were relegated in next to bottom place with 38 points. The competition that season was so close that Derby County, with only six more points, were fourth in the final table.

Ironically, the team relegated in last place was Middlesbrough – managed by Peter McWilliam, who had left Spurs to move to Ayresome Park only a few months earlier. He had been lured away with what was then an astronomical salary of £1,500 a year. The Scot did not want to leave, and told the board that if they would up his wages to £20 a week he would stay. Charles Roberts and his fellow directors refused, so McWilliam reluctantly left for pastures new. They had also let Jimmy Seed move to Sheffield Wednesday rather than increase his wage by a pound to the maximum £8 a week. He was replaced by 'Boy Wonder' Taffy O'Callaghan. Ironically, it was Seed's goals that kept Wednesday in the the First Division at the expense of Tottenham.

Down in the Second Division Spurs had five seasons that were more about taking part than winning. It was a period of gloom, accentuated by the success of Arsenal down the road at Highbury where Herbert Chapman was building his legendary team. Billy Minter, former Tottenham player turned trainer, was promoted to manager when McWilliam took the Middlesbrough bait, but he was out of his depth and happily returned to the back room after two unsuccessful seasons. He made way for Percy Smith, who had played for Preston and Blackburn before managing first Nelson and then Bury.

Smith set about grooming young players to take over from Tottenham's veteran stars. Into the team came Arthur Rowe, a product of the club's Northfleet nursery and somebody who would one day make a huge impact at the club. Smith also snapped up a young inside-forward called Willie Hall, who had just two seasons with Notts County behind him. He was seen as a ready-made replacement for the powerhouse George Greenfield, who was forced by injury into premature retirement.

Within eighteen months both Rowe and Hall were in the England team which defeated France 4-1 at White Hart Lane. Hall had to wait four years for his next international call, this time against Northern Ireland at Old Trafford in November 1938. He plundered what was then a record five successive goals. Three of his goals came within a four-minute spell, still a record for the fastest England hat-trick.

There was no happy ending to the Hall story. He became seriously ill during the War and in 1945 he had the lower part of both his legs amputated. Hall remained a huge favourite at White Hart Lane and in 1949 he was made vice President of the newly formed Spurs Supporters Club.

Hall was a prominent force in the attack that powered Spurs to the First Division as runners-up in 1932-33, and he formed a potent partnership with George Hunt who plundered 138 League goals before becoming, in 1937, the first player to move directly to the unmentionable team down the road at Highbury.

A rare picture of Spurs stars Jimmy Seed, Bert Bliss and Alex Lindsay arriving at an FA disciplinary meeting in 1922 after the Arsenal-Tottenham derby match had been scarred by fisticuffs on and off the pitch. Each club was censured and warned that a repeat would lead to ground closure at both Highbury and White Hart Lane.

In their first season back at the top table Spurs finished third, and had the satisfaction of scoring four more goals (79) than Arsenal, who were on their way to a hat-trick of League championships.

Tottenham marked their return to the elite division with an East Stand development designed by Archibald Leitch that cost £60,000 and brought an extra 5,100 seats and 18,700 terrace spaces. The capacity was now close to 80,000 (the record attendance for White Hart Lane was set on March 5 1938, when 75,038 spectators saw Sunderland beat Spurs 1-0 in the quarter-final of the FA Cup).

Ravaged by injuries including a career-ending one for Arthur Rowe, Tottenham had a nightmare second season at the top table and slid back ignominiously into the Second Division. This spelled the end of Smith's run as manager, and former double international at cricket and football, Wally Hardinge – reserve team trainer – briefly took over in a caretaker capacity.

Next into the hot seat in 1935 was Jack Tresadern, an EastEnder who had played 150 League games for West Ham either side of the First World War. He had been a runner-up with the Hammers against Bolton in the famous first Wembley FA Cup final. He was never comfortable in the job, and resigned to join Plymouth in 1938 just ahead of what would have been an inevitable sacking. This signalled the return of the popular Peter McWilliam, who had been filling in time following his departure from Middlesbrough as a scout for, sshh, Arsenal. By the time of his reappointment the club's registered offices had changed from the original 750 High Road to number 748. White Hart Lane was just about unrecognizable from the ground he had left behind in 1927.

One of the major changes was the introduction of what was to become known, loved and revered as The Shelf, a middle tier in the 'Old' East Stand with standing room for 11,000 spectators. It became synonymous with the soul of Spurs, and the decibel count of the Tottenham choirs over the years could be measured on the Richter Scale, a deliberate mixing of metaphors to capture the awesome sounds emanating from The Shelf. When the ground is ultimately bulldozed into history, the ghosts of Shelf supporters will surely be heard singing their glory-glory anthems.

Stanley Matthews always claimed that his most exciting match with England was played at White Hart Lane. He scored the only international hat-trick of his career against Czechoslovakia at the home of Tottenham on December 1 1937. He had been stung by criticism that he couldn't finish and didn't have a left foot. His three goals were all scored with his left foot, including the last-gasp winner in a 5-4 thriller. England had been reduced to ten men by injury and Matthews switched to inside-right.

When McWilliam returned to manage Spurs in 1938, he concentrated on building up the youth talent at the Gravesend and Northfleet nursery in Kent. Even though push-and-run was twelve years away, the first links in the chain were being put together.

Tottenham's 1921 FA Cup heroes, 1-0 winners against Wolves at Stamford Bridge: (back row, l-r) Trainer Billy Minter, Tommy Clay, Bert Smith, Alex Hunter, Charlie Walters, Bob McDonald; (front row, l-r) Jimmy Banks, Jimmy Seed, Arthur Grimsdell, Jimmy Cantrell, Bert Bliss and goal-scoring idol Jimmy Dimmock

Among the fresh-faced lads learning their trade (and how to push-pass the ball along the ground and then run into space) were free-scoring Les Bennett, Ronnie Burgess, Les Medley and a future master called Bill Nicholson. There was also a teenage goalkeeper by the name of Ted Ditchburn. On his return to The Lane, McWilliam said:

'I see my priority as bringing consistency to the club for the present, and building on our strong youth base for the future. There are some exceptional young players affiliated to the club who are being brought up to think the Tottenham way. We have a fine team of trainers who stress the golden rule that football is a simple game, complicated only by those who try to do intricate things when they are not necessary.

It is important to have a good work ethic to go with individual skills. Man AND ball have to do the work. Our young players are taught to pass the ball accurately and then get themselves into position to take a return pass if necessary. It is all about finding space and using it.

This is what we teach our youngsters at Gravesend, and there are at least half a dozen whom I confidently expect to be playing themselves into the League team in the next two or three years. I see a very productive time ahead for Tottenham. It will not happen overnight, but it WILL happen. I ask for patience from our supporters while we build for the future.

Meantime we must get that consistency at first-team level that has been missing in recent years. It is not acceptable to play brilliantly one week and then be mediocre in the next game. We must get the balance right.'

Horrific history was about to repeat itself for McWilliam, disrupting his master plan. When he took over the first time in 1912, the First World War broke out two years later. This time he had been back in the manager's chair for a little over eighteen months when the Second World War was declared on September 3 1939. He had put the pieces together for a jigsaw that would be completed after the war, but was not around to see his work continued. McWilliam retired in 1942 at the age of 64, leaving club secretary Arthur Turner to again take the reins in an emergency. When the history of Tottenham is discussed, Peter McWilliam deserves a prominent place in the debates, and bear in mind that he was a huge influence on both Arthur Rowe and Bill Nicholson.

There was limited wartime football, and Turner's main job was making sure he had eleven players to put out on the field. His record as manager during this dark period was Played 49, Won 27, Drew 11, Lost 11. Amazingly, 'Affable Arthur' juggled and improvised to keep the club running through two World Wars and there was never a time when he did not manage to field a full team. This wonderfully loyal Hotspur

The German team give the Nazi salute at White Hart Lane before their 3-0 defeat by England in 1935. No sign of Mark Bosnich. Whisper it, but they are the team featuring on the front cover playing at The Lane.

Willie Hall (left), the Tottenham hero who scored five successive goals for England against Northern Ireland at Old Trafford in 1938. He became seriously ill during the War and in 1945 he had the lower part of both his legs amputated. Hall remained a huge favourite at White Hart Lane and in 1949 he was made vice President of the newly formed Spurs Supporters Club.

continued to serve the club up until his death in 1949. He steered Tottenham to two wartime South League titles, often with makeshift teams including guest players who just happened to be on leave in London at the time of the match.

While war was raging there was a temporary truce between Tottenham and Arsenal. Highbury became an Air Raid Precaution control centre, and Spurs extended the hand of friendship and invited Arsenal to share White Hart Lane for wartime fixtures.

It was Arsenal who took part in one of the more bizarre matches ever staged at The Lane. In one of the oddest interludes in English football, Moscow Dynamo came to Britain for what was something of a magical mystery tour. They came, they saw, but did not concur with very much about the game in Britain. Little was known about them when they arrived in November 1945, and little more was known when they suddenly disappeared home without warning just over two weeks later.

They would not allow anybody to watch them train, would eat only meals prepared at the Russian Embassy, insisted on bringing their own referee, and demanded the use of substitutes, which was then pretty near unheard of in British football.

Such was the interest in the 'Mystery Men of Moscow' that 82,000 spectators crammed into Stamford Bridge for their first match. The Dynamo team presented embarrassed Chelsea players with bouquets of flowers before the kick-off, and then with a precise, almost robotic passing game came back to deflower the Chelsea defence and force a 3-3 draw after trailing 2-0. Most neutral witnesses agreed Dynamo were the better team.

Next they went to Wales and destroyed Cardiff 10-1, before returning to London for a prestige match against an Arsenal side including guest players Stanley Matthews and Stan Mortensen. The game was played at Arsenal's temporary home of White Hart Lane. Nobody, including the 55,000 crowd, saw much of the game. A thick pea-souper of a fog shrouded the ground, and few reporters were quite sure how Dynamo managed to come from 3-1 down to win 4-3. Visibility was down to five yards, and the Russian referee patrolled one side of the pitch, with his two linesmen on the far touchline.

The Russians then travelled to Glasgow, where they continued in a fog of their own making. They drew 2-2 with Rangers in front of a 90,000 crowd in a game threaded with ill temper. Without warning, the Dynamo team flew home and shunned a scheduled final match against an FA XI at Villa Park. It was later reported that as they had gone through the tour unbeaten, each of the players was made a Hero of the Soviet Union.

A few weeks later the Gunners returned to their Highbury home. A plaque stating Arsenal's gratitude for Tottenham's hospitality was placed in the Spurs boardroom when the war was finally over. But once the war shooting finished and the football shooting started, they quickly became just as big and bitter rivals as before. Let's be honest, it's more exciting and acceptable for them to be foes than friends.

I can hear chorused approval from the ghosts of The Shelf.

WHEN the Tottenham players reported back for League duty at White Hart Lane after the war they found themselves under the management of a man who had been a legend … with the Arsenal. Enter Joe Hulme, whose flying right wing exploits in the Herbert Chapman era had made him a hero at Highbury.

Hulme steered Spurs to the 1948 FA Cup semi-final, where they were beaten at Villa Park by Matthews-inspired Blackpool. But he was never totally accepted by the old enemy, and when he moved on in 1949 to a distinguished career in journalism it was a Spurs-through-and-through-man – Arthur Rowe – who took over as manager.

As author of this book, I have deliberately kept a low profile while allowing the facts to tell the story of The Lane of Dreams. But I need to briefly come out into the open to explain how I became friendly with the man who was to revolutionize the Tottenham way of football. I caught up with Arthur in my *Daily Express* reporting days when he was 'curator' of the short-lived PFA-supported Football Hall of Fame in Oxford Street in the early 1970s (a venture that quickly died because of lack of public interest).

A gentle, kindly man, Arthur was easy to talk to and we had many long conversations about his career in the game in general and his management of Spurs in particular.

He revealed that the art of push and run football – the signature style of Spurs – was born against the walls of North London. Tottenham-born Arthur, the chief architect of the meticulous method, remembered playing with a tennis ball against the wall as a schoolboy and suddenly thought to himself: "That's how easy and simple the game should be!"

I caught Arthur in reflective mood twenty years after he had entered the land of football legend by steering Spurs to back-to-back Second and First Division titles. Speaking quietly, with a discernible Cockney accent, he told me:

> ❝My philosophy was that the easier you made the game the easier it was to play it. So I used to tell the players to push the ball to a team-mate and then run into space to take the instant return pass. It was making the most of the 'wall pass' or the 'one-two.' Make it simple, make it quick. It was easier said than done, of course, but I got together a squad of players with

Arthur Rowe, the Tottenham manager who perfected the poetry of Push and Run.

the football intelligence to make it work. We used to operate in triangles, with Eddie Baily, Ronnie Burgess and Les Medley particularly brilliant at the concept out on the left. It was amazing to watch as they took defenders out of the game with simple, straightforward passes and then getting into position to receive the return. Over on the right Alf Ramsey, Billy Nicholson and Sonny Walters were equally adept at keeping possession while making progress with simple passes.'

Arthur, as modest and likeable a man as you could wish to meet, was never one to want to take credit for his own genius. He would always stress that the real father of Push and Run was his old Tottenham mentor Peter McWilliam, who had been a noted tactician in two spells in charge at White Hart Lane.

McWilliam was building the 1921 Tottenham FA Cup winning team when Arthur joined Spurs as a schoolboy. The Scot helped launch Arthur's playing career with the Spurs nursery team Gravesend and Northfleet. He developed into a thinking man's centre-half for Tottenham throughout the 'thirties until a knee injury forced his retirement after an international career confined to one England cap. He travelled through Europe as a full-time coach and was on the verge of accepting the Hungarian team manager's job when war was declared. There is a school of thought that it was his ideas passed on to young Hungarian players that was the foundation for the Magical Magyars of the 1950s, who buried England under an avalanche of 13 goals in two mesmeric matches.

His son, Graham, who lives in Los Angeles where he works as a financial adviser, made perfectly pertinent points about his father's impact on football in a 2006 letter to the sports section of the esteemed *Financial Times*. I tracked down Graham in California, and I am grateful for his permission to publish his letter here:

'Sir, In his piece 'Magyars mourn their lost magic' Jonathan Wilson states: 'Half a century ago Hungary were not merely the best in the world but possibly the best team there has ever been.'

I disagree with his assessment of the Hungarian soccer team. The great Hungarian team of 1953 played the same fast, short-passing game that humiliated England and was played by Tottenham Hotspur from 1949 to 1953. During that reign they won the then Second Division championship, followed by the First Division title, and followed that by being runners-up to Manchester United and FA Cup semi-finalists.

In 1952 they toured North America playing an attractive style of football called 'push and run', a fluid, fast-moving style that entertained capacity crowds wherever they played. That Spurs team was managed by my father, Arthur Rowe, who had won championships while in charge of Chelmsford City, a Southern League club, from 1946 to 1949.

After a stellar career as a Tottenham player in the 1930s, my father took a coaching position in Budapest, Hungary, before returning to England in 1939 to join the army.

In Budapest were sown the seeds of the 'push and run' approach, which for the next 13 years, incubated and ultimately manifested itself in that great Hungarian team. But it was a style that was first played by the glorious Spurs team of 1949-53.

In an *FT* article of July 1 1998, Peter Aspden wrote of 'the beautiful version of the game, invented by the Hungarian side of the 1950s'. The Hungarians did not 'invent' the beautiful version of the game. If anyone 'invented' it, it was my father.

On my wall at home there is a photograph of my father with Ferenc Puskas, the peerless member of the Hungarian team of the 1950s, and my thoughts turn to what kind of a game might have been played between those two great teams. What a feast it would have been. *Graham A. Rowe, Los Angeles.*

Yes, what a feast. It would have been a banquet of football at its purist and best; definitely the Beautiful Game.

On his war-forced return to England from Hungary, Arthur became an army physical training instructor and then manager of non-League Chelmsford, making him ideally placed to take over at White Hart Lane as successor to Joe Hulme in 1949.

His first major signing was Southampton right-back Alf Ramsey, a player he knew shared his keep-it-simple principles. Nicknamed 'The General' because of his fanaticism for talking football tactics, Ramsey took the secrets of simple football with him into management, and there was something of the push and run style about the Ipswich side he steered to the League championship and the England team he led to the World Cup in 1966.

Spurs waltzed away with the Second Division title in Rowe's first full season in charge, but sceptics said their "playground push and run" tactics would be exposed in the First Division. Wrong!

They powered to the top of the table, eventually taking the League championship with 60 points, four ahead of Manchester United and the highest total since Arsenal's record 66 twenty years earlier. It was their attack, led aggressively by Channel Islander Len Duquemin, that took the eye, but the defence was a vital part of the jigsaw. It featured

Arthur Rowe (extreme left, back row) proudly poses with his Push and Run Spurs after they had captured the League championship in 1951. Alf Ramsey and Bill Nicholson, who would go on to become master managers, sit alongside each other on the left of the second row.

the safe hands and acrobatics of goalkeeper Ted Ditchburn, the towering presence of centre-half Harry Clarke, the perfect balance of full-back partners Alf Ramsey and Arthur Willis, and two of the finest half-backs in the League in Bill Nicholson and skipper Ronnie Burgess.

Eddie Baily's inch-perfect passing from midfield was a key factor as Spurs took apart the best defences in the land, scoring seven goals against Newcastle, six against Stoke, five against West Brom and defending champions Portsmouth and four in three of the first four matches of the season.

Push and run became more like push and punish. It was wonderful to watch, provided you were not the team on the receiving end.

In my privileged position as chief football reporter with the *Express*, I was able to ask Arthur Rowe, Alf Ramsey and Bill Nicholson who was the most influential player in that push and run team. Each answered without hesitation: "Ron Burgess."

Bill Nick even went so far as to add: "Ronnie was the greatest player ever to pull on a Tottenham shirt. Yes, with a gun to my head I would even have to put him ahead of Dave Mackay."

That was some admission, and when I asked Ronnie Burgess the same question while he was managing Watford in the 1960s he told me in his lilting Welsh accent: "There was no individual more important than the rest. We had that vital all-for-one-and-one-for-all spirit, which I suppose was a spill-over from the war. We'd all been in the forces during the war and knew the importance of teamwork. If you have to single out one man, then it has to be Arthur Rowe. It was his philosophy that we followed. Keep it simple, keep it quick, keep the ball on the ground."

Legend has it that Burgess, a powerhouse of a player, trod on every blade of grass on every pitch on which he played. He was at left-half, with Bill Nicholson a perfect balance with his more disciplined and careful approach on the right.

Behind Nicholson was the immaculate Alf Ramsey, a model of calm and consistency. Tommy Docherty once said spitefully of him that he had seen milk turn faster, but it has to be remembered that Alf was thirty by the time of the push and run era and had learned the art of conserving his energy by clever positioning and intelligent marking.

Arthur Willis, workmanlike at left-back, was an ideal foil for the more artistic Ramsey, with Charlie Withers as a more-than-capable stand-in. Harry Clarke – recruited from Lovells Athletic in the Southern League – stood oak tree solid in the middle of the defence. He had a great understanding with goalkeeper Ted Ditchburn, who would have won dozens more than his six England caps had it not been for the powerful presence of Frank Swift.

The attack piston on which Spurs fired was provided by effervescent Eddie Baily, the Cockney 'Cheeky Chappie' who proudly patrolled in midfield with a Napoleonic air of authority. His uncanny ability to lay a pass on a handkerchief made goal scoring much easier for twin strikers Len 'The Duke' Duquemin and the often lethal Les Bennett.

These were the wonderful days of flying wingers and they did not come much better or more of a handful for full backs than Sonny Walters and Les Medley. Both were encouraged to make their touchline dashes by fans belting out choruses of the following song based on the old Bing Crosby classic McNamara's Band (which was first composed in Limerick in 1885 to mark the fact that the St Mary's Drum and Fife Band featured four McNamara brothers; not a lot of people *want* to know that!):

We are Spurs Supporters and we love to watch them play
We go to all the home games and we go to those away
With us supporters following them we know they will do right
We loudly cheer when they appear, the lads in blue and white

We're very proud of our football ground it's known throughout the land
And while we wait for the game to start we listen to the band
And when we see the teams come out you should hear the roar
We know it won't be long before the Spurs they start to score

The ref his whistle proudly blows, the linesmen wave their flags
The Duke is ready to kick off as he hitches up his bags
We cheer Sonny Walters as he toddles down the line
And the ball like magic is in the net and makes us all feel fine

There's Ronnie Burgess with his skill holding up the line
With Alf, Bill, Harry and Charlie way up there behind
And not forgetting good old Ted whose hands are sure and strong
And Eddie and the Leslies who are always up-a-long

And when the game is over, when the game is through
We cheer the winners off the field and the gallant losers too
The Cockerel proudly wags his tail, he gave the Spurs their name
In honour of the Lilywhites who always play the game

Now come on all you supporters and join our merry band
No matter what your age is, we'll take you by the hand
We'll pin a cockerel on your chest, it shows the world that we
Are members of that loyal band, the S.S.C.!!!!

There was something almost inevitable about Tottenham's great escape from the Second Division in the early weeks of the 1949-50 season. There was an attitude about the team that set them apart from the opposition; it was almost as if they were strutting their stuff and saying: "With this sort of football, we deserve a place at the top table." Yes, there was a touch of arrogance about it, and much of the cocksureness emanated from pass master Eddie Baily. A fellow East Ender of mine and an old and treasured mate, Eddie spent a couple of wind-down seasons at Leyton Orient when I was sports editor of the local paper. We used to chinwag for hours about the "good old days," and he described the push and run side as "the perfect football machine."

Never one to hold back on an opinion or three, Eddie told me:

❛We were far too good for the Second Division, and played our way to promotion with ease. I remember we were top of the table from September and had a run of twenty-three matches without defeat. These days I suppose I would be called a playmaker, but then I was just a good old-fashioned deep-lying inside-forward. My job was to provide the passes for the goalscorers, and I think you'll find I had a foot in the majority of the goals we scored. That's not me being big headed. That was fact.

An important aspect is that we had a very good dressing-room spirit. There were no stars. We all took equal praise when winning, and shared the blame if things went wrong. Max Miller was the big comedian of the time, and I was given his nickname 'Cheeky Chappie' because I was always clowning

We were the thinking man's team. Players like Alf, Bill Nick and Ronnie Burgess were obsessed with tactics, and of course dear Arthur Rowe was the man who led us with clear and concise instructions. There was no mumbo jumbo. We just got on with playing the game in a simple direct way that bewildered the opponents.❜

A goal that Eddie scored against Huddersfield in the 1951-52 season is still talked about by fans who know their Tottenham history. His corner kick whacked against the back of the referee, knocking him to the floor. He collected the rebound (illegally touching the ball twice) and crossed for Duquemin to head into the net. The ref, still scrambling to his feet, awarded a goal that gave Spurs victory and pushed Huddersfield towards relegation. Eddie was to feature again with Spurs as he started a new life as a coach. More of that later. Back to the team he helped make tick.

By Christmas 1950 they were top of the First Division following a sequence of eight successive victories. Among their devastating performances was a 7-0 destruction of FA Cup giants Newcastle United. They achieved that without skipper Ronnie Burgess, who sat in the stand nursing an injury. "That was the finest exhibition of football I have

Ron Burgess, skipper and midfield motivator of the Push and Run Spurs

ever seen," he said later. "It was only by becoming a spectator that I realized just how special this side was. We paralysed Newcastle with our push and run tactics that a lot of so-called experts had said would not work in the First Division."

Sitting on the touchline bench was Arthur's schoolboy son, Graham, who recalled: "Tottenham played football out of this world against Newcastle. If there had been television cameras around in those days, they would still be showing the match today as a classic and as an example of how to play the game to perfection.

"My father was a modest man who did not like or seek the limelight. He was happy to let his team do the talking for him on the pitch, and they were very eloquent. Anybody who saw that push and run side will, I know, never forget it."

In this truly golden season White Hart Lane attendances averaged 55,486 as Tottenham captured their first League championship. They notched 82 goals and were beaten only seven times. In their post-Championship campaign it looked as if they were going to lift the title again as they finished like trains, taking 20 points from the last dozen matches. But Matt Busby's Manchester United hung on to win the crown after finishing runners-up four times in the previous five years. Tottenham beat Chelsea 2-0 on the final day of the season for the considerable consolation of pipping Arsenal to second place.

It was the FA Cup that brought Tottenham greatest success the following season, when they finished an unimpressive tenth in the First Division. They battled through to the FA Cup semi-final after surviving four away ties. Waiting for them at Villa Park, as in 1948, were Matthews/Mortensen-motivated Blackpool.

Victory was handed to Blackpool on a plate by, of all people, safe-as-houses Alf Ramsey, who in a rare moment of carelessness played a back pass intended for Ted Ditchburn into the path of Blackpool goal poacher Jackie Mudie. It became a skeleton in Alf's closet, and I hardly dared mention it in the many hours we spent together during the 1960s. He once confided, after a G and T too many, that the memory of it kept him awake on many nights, playing over and over again what he *should* have done. But his poker face never conveyed to the Tottenham fans that he was even more devastated than they were. Alf was always harder to read than a closed book.

Remarkably, Spurs managed to produce their flowing football on a White Hart Lane pitch that was little more than a mud-heap during the winter months and was a disgrace when compared with John Over's original billiard table surface. The erection of stands right around the ground was good news for the spectators but not for the groundsmen, who were dismayed to find their grass refusing to grow properly without full sunlight. The players joined Arthur Rowe in pleading for a surface suited to their on-the-carpet passing style. When the pitch was finally dug up in 1952, workmen were amazed to find the remains of the old nursery so lovingly tended by George Beckwith. There was a concrete water container, snaking rows of iron piping and greenhouse foundations.

The following year floodlights were erected, set high on four corner poles. Racing

Club de Paris accepted an invitation to become the first visitors to appear under the lights and were beaten 5-3 in what was something of an exhibition match. Spectators complained about dark patches on some poorly lit parts of the pitch, and the lights were upgraded in 1957. This meant a transfer of the cockerel – quiet, noble witness of all comings and goings at The Lane – from the West Stand to the East Stand.

Unfortunately, the stress and strain of managing Spurs took its toll on Arthur Rowe and he reluctantly had to stand down in 1954, with the team he had created, cajoled and championed showing the sign of advancing years. His last signing for the club was a player who was to become a Lane legend – Danny Blanchflower, bought from Aston Villa for £30,000 and in Arthur's expert estimation the perfect player to carry on the push and run philosophy.

Push and run was poetry in motion, and it was Arthur's lasting legacy. They should build a statue to him at The Lane in memory of the man who pumped the pride and the passion back into Tottenham.

Jimmy Anderson, a life-long member of the Tottenham backroom team since 1908, was put in charge when Arthur became ill and the Rowe magic was suddenly missing.

The challenge of management had come too late for Jimmy, and he struggled to motivate his wearying stars, although he had a 1955-56 FA Cup semi-final place to brighten the gloom that had dropped over White Hart Lane. This time Spurs went down 1-0 to Don Revie-inspired Manchester City, again at Villa Park.

Anderson publicly fell out with the articulate Blanchflower, who had his own strong views about how the game should be played and the club managed. He made it clear that in his opinion Jimmy was not the man for the job. His candid views upset a lot of people, but Danny was one of those people who could never be less than honest

There were signs of better things to come when big Maurice 'The Ox' Norman signed from Norwich as reinforcement for a creaking defence, and another beefy giant – Bobby Smith – arrived from Chelsea to help power Tottenham to runners-up place in the 1956-57 title race. Bill Nicholson, who was virtually running the playing side of the club as Anderson battled with poor health, coached the team while also holding the job of assistant coach to England manager Walter Winterbottom. It was Bill Nick's clever and suffocating tactics during the summer of 1958 that had earned England a goalless draw against Pelé-propelled Brazil in the World Cup finals in Sweden.

On the morning of Saturday October 11 1958 – a date that should shine out from every Tottenham calendar – Bill Nicholson was officially appointed manager in succession to the fatigued Anderson.

In the afternoon he was given the most remarkable start there has ever been to a manager's career. Providing the opposition were Everton, who were struggling three from the bottom of the First Division, a point behind sixteenth-placed Spurs. The first decision Nicholson made in his new role was to recall Tottenham's impish inside-

The Way We Were. Tottenham's mighty centre-forward Bobby Smith lets Wolves goalkeeper Malcolm Finlayson know he's around in the days when players could touch goalies without risk of being sent to The Tower. Look, The Lane is jam-packed.

forward Tommy Harmer, known to the White Hart Lane fans as 'Harmer the Charmer.' But that afternoon Everton found him more like 'The Harmer' as he pulled them apart with an astounding individual performance. He had a hand – or rather a well-directed foot – in nine goals and scored one himself as Everton were sunk without trace under a flood of goals. The final scoreline was 10-4. It might easily have been 15-8!

Harmer was the 'Tom Thumb' character of football. He stood just 5ft 2in tall and was a bantamweight who looked as if he could be blown away by a strong wind. But he had mesmeric control of the ball and when conditions suited him could dominate a match with his passing and dribbling. Born in Hackney on February 2 1928, he joined Tottenham from amateur club Finchley in 1951 and over the next eight years played 205 League games and scored 47 goals.

For the record, Bill Nicholson's first selection as Spurs manager:

Hollowbread, Baker, Hopkins, Blanchflower, Ryden, Iley, Medwin, Harmer, Smith, Stokes, Robb.

There was a hint of what was to come in the opening moments when Spurs took the lead through Alfie Stokes after an inch-perfect diagonal pass from Harmer had split the Everton defence. The Merseysiders steadied themselves and equalised eight minutes later when Jimmy Harris side footed in a Dave Hickson centre.

The unfortunate Albert Dunlop, deputising in goal for the injured first-choice 'keeper Jimmy O'Neill, then suffered a nightmare thirty minutes as Spurs ruthlessly smashed five goals past him through skipper Bobby Smith (2), schoolmaster George Robb, Stokes again and Terry Medwin.

The foundation for all the goals was being laid in midfield where Harmer and Danny Blanchflower, both masters of ball control, were in complete command.

Jimmy Harris gave Everton fleeting hope of a revival with a headed goal to make it 6-2 just after half-time, but bulldozing Bobby Smith took his personal haul to four and the irrepressible Harmer helped himself to a goal that was as spectacular as any scored during this gourmet feast.

Bobby Collins lost possession just outside the penalty area, and the ball bobbled in front of Harmer. He struck it on the half volley from twenty yards and watched almost in disbelief as the ball rocketed into the roof of the net. It was the first time Tommy had scored a League goal from outside the penalty area.

Everton refused to surrender and the industrious Harris completed his hat-trick from a centre by dashing centre-forward Dave Hickson. Then Bobby Collins, just an inch taller than Harmer, showed that this was a magical match for the wee people when he hammered in a 25-yard drive as both teams crazily pushed everybody forward.

All the goals were scored by forwards until Spurs centre-half John Ryden, limping on the wing, scrambled in Tottenham's tenth goal – the fourteenth of the match – in the closing minutes. Bill Nicholson, finding it hard to believe what he had witnessed, was close to speechless. It was quite some time later when he told me:

> 'I have never believed in fairy tales in football, but this came close to making me change my mind. In many ways it was a bad advertisement for football because so many of the goals were the result of slip-shod defensive play. But I have to admit it was magnificent entertainment. Little Tommy Harmer played the game of his life. On his day he was as clever a player as I have ever seen, but he was too often handicapped by his small physique. On this day, he was a giant.'

Jimmy Harris commented:

> 'It was a good news, bad news day for me. I was able to tell people that I had scored a hat-trick against Spurs, and would then mumble the bad news that we had lost 10-4. It's no exaggeration to say we could have had at least four more goals. I don't know who were the more bewildered by it all – the players or the spectators, who got tremendous value for their money. Tommy Harmer was the man who won it for Tottenham. It was as if he had the ball on a piece of string.'

Hero Harmer said:

> 'I had been out of the League team for the previous four matches and was half expecting to be left out again when I reported for the match with Everton. But Bill Nick told me I was in, and it became one of those games when just everything went right for me. I particularly remember my goal because it was about the only time I ever scored from that sort of range.'

As Tommy came off the pitch to a standing ovation, he said to Bill Nicholson: "I hope you're not going to expect ten goals from us every week, Boss!"

Only three players from the Spurs team that scored the knockout ten goals survived as regular members of the Double-winning side of 1960-61 – right-back Peter Baker, artistic right-half Danny Blanchflower and centre-forward Bobby Smith. The fourteen goals equalled the aggregate First Division record set in 1892 when Aston Villa annihilated Accrington Stanley 12-2.

This was just the start. The Glory-Glory days were around the corner.

IT was the summer of 1960 when eloquent Irishman Danny 'The Blarneyman' Blanchflower told veteran Tottenham chairman Fred Bearman: "We're going to win the League for you this coming season, Mr Chairman, and for good measure we will throw in the FA Cup, too."

The elderly Spurs boardroom boss could be forgiven for thinking it was a piece of Blanchflower blarney. He was often using his wit and imagination to embroider stories until they were into fairyland. Mr Bearman was older than the century, and he knew better than most that the League and Cup double had become football's "impossible dream".

It had been beyond the reach of Herbert Chapman's great pre-war Arsenal and Huddersfield teams, too difficult a target for an Everton side fuelled by the goals of Dixie Dean and then Tommy Lawton, and a bridge too far for the smooth, sophisticated Spurs push and run side of the early 1950s. And just in the previous three years Wolves and then Manchester United had got within shooting distance of the two supreme prizes, only to fall at the final hurdle.

Mr Bearman wanted to believe his club captain but must have harboured deep doubts. Superstitious Spurs supporters, buoyed by the fact that there was a '1' in the upcoming year, also wanted to believe that a major trophy was coming their way. The League championship? Possibly. The FA Cup? Maybe. Both of them? Not a hope. The build-up involved in trying to capture the two trophies needed such contrasting preparations that it was too easy to fall between the two and finish empty-handed.

The race for the League title was a marathon that called for stamina, consistency, and a total commitment to trying to win week in and week out. The FA Cup was like a sudden-death sprint through a minefield with no knowing what explosions waited around the corner. The tripwire could be hidden at such unfashionable soccer outposts as Walsall (ask Arsenal), Bournemouth (ask Manchester United and Spurs), Yeovil (ask Sunderland), or Worcester (ask Liverpool).

No team in the 20th Century had achieved the elusive double, but Danny Blanchflower was *not* joking. He was quietly insisting that it could be done, and set about convincing

Super Spurs have just clinched the Double and Danny Blanchflower is on top of the world – riding on the shoulders of Peter Baker and Bobby Smith. Also in the picture Cliff Jones (left), Bill Brown, Terry Dyson, the back of Les Allen's head, John White, Dave Mackay and Big Maurice Norman. Only Ron Henry is missing.

anybody in earshot at White Hart Lane during the build-up to the season. As he spoke from a position of responsibility and influence in his role as Spurs captain he had to be listened to, but few really shared his belief at the start of what was to become an historic 1960-61 season.

When Spurs set a new First Division record by winning their opening eleven matches on the trot (or more at a smooth canter) Blanchflower found his was no longer a voice in the wilderness. Good judges began to wonder if – as Danny had been insisting from day one – this could be the year for the Double. Spurs were looking *that* good.

Aston Villa were crushed by six goals, Manchester United by four, and mighty Wolves were hammered by four goals on their own territory at Molineux. They were victories that brought gasps of astonishment and admiration right around the country, because Man United and Wolves were still living on their reputations of the previous decade of being the kings of English football.

It was records all the way as Tottenham romped to the League championship with eight points to spare over runners-up Sheffield Wednesday. Their 31 victories was a League record, as was their total of sixteen away wins. The 66 points collected with style and flamboyance equalled the First Division record set by Herbert Chapman's Arsenal in 1930-31.

While winning the First Division marathon they also managed to survive in the minefield of the FA Cup, getting a scare in the sixth round at Sunderland, but winning the replay 6-0 at White Hart Lane.

The Final against a Leicester City team handicapped by injury problems was something of an anti-climax, but Spurs managed to win 2-0 to prove Danny Blanchflower as good a prophet as he was a footballing captain. Bobby Smith and Terry Dyson scored the victory-clinching goals past the goalkeeper who was to become a legend, Gordon Banks.

On the way to the League title, all five of Tottenham's first-choice goal-hunting forwards reached double figures – Bobby Smith (28), Les Allen (23), Cliff Jones (15), John White (13) and Terry Dyson (12).

It was in midfield where they won most matches thanks to the combination of skill and strength springing from skipper Danny Blanchflower, schemer John White and thunder-tackler Dave Mackay. Blanchflower was the poet of the side, Mackay the buccaneering pirate, and White the prince of passers.

Jimmy Anderson had fought with the influential and intellectual Blanchflower; Bill Nicholson had wisely forged an understanding with him, and took him into his confidence. He restored the artistic Irish playmaker at right-half in the shirt he had worn with such distinction in the push and run era, and he gave him back the captaincy that he had relinquished under the Anderson regime. It was one of Nicholson's qualities as a manager that he could listen as well as put his own theories in an uncomplicated way that did not bamboozle his players.

Nicholson had always been an admirer of the Scottish school of football and went north of the border to sign three players that he felt could put the finishing touch to the team he had inherited: goalkeeper Bill Brown, left-half Dave Mackay and inside-right John White.

In John White, Nicholson had bought a pulse for his team. In Mackay, he had purchased a heart.

Cynics could sneer that Nicholson was a chequebook manager. But Tottenham's money could easily have been squandered if handled by a less discerning manager. He always spent with care and caution, almost as if the money was coming out of his own pocket.

There has rarely, if ever, been a more conscientious and caring manager. He matched even fanatical Wolves boss Stan Cullis for dedication to duty. It used to be whispered at Tottenham that he was the one man who could get away with bigamy. He had one marriage to his lovely wife, Grace, and another one to Tottenham Hotspur. So that he could always be on call he was content to live in a modest little terraced house within goal-kicking distance of White Hart Lane. Grace used to cycle to the shops, and Bill often used to walk to the ground.

Harry Miller, my best mate in my Fleet Street days, was my rival on the *Daily Mirror* while I was chasing headlines and deadlines on the *Daily Express*. Every Sunday morning we used to call into the Tottenham ground together for an hour-long natter with Bill, who used to be in his office catching up on paperwork.

To the outsider, Bill Nick was the epitome of a dour Yorkshireman – tough, guarded, stubborn and unsmiling. But anybody able to break through his defensive barrier found a warm, sensitive man with a nicely tuned sense of humour.

The eighth of nine children, he gave up working in a Scarborough laundry to move south to join Spurs in 1936 as a sixteen-year-old groundstaff boy at a wage of £2 a week. It is legend how he served the club for more than sixty years, and eventually had the approach road to White Hart Lane named after him: Bill Nicholson Way.

He broke down and cried at the wedding of one of his two daughters. "I suddenly realized I had not seen the girls grow up," he said. He had given his life to football in general, and Tottenham in particular.

A tidy and determined player, Bill Nick was treated less than kindly by the England selectors, who awarded him just one cap against Portugal. He scored with his first kick in international football yet never got a second chance in an England shirt. The ever-consistent Wolves captain Billy Wright was recalled, and Nicholson joined the one-cap wonder club. His polished, yet at times pedestrian performances were just not

Bill Nicholson, The Master, at home

eye-catching; fellow professionals, however, looked up to him as a player's player.

"Bill didn't take the eye of the spectators," said Eddie Baily. "But his team-mates knew he was doing all the right things for the team. Alf Ramsey was creaking a bit behind him, and Bill was often his legs, getting him out of trouble. He was the most dedicated footballer I ever had the joy of playing with."

Eddie and Bill later teamed up again when Baily was appointed Tottenham coach following the sudden death of Harry Evans, who had been Nicholson's trusted and talented right hand man in his first three years in charge at The Lane.

When I asked Bill how he felt about never getting another England call-up, he said with typical shining honesty: "I understood. Billy Wright was a better player than me."

Bill Nick always shunned personal publicity, and he used to wince when he saw the new cult developing of managers taking a stage that once belonged exclusively to the players. He used to be at his most articulate in defeat, cutting down any players he felt were getting an inflated opinon of their own ability. In victory, he was content to let his team's performance do the talking for him.

He could be brutally candid, and never gave praise that had not been earned. His players found his compliments hard to come by because he was a perfectionist who demanded the highest level of performance at all times. He was not interested enough in self-projection as a manager to earn the public's affection, but in the autumn of his life – after being reinstated at the club following a clumsily handled end to his managerial career – he became the father figure at Tottenham, and was warmly regarded by everybody who had close contact with him during those 'Glory, Glory' days.

There is still a campaign going on to get him a posthumous knighthood, for which he was shamefully overlooked during his life. But all those well-intentioned petitioners are wasting their time and energy. If they give one to Bill Nick, what do they do about the likes of Bill Shankly, Arthur Rowe, Jock Stein, Stan Cullis ... I could go on and on. Bill would hate the fuss.

His greatest strength as a manager was his tactical understanding of a game that he always believed should be kept simple. Remember, he had been heavily influenced by first Peter McWilliam and then Arthur Rowe. While too many coaches were trying to turn football into a sort of master-class chess, he kept it more like draughts. His teams played football that was easy to understand and beautiful to watch. And it was also stunningly effective.

The Nicholson record speaks for itself: League and FA Cup double (1960-61), FA Cup (1961, 1962 and 1967), European Cup Winners' Cup (1963), Uefa Cup (1972), League Cup (1971 and 1973). But in a way it was all downhill after the Double Year. He was like a man who had fallen in love with the most beautiful girl in the world, and spent the rest of his years trying to find an exact copy. He never quite managed to recreate a team on a par with the 'Super Spurs' of 1960-61.

This was Bill Nick on that Tottenham team in a moment of rosy reflection:

> 'Everything was right. The balance of the team. The attitude of the
> players. We managed to find the perfect blend and everybody gave 100
> per cent in effort and enthusiasm. We had the sort of understanding and
> cohesion that you find in only the finest teams, and we tried to keep our
> football as simple as possible – imaginative but simple. I kept pushing
> an old theory: 'When you're not in possession, get into position.' The
> man *without* the ball was important, because he could make things
> happen by getting into the right place at the right time. Running off the
> ball was as vital as running with it. Simple, simple, simple.'

His Double team was never defence minded – as is revealed by the fact that they
conceded 50 League goals on their way to the First Division championship. But they
were sufficiently steady at the back to allow heavy concentration on attack. Goalkeeper
Bill Brown, one of the more efficient Scottish goalkeepers, had excellent reactions
and a safe pair of hands, which made up for his occasional positioning misjudgement.
He had a good rapport with the 6 foot 1 inch Norfolk-born giant Maurice Norman,
a dominating centre-half who won 23 England caps. He was flanked in a fluid 3-3-4
formation by full-backs Peter Baker and Ron Henry, both of whom were disciplined
and determined and had unyielding competitive attitudes.

Dave Mackay was always quick to take up a defensive position alongside Norman
when needed and his tackles were like a clap of thunder. They used to say in the game
that anybody who felt the full weight of a Mackay challenge would go home feeling as
if he was still with them. Danny Blanchflower was not noted for his tackling but was
a shrewd enough positional player to manage to get himself between the opponent in
possession and the goal. He would defend with the instincts of a sheepdog, cornering
the opposition by steering them into cul-de-sacs rather than biting them. He left that
to the Great Mackay.

The Tottenham attacking movements in that Double year were full of fluency and
fire, a blaze lit in midfield by three of the greatest players to come together in one club
team (up there with Best-Law-and-Charlton and Moore-Hurst-Peters). Blanchflower,
an inspiring skipper for Northern Ireland as well as Tottenham, was the brains of the
team who had an instinctive feel for the game and an ability to lift the players around
him with measured passes and intelligent tactical commands.

He was the sort of confident captain who would sort things out on the pitch in the heat

Dave Mackay leaps into the new 1962-63 season at the Tottenham training ground at Cheshunt, watched by Cliff Jones, Ron Henry and Jimmy Greaves.

of battle rather than wait until the after-match dressing-room inquest.

Mackay, the Scot with an in-built swagger and a he-man's barrel chest, was the heart of the side, always playing with enormous enthusiasm, power and panache. John White, an artist of an inside-forward in the best traditions of purist Scottish football, was the eyes of the team, seeing openings that escaped the vision of lesser players and dismantling defences with precision passes and blind-side runs that earned him the nickname, 'The Ghost of White Hart Lane'. This talented trio were essentially buccaneering, forward-propelling players, but were sufficiently geared to team discipline to help out in defence when necessary.

Spearheading the attack in that memorable start to the swinging 'sixties was burly, bulldozing centre-forward Bobby Smith, a 15-cap England centre-forward who mixed subtle skill with awesome strength. He was the main marksman in the Double year with 33 League and Cup goals.

The mighty Smith was in harness with Les Allen, father of future Spurs hero Clive. He was a clever and under-rated player who was the odd man out when Jimmy Greaves arrived the following season. Les contributed 23 goals to Tottenham's championship season. Smith, Allen and Greaves all started their careers with Chelsea.

Out on the wings Spurs had Terry Dyson – tiny, quick and taunting, the son of a Yorkshire jockey – and the marvellous Cliff Jones, one of the 'Untouchables' of Welsh international football, who could take the tightest defences apart with his fast, diagonal runs. In reserve Spurs had players of the calibre of Welsh terrier Terry Medwin, fearless Frank Saul, cultured wing-half Tony Marchi and utility player John Smith, all of whom made occasional appearances during that golden season.

Danny Blanchflower, who became a colleague of mine on *Express* newspapers when he seamlessly followed playing the game with writing about it, told me:

> ❛When I predicted to our chairman before the start of the season that we would achieve the double I said it quietly and confidently … but not confidentially, because I wanted to get the message out. It was not a boast but a belief. I am a great believer that confidence, like fear, can be contagious, and I wanted our players to catch my belief.
>
> "I was impressed by the individual ability running through our squad, also its teamwork, and its whole personality. You could say we were one of the last of the good teams in which players were allowed to do things their own way, without restrictions from the coaching manual.
>
> "I sensed people grew to like us because we were a cosmopolitan team as well as a very good one. We had Englishmen, Welshmen, Scots and Irishmen, big guys, little guys, fat men and thin men. Also, we scored

goals in so many different ways. I know if I had been a spectator I would have wanted to watch us. We were exciting, explosive and – virtually throughout the season – exceptional.**'**

So that I give individual credit to the team that did the Double, I reproduce here a Who's Who of Tottenham's team composed in partnership with Jimmy Greaves, who was top First Division scorer in the 1960-61 season with 41 goals – uh, for Chelsea ...

BILL BROWN

Born Dundee October 8 1931. Tottenham goalkeeper in 222 League matches between 1959 and 1965 after joining them from his local Dundee club during Bill Nicholson's first season as manager. He was capped 28 times by Scotland, and wound down his career with Northampton Town. Throughout his career he worked part-time on building up a printing business, eventually emigrating to Canada where he passed on in 2004.

> GREAVSIE ASSESSMENT: "As is well known, I rarely have a good word to say about Scottish goalkeepers, but Bill was an exception. He had a good pair of hands, was very agile, and had the courage of a lion. There were few to match him on his day, but he was known to have his dodgy moments, particularly dealing with crosses when he sometimes got caught in two minds as to whether to leave his goal-line. He had a good rapport with centre-half Maurice Norman, and between them they usually managed to clear the danger. I remember that he was often preferred to Pat Jennings when the big feller first joined us from Watford. Pat was struggling to conquer his nerves in those early days before he became one of the all-time great goalkeepers. Until he settled down, Bill Nick had to keep calling on faithful old Brownie. He rarely let Spurs down."

PETER BAKER

Born Hampstead, London, December 10 1931. Played 299 League games for Spurs, and scored three goals. Signed for Tottenham from Enfield in 1952 at the age of 20, during the Arthur Rowe era and served the club for nearly 14 years. After eventually losing his place in defence to Cyril Knowles (who was more comfortable on the left), he wound down his career in South Africa with Durban City. Educated in Arsenal territory at Southgate County School, he became a regular in the Bill Nicholson Double side and was the only player in the defence not rewarded with an international cap.

The historic Double winners, back row left to right: Bill Brown, Peter Baker, Ron Henry, Danny Blanchflower, Maurice Norman, Dave Mackay; front row: Cliff Jones, John White, Bobby Smith, Les Allen, Terry Dyson.

GREAVSIE ASSESSMENT: "Peter was very much under-estimated. His hard, uncompromising style balanced perfectly with the more skilled approach of his partner Ron Henry. I can never recall a winger giving him a roasting, and this was in an era when every team carried two wingers playing wide on the flanks. He could be tough to the point of brutal when necessary and many's the time he ended dangerous raids with perfectly timed tackles. Fair haired and very upright, Peter had been well schooled in the Push and Run methods and always tried to use the ball positively by finding a better placed team-mate."

RON HENRY

Born Shoreditch, August 17 1934. Played 247 League matches for Tottenham between 1954 and 1965 before becoming a highly regarded youth coach. He was at left-back in all 42 of Tottenham's League matches in the 1960-61 season. Early in his career with Redbourne he had been a skilful left winger, and then switched to wing-half and later, on turning professional with Tottenham, settled down at left back. He made his League debut at centre-half against Huddersfield in 1955, but it was not until the 1959-60 season that he took over the No 3 shirt from Welsh international Mel Hopkins. Capped once, in Sir Alf Ramsey's first match as England manager against France in 1963.

GREAVSIE ASSESSMENT: "I would rate Ron among the top six left-backs I have played with or against, and that includes my international experience with England. Ron would always use the ball intelligently and was a master of positional play. He and Peter Baker went together like bacon and eggs. It was a pity that Ron got his one and only cap in Alf Ramsey's nightmare opening match. We got trounced 5-2 by France, and Ron was unlucky to be one of the players who carried the can. He deserved a longer run with the international team."

DANNY BLANCHFLOWER

Born Belfast, February 10 1926. Played 337 League games for Tottenham between 1954 and 1963 after service with Glentoran, Barnsley and Aston Villa. One of the most creative and authoritative players ever to set foot on a football pitch, he was a born leader who, as well as skippering Spurs through their 'glory-glory' years, also captained the Northern Ireland team that reached the quarter-finals of the 1958 World Cup. Danny was twice voted the Footballer of the Year before a recurring knee injury forced his

Going down Memory Lane, two great Tottenham thinkers. Bill Nicholson and his faithful skipper Danny Blanchflower are pictured together here in 1987.

his retirement in 1963. He became a respected broadcaster and journalist with an acid wit and something fresh to say on every subject. He managed the Northern Ireland team and had a brief but rarely satisfactory reign as Chelsea manager. His *Sunday Express* columns were always readable and perceptive. Danny passed on in 1993.

GREAVSIE ASSESSMENT: "Danny was the poet of Spurs. He gave the team style and was a captain in every sense of the word, inspiring the players around him with his almost arrogant performances and lifting them with words of wisdom. His contribution to the team was as important as Bill Nick's, with an influence that went much farther and deeper than his performances on the pitch. He was the dressing-room tactician, the training ground theorist, the man who talked up for players during moments of crisis and misunderstanding. And what a beautiful player. He rivalled even my old England team-mate Johnny Haynes for firing a pass through the heart of a defence. He was a great reader of the game, and had an in-built radar system that guided him to the right places at the right times. He could lift and motivate players before vital matches with Chuchillian-class rallying speeches and had a wit that was as sharp as a razorblade. The man was different class."

MAURICE NORMAN

Born Mulbarton, Norfolk, May 8 1934. Played 357 League matches for Spurs between 1955 and 1965, following one full season with his local club, Norwich City. He was England's centre-half in 23 international matches and was shortlisted for World Cup duty in 1966 when his career was finished by a broken leg received in a Spurs friendly against the Hungarian national team. At 6ft 1in and 13 stone, he stood like an immovable mountain in the middle of the Spurs defence. He had joined Tottenham as a full-back, but it was his switch to centre-half that established him as one of the most reliable defenders in the League. Made his international debut against Peru in 1962, and was England centre-half throughout the 1962 World Cup finals (Brazil eliminated them in the quarter-finals).

> GREAVSIE ASSESSMENT: "We used to call him 'Big Monty' or 'Mighty Mo'. He was an ox of a man. Big in build, big in heart and big in personality, with a lovely slow 'have-you-got-a-loight-boy' drawl. Strangely enough he was not that commanding in the air, but he was so tall that he usually got to the high balls before rival forwards had started jumping. He helped make goalkeeper Bill Brown's job easier with his expert covering and support play. On those occasions when the usually dependable Brown made a mess of a cross you would usually find Big Mo thumping the ball away. There have been more polished and skilful centre-halves than Maurice, but I have yet to come across one as physically strong as the likeable Swede-basher from deepest Norfolk. But for tragically breaking a leg in a meaningless friendly match I am sure he would have been England's centre-half in the 1966 World Cup finals and Jack Charlton might never have got his chance. That's football for you. Full of cruel twists and lucky breaks."

DAVE MACKAY

Born Edinburgh, November 14 1934. Scored 42 goals in 268 League appearances for Tottenham after joining them from Hearts for £30,000 in March 1959. His entire career in football was about winning. He was capped at schoolboy, under-23 and full international level by Scotland; while with Hearts he won Scottish League Cup, Scottish

Cup and Scottish League championship medals; then with Spurs he collected three FA Cup winners' medals, a League Championship medal and a European Cup Winners' Cup medal, although missing the final because of injury. Later, with Derby County, he won a Second Division Championship medal; and as manager he steered Derby to the First Division title in 1974-75. He also managed Swindon, Nottingham Forest and Walsall before becoming a successful coach in the Middle East. His greatest victory was over adversity. He twice made comebacks after breaking a leg. Not for nothing was he known as the 'Miracle Man' of football.

> GREAVSIE ASSESSMENT: "If somebody put a knife to my throat and insisted that I name *the* greatest player in that marvellous Spurs side it would have to be Dave Mackay. He had just about everything: power, skill, drive, stamina, the sort of heroism that would have won medals in wartime, and – above all – infectious enthusiasm. Power? I used to shudder at some of his tackles on rival players, and he used to go in just as hard after twice breaking a leg. I often offered up a silent prayer of thanks that he was with me and not against me. He also had delicate skills to go with his enormous strength. Bobby Moore was one of the few defenders I could think of who could rival him for ball control in a tight situation. Dave was the king of the first-time pass, drilling the ball through to a team-mate as accurately and casually as if in a training session, despite being under pressure from an opponent. Dave took over from Danny as Spurs captain, and I can safely say that I played under the two greatest skippers that ever carried a ball on to the pitch. I have never known anybody have such physical presence on a football field as the Great Mackay. You could almost hear the skirl of the pipes as he stuck out his barrel chest and led his team into battle. There were times when he frightened me to death with his take-no-prisoners attitude, and I was on *his* side! There will never be another like him."

TERRY MEDWIN

Born Swansea, September 25 1932. Scored 65 goals in 197 League matches for Spurs between 1956 and 1962, after establishing himself as a Welsh international winger while with his hometown club, Swansea. He was capped 30 times by Wales and might have played many more games for Spurs but for a succession of injuries that finally forced his premature retirement after he had helped Tottenham retain the FA Cup at Wembley in 1962. Played 14 League games during the 'Double' campaign. He later became a top-flight coach, notably with Fulham.

The Tottenham players having a ball in summer training in 1963, left to right: Tony Marchi, Greavsie, Peter Baker, Danny Blanchflower, Dave Mackay (covered), probably John White, Bobby Smith, Terry Dyson and Cliff Jones.

GREAVSIE ASSESSMENT: "Terry came out of that marvellous Swansea finishing school that also produced players of the calibre of the Allchurch brothers, Mel Charles, Mel Nurse and, of course, my old mate Cliffie Jones. Terry was a very correct player, a student of the game who did everything with care and accuracy. His ball skill was of the highest order; he was always a menace to defences with his quick changes of pace, and he used to get up well to head the ball. It is a measure of the strength in depth of that Spurs squad that he was not a regular first-team player, yet was an automatic choice for Wales."

TERRY DYSON

Born Malton, North Yorkshire, November 29 1934. Played 184 League games for Spurs and scored 41 goals. The son of famous jockey 'Ginger' Dyson, he came to White Hart Lane from non-League Scarborough in 1955. He was a member of the first-team squad until 1965 when he moved on to Fulham and then Colchester and Guildford City. A regular in the Double-winning side, he scored two goals that clinched victory in the European Cup Winners' Cup final in 1963. In 1961 he became the first Spurs player to score a hat-trick in the derby against Arsenal (Spurs won 4-3). He later became an assessor of schoolboy footballers for the Football Association.

GREAVSIE ASSESSMENT: "The two Terrys, Dyson and Medwin, used to play musical chairs with the No 7 shirt. Both were determined competitors who never let the side down, but I think Dyson's grit and whole-hearted endeavour just gave him the edge over Medwin, who was desperately unlucky with injuries. Terry D. would run his legs off for the team, and often popped up with vital winning goals. He had the most memorable match of his career in the Cup Winners' Cup final. He continually had the Atletico Madrid defence in disarray with his thrusting runs, and his two goals turned the match. He was big enough to admit he did not have the skill of some of those tremendous players around him, but he more than made up for it with his effort. Terry was equally effective on either wing, and often wore the No 11 shirt, with Cliffie Jones switching to the right."

JOHN WHITE

Born Musselburgh, Lothian, April 28 1937. Scored 40 goals in 183 League games for Spurs after joining them from Falkirk in 1959 for a bargain price £20,000. He was capped

22 times by Scotland and was an 'ever present' for Spurs during the Double season. In his youth he had been turned down by both Glasgow Rangers and Middlesbrough as being too small, but he quickly showed that his frail appearance was misleading when starting his career with Alloa Athletic and then Falkirk. Bill Nicholson bought him on the advice of both Dave Mackay and Danny Blanchflower, who had seen him in action for Scotland. He took time to settle to the pace of English League football, but once attuned he became one of the finest schemers in the game. The year after helping Spurs capture the European Cup Winners' Cup in 1963 he was struck down and killed by a bolt of lightning while sheltering under a tree during a solo round of golf.

> GREAVSIE ASSESSMENT: "John was a great, great player when he died, and I am convinced he was going to get better. He was so aptly nicknamed 'The Ghost of White Hart Lane.' It was his ability off the ball that made him such a phenomenal player. He would pop up from out of nowhere just when he was needed most to make a pass or collect the ball. Like Danny Blanchflower, he had the gift of being able to give the exact weight to a pass, so that the ball would arrive where and when you wanted it. John had the energy to run all day and could cut a defence in half with just one cunningly placed ball. With White together in midfield with Blanchflower and Mackay Spurs just could not go wrong. I felt privileged to have John providing me with passes that made my life so much easier."

BOBBY SMITH

Born Lingdale, Co. Durham, February 22 1933. Scored 176 goals in 271 League matches for Spurs after joining them from Chelsea in 1955. Wound down his League career with Brighton, his 18 goals in 31 matches helping them win the Fourth Division Championship in 1965. He scored 13 goals in 15 appearances as England centre-forward, all but one of them in partnership with Jimmy Greaves. In the Double season he was top First Division marksman for Spurs with 28 goals and he netted in each of the successive FA Cup final victories.

> GREAVSIE ASSESSMENT: "Bobby was my favourite centre-forward partner. He was never given the credit he deserved for his high level of skill. People seemed to think he was all brute force. Strength certainly played an important part in his game, and he used to make full use of his heavyweight physique. But he also had subtle touches and could lay off delicate passes. I fed off him at Spurs and with England and I am pleased

Five of the Tottenham Double heroes, above John White and Bobby Smith; below Ron Henry, Terry Dyson and Maurice Norman.

to acknowledge the part he played in my goals accumulation. He used to win the ball for me in the air, removing a defender or two with the sheer force of his challenge, and I was left with the relatively simple job of netting with a tap shot. Smithy did not think he was in the game until he had let the goalkeeper know he was on the pitch by hammering into him at the earliest opportunity. This was in the days when forwards were allowed to make physical contact with goalkeepers. Nowadays, if you so much as breathe on them it's a yellow or red card. It's made life easier for the goalkeepers, but the game less of a spectacle for the fans. I think Bobby would feel redundant in a match if he were playing in the modern game. Mind you, he would survive on skill alone – but he would not be the same old Smithy without letting everybody know who was boss by a show of a strength."

LES ALLEN

Born Dagenham, Essex, September 4 1937. Scored 47 goals in 119 League matches for Spurs. Started his career as an amateur with Briggs Sports while working as an apprentice with the local Ford factory. Signed for Chelsea in 1954 and netted 11 goals in 44 League appearances before joining Tottenham in December 1959. Making way for the arrival of Jimmy Greaves, he joined Queen's Park Rangers and helped them become the first Third Division side to win the League Cup at Wembley. He scored 55 goals in 128 League games for QPR before starting a management career during which he was in charge at Loftus Road and at Swindon, and then in Salonika, Greece. He later became a skilled model maker, and in retirement shared his time between his homes in Essex and Cyprus.

GREAVSIE ASSESSMENT: "The Allen family are famous for their footballing feats in the Dagenham manor where I grew up. There was Les and his brother Dennis, and then Les's sons Clive and Bradley and nephews Martin and Paul all became professionals. Before I arrived on the scene at Spurs Bobby Smith had a prolific partnership with Les, and together they played a major part in clinching the League and Cup double triumph. Les was alongside me when I made my League debut for Chelsea in 1957, and again when I played my first match for Spurs. He was a neat, constructive centre-forward or inside-forward with a fine turn of speed, an accurate right foot shot, and excellent positional sense. He was unlucky not to get international recognition."

CLIFF JONES

Born Swansea February 7 1935. Scored 135 goals in 318 League matches for Spurs after joining them from Swansea for £35,000 in Februry 1958. He won a then record 59 Welsh international caps and had the final shots of his career with Fulham, for whom he signed in 1968 after collecting a string of honours with Spurs. He stood 5ft 7in tall, weighed just over 10 stone, and moved like a whippet along either wing for Spurs and Wales. Football was in his blood. He was the son of pre-war Welsh international Ivor Jones, and the nephew of former Arsenal and Wales inside-forward Bryn, and the brother of long-serving League professional Bryn Jnr. His cousin, Ken Jones, was an ex-pro who became one of the country's leading sports columnists.

> GREAVSIE ASSESSMENT: "At his peak, Cliffie was without doubt one of the world's greatest wingers. When he was in full flight I doubt if there was a more dangerous forward on the ball. He used to run with the pace, determination and bravery of a Welsh wing three-quarter. He was brave to the point of madness in the penalty area. Cliffie used to rise like a salmon at the far post to head spectacular goals that were remarkable when you realize he was a smallish bloke with a slim frame. When you talk about great wingers like Matthews, Finney and Best you can mention Jonesie in the same breath. He was as effective as any of them, and on either wing."

These, then, were the players who collectively achieved the greatest season in Tottenham's history. But there were a lot of golden moments still to come during Bill Nicholson's reign at White Hart Lane, and they kicked off with the arrival of a player who cost one pound under £100,000. Enter Greavsie.

Before we leave the double side, a lament to Danny Blanchflower:

Oh Danny Boy, the Spurs the Spurs are calling
From stand to stand and down the Shelf side
The summer's gone, but memories are flying
Of the glory-glory days that have never died.
But come ye back when the pitch is in meadow
Or when The Lane's hushed and white with snow
'Tis we'll be there in sunshine and shadow
Oh Danny boy, oh Danny boy, we love you so.

– Norman Giller 2009

BILL Nicholson did not want to burden Jimmy Greaves with being the first £100,000 footballer, and so he negotiated a £99,999 fee to bring him home from Italy where he had spent a miserable five months after joining them from Chelsea in May 1961.

It was the start of a mutual love affair between Jimmy and the Tottenham fans as he set about building a mountain of goals that lifted him into a lasting place in Lane legend.

These 1960s were about much more than just England's long-awaited triumph in the World Cup. The decade heralded the first success in Europe of British clubs – led by Tottenham; saw the long overdue introduction of substitutes, ushered in the ee-aye-adio revolution on Merseyside; and witnessed the kicking out of the maximum wage to lead the way to today's professional footballers swimming in money. The sixties were all about the Beatles, rock 'n' roll, Mini-cars, mini-skirts, the psychedelic, Ali-psyche and, of course, George Best.

It was a swinging time for everybody apart from those footballers who found themselves redundant as clubs made swingeing cuts to help pay their suddenly inflated wage bills. Spurs prudently paid each of their first-team players £65 a week.

Fulham's bearded wonder Jimmy Hill led the PFA's campaign to kick out the £20 maximum wage as the eloquent union chairman, and it was his Craven Cottage team-mate Johnny Haynes who made the quickest profit. Comedian Tommy Trinder, chairman of Fulham, announced to the press in 1961 that he was making England skipper Haynes British football's first £100-a-week footballer. "It was," admitted Johnny, "the funniest thing Tommy ever said."

The players owed a big vote of thanks and a few bottles of bubbly to England inside-forward George Eastham, who stood alone against the football barons. He battled in the High Court against what was described as "a slave contract" and the restraint of trade. Eastham started his one-man war while at Newcastle and finally won it after moving to Arsenal in November 1960. He was the Bosman of his time, and does not get enough credit for his courage in taking on, and beating, the establishment.

The Football League caved in after the players once again threatened strike action, and this time they really did mean it. In the space of a week in January 1961 the maximum wage was kicked out and the restrictive contracts scrapped. Suddenly the likes of Greavsie, Denis Law, Joe Baker and Gerry Hitchens found they could earn in England the same sort of money that had tempted them to be lured by the lira to Italy.

Here's Greavsie talking about those early days as a Spurs player and his move from Milan to Tottenham in that historic £99,999 deal:

❛I considered myself the luckiest footballer on earth the day Bill Nick arrived in Milan to sign me for Tottenham. Not only was he rescuing me from what I reckoned was the prison of Italian football, but he was also giving me the chance to join what I believed was the finest club side in Europe. It was in the previous season that Spurs had pulled off that historic Double. I had played against them with Chelsea, and I can vouch for the fact that they were, to use a Cockney understatement, 'a bit tasty.'

They purred along like a Rolls Royce, with Danny Blanchflower, John White and Dave Mackay at the wheel. When they wanted to touch the accelerator there was Cliff Jones to break the speed limit down either wing; and if they needed a full show of horsepower, Bobby Smith was put in the driving seat. These were the nucleus of five world-class players around which Bill Nick had built his team. He had got the perfect blend and I remember thinking when I played against them, 'Blimey, there's not a weakness in this team. They can win the lot.'

'The lot' in those days meant the League Championship and FA Cup, two trophies that were harder to win then because – and of this I am convinced – the game was a lot tougher and more demanding. In comparison, today's football has become a virtual non-contact sport. And remember we were all on a twenty quid a week maximum wage at the time, which is why I nipped off to Italy.

Just to give you an idea of the overall standard of the First Division in 1960-61: I was playing in a Chelsea side that included such international-class players as Peter Bonetti, Frank Blunstone, Peter Brabrook, Bobby Evans, Bobby Tambling and Terry Venables. I managed to bang in 41 goals that season. We finished in twelfth place in the table.

Wolves, dripping with international players, scored 103 First Division goals and could do no better than third. Defending champions Burnley, blessed with the talents of Jimmy McIlroy, Jimmy Anderson, Alex Elder, Jimmy Robson, Ray Pointer, John Connelly, Brian Miller and Gordon Harris, netted 102 First Division goals, and were back in fourth place. We were all puffing and panting trying to keep up with Spurs.

Runners-up Sheffield Wednesday had England internationals Tony Kay, Peter Swan, Ron Springett and John Fantham at their peak. Blackpool missed relegation by a point, despite being able to call on such skilled players as Tony Waiters, Jimmy Armfield, Ray Parry, Ray Charnley and the one and only Stanley Matthews. Each team also had at least two hatchet men, with instructions to stop the clever players playing.

The like of 'Bites Yer Legs' Norman Hunter, Tommy Smith and Chopper Harris were

The Master on the ball at White Hart Lane, the one and only Greavsie

coming through the ranks and about to make themselves felt. Just talking about them brings me out in bruises. In today's game they would have been red carded every time they stepped on a pitch if they tried to tackle as they did in those 1960s when football was not for the faint-hearted.

There was class running right the way through the First Division – and not a foreign player in sight. This was the quality of the opposition that the 'Super Spurs' side had to overcome to pull off the League and Cup Double that had eluded every great team throughout the 20th Century. They did it with a style and flair that made them one of the most attractive teams of all time. There were defensive deficiencies, but you never heard a murmur of complaint from the spectators, who were always given tremendous value for money.

For me to join the team in 1961 was like being given a passport to paradise. I considered it like coming home. I was a Spurs fan when I was a kid, and it was odds-on my joining them from school until a lovely rascal of a Chelsea scout called Jimmy Thompson sweet-talked my Dad into encouraging me to go to Stamford Bridge.

I wondered how the Tottenham fans would react to me moving to their manor at White Hart Lane, and realized they were quite keen on the idea when I played my first game in a Spurs shirt in a reserve match at Plymouth. There was a record crowd for a reserve game of 13,000 and I know many of them were Spurs supporters, because over the years I have met loads that say they were there!

My other concern was how the Spurs players would take to me. They had been reading the day-to-day accounts of my exploits in Italy, where I had been waging a verbal war in a bid to get back into British football. Those who knew me only by reputation must have been thinking I was a real troublemaker, and – having just won the 'impossible' Double without me – understandably looked on me as an intruder who could possibly rock their happy and successful boat.

Thank goodness it didn't take me long to kick their doubts into touch. I got lucky and kicked off with a hat-trick against Blackpool in my first-team debut, and I settled into the side – both on and off the pitch – as if I had been at Tottenham all my life.

I am never comfortable talking about goals that I scored, but I have to admit that one of the goals in my first match was a little bit special. Dave Mackay took one of his long throw-ins, Terry Medwin flicked the ball on, and I scored with what the newspapers described as 'a spectacular scissors kick.' From that moment on I was accepted by the Tottenham fans and players as 'one of them'.

All these years later I can say that the Tottenham team of that period was the best side I ever played with, and that takes into account England matches.

I get goosebumps just thinking about some of the football we used to play: it was out of this world, and I consider myself as fortunate as a pools winner to have had the chance to be part of the dream machine.**'**

Tottenham made a monumental bid for the major prize – the European Cup – in Jimmy's first season, during which the 'Glory-Glory-hallelujah' choruses raised the White Hart Lane roof. There are conflicting opinions as to when the 'Battle Hymn of the Republic' was adopted as the club's theme song. Some insist it was being sung by Spurs supporters at Molineux in April 1960 as Tottenham powered to a 3-1 victory that stopped Wolves being first to the League and Cup Double.

Older supporters vaguely remember it being sung back in the early 1950s after a cartoon had appeared in the Tottenham match programme showing Arthur Rowe day dreaming of the Double. The caption read: "While the Spurs go marching on …"

There was an explosion of noise every time Spurs played European Cup ties at White Hart Lane in 1961-62 as they saw off Gornik, Feyenoord and Dukla Prague. There was also good humour to go with the fanatical support. A small group of Spurs supporters always dressed as angels, carrying witty placards and waving them – without malice – at opposition fans. There was never a hint of hooliganism. That scar on the face of soccer was a decade away.

Tottenham were desperately unlucky to lose a two-leg European Cup semi-final against eventual champions Benfica, propelled by the rising master Eusebio. To this day, Greavsie insists that a 'goal' he scored, which would have put Spurs into the final, was wrongly flagged offside.

They quickly picked themselves up after their exit from Europe and the following month retained the FA Cup, with Jimmy Greaves scoring an exquisite goal in the third minute to put them on the way to a 3-1 victory over Burnley.

My Greavsie bias coming out again, but I think it rates with the finest goals scored at old Wembley. He was fifteen yards out and *passed* the ball along the ground into the net through a forest of players' legs and with all the unerring accuracy of a Jack Nicklaus putt. Jimmy, never one to boast in his playing days, said just before the players left the dressing-room, "I'm going to get an early one today lads." If it had been a fluke it would have been an outstanding goal, so the fact that Greavsie meant it puts it up into the classic category.

The Tottenham team: **Brown; Baker, Henry; Blanchflower, Norman, Mackay; Medwin, White, Smith, Greaves, Jonses.**

Goals from Bobby Smith and skipper Danny Blanchflower clinched Tottenham's win after Jimmy Robson had equalized for Burnley. Danny's goal came from the penalty spot in the 80th minute after Tommy Cummings had handled a Terry Medwin shot on the goal-line.

As Blanchflower was placing the ball on the penalty spot his Northern Ireland team-mate and good friend Jimmy McIlroy said to him: "Bet you miss."

Three of the stars of Tottenham's historic European Cup Winners' Cup victory in Rotterdam in 1963: Top left, Terry Dyson, whose two goals made him the man of the match; Top right Tony Marchi, a magnificent deputy for the 'irreplaceable' Dave Mackay; and, right, goalkeeper Bill Brown, a safe and reliable last line of defence.

Danny did not say a word. He calmly sent goalkeeper Adam Blacklaw the wrong way as he stroked the penalty home. As he ran past Burnley schemer McIlory, he said: "Bet I don't!"

The victory earned Tottenham a place in the European Cup Winners' Cup, and the 'Glory-Glory' chanting supporters roared them all the way into the final in May 1963. No British team had won a major trophy in Europe when Spurs travelled to Rotterdam for the final, and hopes that they could break the duck were suddenly diminished when their main motivator, Dave Mackay, failed a fitness test on the day of the match.

The absence of Mackay was a devastating blow because he had been a major force in Tottenham's magnificent success over the previous two seasons. As it sank in that they would have to perform without his battering ram backing a blanket of gloom dropped on the Spurs camp.

Atletico were suddenly considered by neutrals to be warm favourites to retain the trophy they had won in impressive style the previous year, when they mastered a high-quality Fiorentina side.

Mackay's absence plunged manager Bill Nicholson into a morose mood, and he added to the air of pessimism when he ran through the strengths of the opposition during a tactical team talk. He made Atletico sound like the greatest team ever to run on to a football pitch, and he bruised rather than boosted the confidence of his players.

Skipper Blanchflower was so concerned about the sudden gloom and doom environment that he summoned all the players to a private meeting and made one of the most inspiring speeches of his career.

Using a mixture of fact and blarney, word-master Blanchflower pumped confidence back into his team-mates and made them believe in their ability to win. He countered every point that Bill Nicholson had made about the Madrid players by underlining Tottenham's strengths, and he convinced them that they were superior to the Spaniards in every department. It was a speech of Churchillian class and Tottenham went into the final with renewed determination to take the trophy back to White Hart Lane.

This was how Tottenham lined up for the game of their lives, with Tony Marchi stepping into Dave Mackay's place:

Brown, Baker, Henry, Blanchflower, Norman, Marchi, Jones, White, Smith, Greaves, Dyson

Bill Nicholson, one of the finest tacticians in the game, deserved the credit for the fact that Greavsie was in position to give Spurs the lead in the 16th minute. He had spotted, during a spying mission to Madrid, that the Atletico defence was slow to cover down the left side, and he instructed that full use should be made of the blistering speed of Cliff Jones. Moving with pace and penetration, Cliff sprinted to meet a neatly placed pass from Bobby Smith and Greavsie drifted into the middle to steer his accurate centre into the net with his deadly left foot. It was a real pick-pocket job, and Tottenham's fans roared their 'Glory-Glory' anthem as the Spaniards suddenly wilted.

It was on the wings that Tottenham were monopolizing the match, with Jones and tiny Terry Dyson running the Spanish full-backs into dizzy disorder. Atletico, strangely enough, also had a winger called Jones, but he was not in the same class as Tottenham's Welsh wizard.

It was Dyson and Jones who combined to set up goal number two in the 32nd minute, exchanging passes before releasing the ball to Smith, who laid it back for John White to rifle a low shot into the net.

It was a rare but crucial goal for White, who had made his reputation as a maker rather than taker of goals. His signature was stamped on most of Tottenham's attacks as he prised open the Atletico defence with beautifully weighted passes. Blanchflower, White and the tall, stately Marchi were working like Trojans in midfield to make up for the absence of the one and only Mackay. At most clubs, Marchi would have been an automatic choice for the first team, and he played with such skill and determination that his contribution was in the Mackay class. There can be no higher praise.

Atletico Madrid revived their flickering flame of hope in the first minute of the second-half when Collar scored from the penalty spot after Ron Henry had fisted the ball off the goal-line.

For 20 minutes there was a danger that Spurs could lose their way as the Cup-holders forced a series of corner-kicks, but the defence managed to survive the Spanish storm.

Goalkeeper Bill Brown took his life in his hands as he threw himself courageously at the feet of Mendonca to snatch the ball off the forward's toes. Chuzo broke free and Tottenham's fans sighed with relief as he shot the wrong side of the post; then Ramiro drove the ball just off target. This was when everybody connected with Tottenham began to wonder and worry whether they were going to get by without the great Mackay, who in a situation like this would have been breaking Spanish hearts with his thundering tackles and brandishing a fist in a demand for extra effort from all his team-mates.

It was 'Dynamo' Dyson, having the game of a lifetime, who ended the Atletico comeback when his hanging cross was fumbled into the net by goalkeeper Madinabeytia, who had one eye on the menacing presence of big Bobby Smith.

Dyson became a man inspired and laid on a second goal for Greavsie before putting the seal on a memorable performance with a scorching shot at the end of a weaving 30-yard run. His first goal was something of a fluke, but the second was a masterpiece.

As Tottenham's triumphant players paraded the Cup in front of their ecstatic fans, Bobby Smith shouted at Dyson in his typically blunt way: "If I were you, mate, I'd hang up my boots. There's no way you can top that. You were out of this world."

The following season dawned with no hint that it was to see the break-up of the 'Super Spurs.' The heart was ripped out of the Tottenham team in a tragic and painful way, and a black cloud of despondency enveloped the club.

The nightmare was slow and drawn out. It started on the evening of December 10 1963 at Old Trafford, when Tottenham were playing Manchester United in the second-leg of a European Cup Winners' Cup tie. Dave Mackay broke a leg in a collision with Noel Cantwell that surely left the United skipper losing sleep about the validity of his challenge.

Just a few weeks later, Danny Blanchflower was forced to retire because of a recurring knee injury. Tottenham had lost the brains of the team and the heart of the team, and worse was to follow at the end of the season. John White, the eyes of the team, was sitting under a tree sheltering from a storm on a North London golf course when he was tragically killed by lightning. Tottenham had lost the three most vital cogs in their machine.

Bill Nicholson got busy in the transfer market and bought Alan Mullery from Fulham, Laurie Brown from Arsenal, Cyril Knowles from Middlesbrough, Pat Jennings from Watford, Jimmy Robertson from St Mirren and Alan Gilzean from Dundee.

He took a breather, and then went shopping again, this time buying centre-half Mike England from Blackburn and Terry Venables from Chelsea.

Bill Nick was trying to build another 'Super Spurs'. He never quite made it. The new Tottenham team had some memorable moments together in the mid-sixties, but they never touched the peak performances of the Blanchflower-White-Mackay era.

Secretly, Nicholson had tried to bring Edmonton-born England skipper Johnny Haynes to White Hart Lane to team up with his old England side-kick Jimmy Greaves. But the bold attempt fell through, and the Blanchflower-White roles went to Mullery and Venables; good as they were, they were never in the Blanchflower-White class.

Greavsie had become accustomed to the pace set by Danny and John, and he struggled to adapt to their style of delivery. Both were given a tough time by the Spurs supporters, who had been spoiled over recent years. They unkindly but understandably compared the newcomers with their great idols.

Venables was not always happy playing at White Hart Lane after his success as the midfield boss at Chelsea, and when he eventually moved on to Queen's Park Rangers who would have taken any bets that one day he would return and buy the club! Yes, as Greavsie says, it's a funny old game.

One of the new-look Tottenham squad who did win the hearts of the fans was Alan Gilzean, who formed a wonderful partnership with Greavsie. Jimmy found Gilly a joy to play with, and he felt that Alan was never given sufficient credit for his delicate touch play and finishing finesse in the penalty area. He was a master of the flick header, and could bamboozle defences with deceptive changes of pace and clever ball control.

Missing the command of Blanchflower, and the drive of Mackay, the 1963-64 season was relatively barren for Spurs after three years of non-stop success. But they still managed to finish fourth in the League Championship in a season that would be remembered for the start of Liverpool's 'Red Revolution' under the mesmeric management of Bill Shankly.

Ownership of the Spurs had moved from the Bearmans to the Wales late in 1960, with first Fred Wale and then Sidney as chairman. They considered Tottenham a family club, and allowed Bill Nick to get on with the job of managing without interference. Under the Wale influence, the Tottenham directors ran a tight, well-organised ship and among ground improvements during the 1960s was a new floodlight system with impressive pylons, and in 1962 the rear of the Park Lane Stand was fitted with 2,600 seats. A year later, the Paxton Road Stand was given a similar overhaul, with 3,500 seats installed and in 1968 was extended to link up with the West Stand, providing a further 1,400 seats. This was long before the directive for all-seater stadiums.

Bill Nick's latest team saved their peak performances for the FA Cup in the 1966-67 season, culminating in a well-earned FA Cup final triumph over London neighbours Chelsea at Wembley. Of the side that won the trophy in 1962, only Dave Mackay and Greavsie had survived, along with Cliff Jones on the substitute's bench. Greavsie had recovered from the hepatitis that had robbed him of half a yard of pace during the build-up to the 1966 World Cup finals; nobody ever takes that illness into account when discussing Jimmy's contribution to the World Cup triumph, halted by a shin injury received in a group game against France.

The fact that Mackay was there at the 1967 FA Cup final to lead out the Tottenham team as skipper was the sort of story that you would expect to come from the pages of Roy of the Rovers. 'Miracle Man' Mackay had made an astonishing recovery after breaking his leg a second time following his controversial collision with Noel Cantwell at Old Trafford in 1963.

Mackay motivated a team that had Pat Jennings building himself into a legend as the last line of defence. Baby-faced Irish international Joe Kinnear had come in as right-back in place of the energetic Phil Beal, who was unlucky to break an arm after playing an important part in getting Spurs to the final. Joe, a neat, controlled player, was partnered at full-back by Cyril Knowles, a former Yorkshire miner who took the eye with his sharp tackling and some polished, if at times eccentric skills. He was to become a cult hero, with anything he attempted – good or bad – accompanied by chants of 'Nice one, Cyril' from the White Hart Lane faithful.

Standing like a Welsh mountain in the middle of the defence was the majestic Mike England, one of the finest centre-halves ever produced in Britain. He was a class player from head to toe.

Dave Mackay was the immoveable link between defence and attack as he adapted

Terry Venables (left) is looking mightily pleased with himself after Tottenham's 1967 FA Cup final victory over his old club Chelsea, while Alan Mullery gives skipper Dave Mackay a smacker. Pat Jennings is in the background.

his game from buccaneer to anchorman, helping to stoke the fires of the engine room where Alan Mullery and Terry Venables were forging a productive partnership. They never quite touched the peaks that Spurs fans had seen in the 'Glory-Glory' days of Blanchflower-White-Mackay, but – let's be honest – few midfield combinations have ever reached that sky-scraping standard.

Jimmy Robertson was a flying Scot on the right wing, where his speed was a vital asset for the G-men – Gilzean and Greaves, who had a radar-like understanding for where to be to get the best out of each other. For the final, Bill Nick preferred Frank Saul to Cliff Jones for the No 11 shirt. Frank, who had been a fringe player in the Double-winning squad, was more of a central striker than a winger, but he was a direct player with a good nose for goal. Cliff, and Joe Kirkup for Chelsea, were the first players to wear No 12 shirts in an FA Cup final. The Tottenham team:

Jennings, Kinnear, Knowles, Mullery, England, Mackay, Robertson, Greaves, Gilzean, Venables, Saul. Sub: Jones

Facing Tottenham in the first all-London final were Tommy Docherty's elegant but unpredictable Chelsea team. They had gone through an even more drastic rebuilding programme than Spurs, and Terry Venables was part of the upheaval when he moved on to Tottenham to make room the previous year for the arrival of Scotland's 'Wizard of Dribble', Charlie Cooke.

Peter 'Catty' Bonetti was their goalkeeper, as good a catcher of the ball as there was in world football. Allan Harris, preferred at right-back to usual choice Joe Kirkup, was a solid defender and a good balance for the marvelously skilled Eddie McCreadie, who had the ball control of a winger to go with his scything tackles.

Marvin 'Lou' Hinton was a sound centre-half with a good footballing brain, and making the earth tremble alongside him was poker-faced Ron 'Chopper' Harris, Allan's brother and one of the most feared ball-winners in the game. Young John Hollins was a bundle of atomic energy at right-half, and aggressive Scot John Boyle played a utility role in midfield while wearing the No 11 shirt.

Filling the scheming role for Chelsea that had belonged to Venables was the dance master Cooke, a charismatic character known to his friends as 'Bonny Prince Charlie'. All the people who tried to compare Charlie with his predecessor Venables were wasting their breath. They were as alike as grass and granite. Charlie liked to hang on to the ball and run with it as if it was tied to his boot laces, while Terry let the ball do the work with precise passes that could have come out of the Push and Run coaching manual.

Chelsea relied on three main marksmen to get the ball into the net. Bobby Tambling, a faithful Stamford Bridge servant who had recently overtaken Greavsie's club goalscoring record, had a terrific turn of speed and was a deadly finisher. Tommy

Baldwin, who had joined Chelsea in a part-exchange deal that took George 'Stroller' Graham to Arsenal eight months earlier, was nicknamed 'Sponge' because of the way he soaked up work (and off the park, beer!).

Then there was Tony Hateley, a master of the airways whom Tommy Docherty had bought from Aston Villa for £100,000 after his silkily skilled centre-forward Peter Osgood had broken a leg. While weak on the ground, Tony was a powerhouse header of the ball who learned a lot from the old head master Tommy Lawton while at Notts County. One day he would pass on all he knew to his son, Mark Hateley.

Masterminding the Chelsea team was manager Tommy Docherty, one of the game's great personalities. He had a razor-sharp Glaswegian wit and was in complete contrast to the dour and often tight-lipped Bill Nicholson.

On paper, it looked certain to be a cracker of a match. But on the pitch it turned out to be something of a damp squib. The whole day fell a bit flat, mainly due to the fact that both teams were from London. That robbed the match of much of its atmosphere, because the supporters were not in that bubbling 'Oop f'the Coop' day-out mood.

Spurs skipper Mackay had a personal mission to win after having been inactive for so long, and he drove the Tottenham team on like a man possessed. They were always playing the more positive and purposeful football, and deserved their lead just before half-time. Jimmy Robertson crashed a shot wide of Bonetti after Alan Mullery's long-range pile-driver had been blocked.

Robertson, proving one of the most effective of all the forwards, set up a second goal in the 68th minute when he steered a typical long throw-in from Dave Mackay into the path of Frank Saul, who pivoted and hooked the ball high into the net.

Tottenham then slowed the game down to suit themselves, playing possession football so that Charlie Cooke could not get the ball to take command with his mesmerizing control. Bobby Tambling was allowed in for a goal five minutes from the end, but Tottenham tightened up at the back to hold out for victory.

Three months after this triumph, Tottenham drew 3-3 in the Charity Shield against Manchester United at Old Trafford, a match that has gone down in footballing folklore because of a goal scored by Pat Jennings. The Irish international goalkeeper hammered a huge clearance from the Spurs penalty area that went first bounce over the head of Alex Stepney and into the back of the United net. The bewildered look on the faces of the players of both teams was hilarious to see, I was reporting the match for the *Daily Express*, and afterwards Pat told me: "I decided to clear the ball up to Greavsie and Gilly, and a strong following wind grabbed it and took it all the way to the United net. Jimmy and Alan had their backs to me and could not believe it when they realized it was me who had scored. Greavsie said he told Alan: 'D'you realise this makes Pat out top scorer for the season? He'll never let us forget it.'"

The Greavsie era at Tottenham was drawing to a close, leaving a remarkable legacy

Pat Jennings, a White Hart Lane hero forgiven for transferring to the old enemy at Highbury, uses unorthodox methods to stop his countryman George Best during the 1966 First Division match against Manchester United. Can you spot anybody you know in the capacity crowd?

of a club record 220 First Division goals (including a record 37 in 1962-63) and 32 FA Cup goals. Those bare statistics hide the fact that many of the goals were of the spectacular variety, fashioned like a skilled sculptor with clever feints, dizzying dribbles, astonishing acceleration and then finished with a pass rather than a shot into the net.

Those old enough to have witnessed a Greaves goal will confirm that I am not exaggerating when I say we actually felt privileged to have been there to see it. We were keeping company with a genius, a Goya of goals. How many would a peak-powered Greaves score in today's game, with no Norman Hunter-style bites-yer-legs tackling from behind and the relaxed, often-confusing off-side law? And what would he be worth in the transfer market? Let the bidding begin at £29,999,000!

There were calls for Greavsie to be reinstated in the England team when he hit a purple patch with 27 First Division goals in 1968-69, but Jimmy seemed to be almost visibly losing his appetite for the game the following season. Bill Nick told me privately that he was concerned that the Artful Dodger of the penalty area seemed to be showing more enthusiasm preparing for driving to Mexico in a 1970 World Cup rally than playing football. By this time, Jimmy had built up a flourishing sports shop and travel business with his brother-in-law Tom Barton, and football was no longer the be-all-and-end-all for him. Yet he was still by some distance the most dynamic finisher in the 'old' First Division. To try to bring the best out of Greavsie, Nicholson went shopping and bought Martin Chivers as a new playmate from Southampton.

How times change. In my reporting role for the *Daily Express* I met 'Big Chiv' at Waterloo Station and travelled with him by tube to Liverpool Street and then on to Tottenham as he prepared to start his new life at The Lane. These days, reporters cannot get near the prima donna players, who invariably arrive at their new clubs in chauffeur-driven limos with dark-tinted windows and an agent handing out second-hand quotes. Martin, a Grammar school boy educated at the highly regarded Taunton's School in Hampshire, spent the train journey from Southampton to Waterloo tackling *The Guardian* crossword. He told me on the way to The Lane: "This is like a dream for me. I have always been an admirer of the way Spurs play, and it's going to be a thrill as well as a challenge to play alongside Jimmy Greaves."

Sadly, he arrived at Jimmy's side just as the goal master was losing his motivation. The crunch came when Spurs wore their white shirts like flags of surrender against Crystal Palace in a fourth round FA Cup replay at Selhurst Park. Palace striker Gerry Queen dismantled the Spurs defence for the winning goal, and I recall that the headline on my report for the *Daily Express* announced: "Queen Is King at the Palace."

Greavsie, trying to settle to his new partnership with Chivers, was dropped for the first time in his nine years at Spurs. It was his final curtain at Tottenham. A fascinating – and often fraught – new era was being ushered in at White Hart Lane. Here come the 'seventies.

THE 1970s – the age for footballers of flared trousers, kipper ties, platform shoes and bubbly perms – started and finished with Tottenham creating mind-blowing records in the transfer market.

At the dawn of the decade Spurs set up the first £200,000 British transfer deal, World Cup hero Martin Peters moving to White Hart Lane from West Ham for cash plus the idolized Jimmy Greaves. That was pretty sensational, but was dwarfed by the events of the summer of '78 when Tottenham revolutionized the game by importing two Argentine World Cup superstars to open the doors to the invasion of foreign players.

In between these two extraordinary transactions, Tottenham led a yo-yo existence, promising much but producing little. At the lowest point in the '70s they were dumped back into the Second Division, and the decade saw a messy end to the never-to-be-forgotten Bill Nicholson era.

The '01' superstition worked its magic again with victory in the Football League Cup, but in a season in which Spurs were forced to live in the shadow of the old enemy. Arsenal completed the League and FA Cup Double in 1970-71, yet with nothing like the style and sublime skill of the history-making Tottenham team ten years earlier. To rub it in, the Gunners clinched the League title by winning at The Lane. Ouch!

It was Aston Villa's brave run to Wembley from a Third Division base that brought romance and excitement to the League Cup. Villa were fortunate in meeting only one First Division club – a struggling Burnley – in their first five ties, but then came the peak performance that captured the headlines. They were drawn against mighty Manchester United, and they proved their calibre by holding them to a 1-1 draw in the first leg of the semi-final at Old Trafford. Then, in front of a roaring 62,500 crowd at Villa Park, they mastered United to win 3-2 on aggregate,

Tottenham, meanwhile, had conquered Bristol City 3-1 on aggregate in their semi-final and went to Wembley bidding to win the League Cup for the first time. Villa, the first club to lift the trophy in 1960-61 before the tournament was given a Wembley setting for the final, were hoping to follow Queen's Park Rangers and Swindon Town as Third Division winners.

For 80 minutes Villa were the equal of Tottenham in a match that was never a classic but always competitive. Then, with extra-time beckoning, centre-forward Martin Chivers struck twice in the last ten minutes to vanquish Villa.

Martin Peters, according to Sir Alf Ramsey "ten years ahead of his time," arrives at Tottenham, with Greavsie going to West Ham as a makeweight.

The line-up of the triumphant Tottenham team, that eventually finished third in the First Division title race:

Jennings, Kinnear, Knowles, Mullery, Collins, Beal, Perryman, Gilzean, Chivers, Peters, Neighbour. Sub: Pearce.

Steve Perryman had come through the youth ranks to give bite and composure to the midfield. Bill Nicholson, never one to go overboard with praise for players, described him as "a little diamond." As likeable and unassuming bloke as you could wish to meet, Steve stretched his loyalty to Tottenham to a club record 655 League games plus another 211 cup ties over the next fifteen years. He was awarded an MBE for his services to football. Tottenham fans, who identified with his 100 per cent effort and enthusiasm, would have given him a VC. I described him as the Babyfaced Assassin.

Martin Peters brought subtlety and elegance to the team. He was never going to be as explosive as his boyhood idol Greavsie, but he tip-toed through defences to create chances from out of nowhere. Sir Alf Ramsey had described him as being ten years ahead of his time because of his ability to read a game and make use of space that lesser players did not even know existed. His blind-side running was a joy to behold, and his passing always imaginative and accurate. He had an in-built radar system that continually took him ghosting to the near post, while defenders were chasing shadows at the far post. The many goals he scored from his midfield starting point (46 for Tottenham and 20 for England) invariably had a touch of class about them. He was an aristocrat of a player in the true traditions of the great Tottenham giants of the past.

Patrolling along the left touchline was Jimmy Neighbour, a skilled, old-style winger who had the ability to dismantle the tightest defence when at peak form. Jimmy was a modest and likeable lad from Chingford, and all his old team-mates and the older fans were devastated at the news of his early passing at the age of 58 in April 2009.

Martin Chivers was one of the players to benefit from Jimmy's mazy runs and accurate crosses. He had been overshadowed by Greavsie and Gilzean early in his career at The Lane, but with increased responsibility he came into his own, and in the early '70s was as potent and productive as any centre-forward in the League. Powerfully built and as wide as a door, Chiv had a deceptively lazy-looking bearing, but if a possible goal beckoned he would suddenly fire on all cylinders and leave surprised defenders in his wake as he accelerated. He preferred the ball on his right foot, and had a rocketing shot that brought him many of his 118 League goals. He also netted 13 times in 24 England games, and might have plundered many more goals but for a recurring knee injury.

It was Chivers who was chiefly responsible for shooting Tottenham to the Uefa Cup in 1971-72. They battled through to the first ever all-English final, with Wolves waiting for them in the two-leg decider. The game was virtually settled in the first leg at Molineux. Chivers knocked the wind out of Wolves with two scorching goals that added weight to Tottenham claims that he was currently the most dynamic centre-forward in the country. It brought Martin's goals haul for the season to five in three matches against Wolves, who went into the second leg at White Hart Lane trailing 2-1.

A bravely headed goal by Alan Mullery – back after a controversial loan spell at his old club, Fulham – gave Spurs a stranglehold on the tie in the 29th minute of the second leg. Mullery dived in among flying boots to connect with a Martin Peters free-kick, and was the only person in the ground who did not know the ball had hit the back of the net. He was knocked out as he headed the ball and had to go off for treatment. Soon after his return he played a reluctant part in a Wolves equalizer. The ball bounced off him into the path of winger David Wagstaffe, who scored from 25 yards with a swerving left-foot shot. Pat Jennings could only wave at the ball on its way into the net.

Tottenham's defence, with Mike England and Phil Beal mastering the twin threat of John Richards and Derek Dougan, withstood an all-out assault in the second-half, which was given new impetus when Wolves club captain Mike Bailey came into the action from the substitutes' bench after an injury-forced four month lay-off.

The usually adventurous Cyril Knowles at left-back was forced into full-time rearguard duties as Wolves went hunting a goal that would bring them right back into the tie. A string of superb saves by Jennings, a disputed off-side decision against Dougan and disciplined defensive play took the whip out of the Wolves whirlwind. Tottenham's players were visibly tired in what was their 68th competitive match of the season.

Only skipper Mullery, clutching the Uefa Cup – formerly the Fairs Cup – in his arms like a baby, found the stamina for the traditional lap of honour. He had at least 4,000 Spurs fans as companions on the disorganized journey around the perimeter of the pitch. Just two weeks earlier he had asked Sir Alf Ramsey not to consider him any more for the England team because he felt he was playing too much football. "This has made everything worthwhile," he said. "You can't beat winning a trophy to take the tiredness out of your legs."

The Tottenham victory – 3-2 on aggregate – was a personal triumph for Bill Nicholson. Since taking charge of the club in 1958 he had steered Spurs to three FA Cup finals, one League Cup final, one European Cup Winners' Cup final and the Uefa Cup final. And they had won the lot! Bill Nick gave his usual level-headed and fair assessment after his latest conquest:

> ❛We won the cup at Molineux with two marvellous goals by Martin Chivers. Give Wolves full credit for the way they came back at us. They were the better team for much of the second leg. The two matches were a fine advertisement for English football, and I wonder what the rest of Europe think of the fact that this is the fifth successive year that the Uefa Cup has been won by an English club. We look forward to defending it next season.❜

Skipper Alan Mullery parades the UEFA Cup with triumphant Tottenham team-mates Ralph Coates, Alan Gilzean, Martin Peters, Mike England, Pat Jennings, Joe Kinnear, Cyril Knowles and first-leg hero Martin Chivers. Missing from the picture, two Spurs stalwarts, Steve Perryman and Philip Beal.

It was round about this time that Nicholson was losing a battle to hang on to one of the finest young prospects in British football, one Graeme Souness.

Graeme, born in the tough Broomhouse district of Edinburgh on May 6 1953, went to the same Carrickvale school that Dave Mackay had attended a generation earlier. They must have been hewn out of the identical lump of granite, because Souness had all the Mackay motivating mannerisms and liked to boss the pitch in the same intimidating way as his schoolboy idol.

His encyclopedic knowledge of all that Mackay achieved swayed him to join Tottenham at the age of fifteen when any of the Scottish clubs would willingly have opened their doors to him.

I learned earlier than most that Souness was not only a star in the making, but also a head-strong boy who knew his own mind. Jim Rodger, the sleuth of a reporter on the *Scottish Daily Express,* was so close to Tottenham manager Bill Nicholson that he knew all the Spurs secrets and kept most of them close to his chest, never sharing them with readers or colleagues. He earned a mutual trust with chairmen, managers and players that got him an ear in boardrooms and dressing-rooms throughout football.

Jim, almost as wide as he was tall, was a legend in Scotland, on nodding terms with Prime Ministers and princes as well as most of the people who mattered in football. He telephoned me in the Fleet Street office of the *Express* one day in 1970 and whispered in the conspiratorial tone that he always used, 'Get over to the North London digs of Graeme Souness and talk him out of doing anything silly. Bill Nick thinks he's going to walk out on the club.'

'Graeme who?' I said. 'I wouldn't know what he looks like, let alone where he lives.'

'He's the hottest young prospect in the country,' Jim said in a scolding tone, and proceeded to give me Graeme's address. 'You'll be doing Bill Nick a big favour if you can tell him to just be patient and wait for his chance. He could not be with a better club. If you get him, put him on the phone to me. I'll talk some sense into him.'

That was how 'Rodger the Dodger' operated, working almost as a secret agent on behalf of managers across Britain and then being rewarded with some of the hottest exclusive stories in the game.

In those days I was more concerned with trying to dig out stories on first-team players at all the London clubs, and could not see the point of chasing after a youngster whose career had hardly started. But as I had so much respect for my Glasgow colleague, I drove to Graeme's digs, only to be told by his landlady that he had gone home to Scotland an hour earlier.

'What a waste of time,' I thought. 'As if anybody apart from Jim Rodger is going to be the slightest bit interested in this story.' Wrong!

It got to the point over the next few days when questions were asked in the House of Commons, as the story crossed from the back to the front pages. Graeme, then seventeen, had spent two years at Spurs as an apprentice who considered himself more of a sorcerer. He had gone back to Edinburgh because he said he felt homesick.

Tottenham reacted by suspending him without pay for two weeks. Graeme's local MP took up the case, and questioned in the House what right a football club had to deal with 'a minor' like this when his only 'crime' was to suffer from homesickness. 'Is homesickness something that should be punishable?' demanded the MP, managing to make Souness sound as hard done by as Oliver Twist. The story became the property of columnists with poison pens, and Bill Nicholson, a fatherly manager if ever there was one, was unfairly pilloried. Souness, without having kicked a ball in senior football, was suddenly the best-known young player in the land.

The suspicion at Spurs was that their hot young property had been 'got at' and was being tempted away from Tottenham.

'I have never known such an ambitious and impatient young man,' an exasperated Nicholson told me. 'He has a wonderful future in the game, but he wants to run before he can walk. He can't understand why I'm not already considering him for the first-team. He wants to jump ahead of established professionals like Alan Mullery, Martin Peters and Steve Perryman. His chance will come, but he must show patience. If he's ever picked for Scotland I wonder if they will find a cap big enough for his head.'

A suitably repentant Souness returned to Tottenham, but he wore out the carpet to Bill Nicholson's office to the point where the veteran Spurs boss decided, reluctantly, he had no option but to let him go. He had made one brief first-team appearance in a Uefa Cup tie (substituting for Martin Peters in a match in Iceland) before being sold to Middlesbrough in December 1972 for £27,000, which was a hefty fee in those days for a virtually unknown and untried player. For ever after, Bill Nick considered Souness 'the one that got away.'

Souness was history at The Lane by the time Tottenham's defence of the Uefa Cup ended in the semi-final in the 1972-73 season, eliminated by a rampant Liverpool team on its way to a League Championship and Uefa Cup double. Consolation came in the shape of the League Cup again, this time with Norwich City the beaten team in an uninspiring final.

The highlight for Tottenham on the way to Wembley was beating the form team Liverpool 3-1 in the deciding semi-final leg at White Hart Lane to reach their second final in three years. It was one of those special Lane evenings, the action and the atmosphere making the skin tingle. They saw off Wolves 4-3 on aggregate in the semi-final, which softened the blow of going out to Brian Clough's Derby County in the fourth round of the FA Cup.

Substitute Ralph Coates provided the only memorable moment in the final against a Norwich team bidding for a hat-trick against London glamour sides. They accounted

Many knowledgeable Tottenham fans rate Mike England the greatest of all Spurs centre-halves. Here he is proving his superiority over Chelsea centre-forward Tony Hateley in the 1967 FA Cup final.

for Arsenal in the quarter-final and Chelsea in the semi-final. Their second-leg tie against Chelsea had been abandoned because of fog, and some critics cruelly suggested that they were still in a fog when they got to Wembley to face Tottenham. Norwich played with a strangely negative attitude, and the game got bogged down in a midfield traffic jam.

Coates, a £190,000 signing from Burnley in May 1971, had never quite lived up to his potential at White Hart Lane, and he was desperately unhappy to be relegated to the substitutes' bench. But he gave his answer to the critics in the best possible way after being summoned into the goalless match midway through the first-half following an injury to Tottenham loyalist John Pratt.

Finding rare space in the congested midfield, Coates raced forward and cracked in a low right foot shot from the edge of the penalty area that sizzled wide of goalkeeper Kevin Keelan's despairing dive. It was the only goal of a game that was described by one veteran reporter as, 'the dullest match ever witnessed at Wembley.'

Hero Coates, who settled down to score 23 goals in 229 League matches in a seven-year stay at Spurs, said:

> **'**I needed this goal as much for my own confidence as for the team. It was a bitter blow when I was told I would be on the subs' bench. Norwich packed so many players into their own half that there didn't seem to be any room out there to breathe, let alone run. Happily, I got one sight of goal and let fly. It was one of the most satisfying goals I've ever scored.**'**

The winning team:
Jennings, Kinnear, Knowles, Pratt, England, Beal, Gilzean, Perryman, Chivers, Peters, Pearce. Sub: Coates.

In the same month that he helped Spurs win the League Cup, the peerless Pat Jennings proved just why he was rated one of the world's greatest goalkeepers by making two penalty saves in a First Division game against League leaders Liverpool at Anfield. No wonder he was elected Footballer of the Year that season.

Author warning: Tottenham fans of a nervous disposition might want to skip the next few pages. It does not make pretty reading.

Bill Nicholson called it "the saddest night of my life" – the night that Tottenham played Feyenoord in Rotterdam in the second leg of the Uefa Cup final on May 29 1974. It was what happened *off* the pitch rather than on it, where Spurs were soundly beaten 2-0 to give Feyenoord a 4-2 aggregate victory.

The Uefa Cup had been the exclusive property of Football League clubs for six successive years, but Feyenoord deservedly became the first Dutch winners of the trophy after a final that turned into the blackest event in Tottenham's proud history.

Spurs had been flattered by a 2-2 draw in the first leg at White Hart Lane. A goal just before half-time from centre-half Mike England and an own goal by Van Daele cancelled out goals by the highly skilled tandem team of Van Hanegem and De Jong.

Feyenoord were comfortably the better team in the second-leg, and a section of so-called Spurs supporters could not stomach seeing their team being made to look strictly second best.

The Dutch masters clinched victory with their second goal two minutes from the final whistle. This sparked a riot by Spurs followers that led to 70 arrests and to 200 spectators being treated for injuries.

Bill Nicholson, choking back tears, appealed over the public address system for sanity. "You hooligans are a disgrace to Tottenham Hotspur and a disgrace to England," he said. "This is a game of football – not a war."

That night Bill Nick was close to walking out on the club that had been his life. He said in an emotional after-match statement:

> ❛This is the saddest night of my life. It makes you wonder if it is all worth it when you see people behaving like animals. It is not just a football problem. It is a social problem, and hooliganism is eating into our great game. Questions should be asked as to whether there is enough discipline in schools. Feyenoord were worthy winners, and I am extremely embarrassed that a minority among our supporters – people we should disown – were unable to accept the fact that we were beaten by a better side.❜

Bill Nick festered and fretted throughout the summer, waiting for the new season for the first time in his career without enthusiasm. He felt his beloved Spurs had been badly wounded by the incident in Rotterdam, and he was disillusioned by the way widespread hooliganism was scarring the face of the once Beautiful Game.

He had suddenly lost the ability to motivate his players, and he slipped into a deep depression as Spurs got off to their worst start ever with four successive defeats. On August 29 1974, 'Mr Tottenham' handed in his resignation, bringing to an end 39 years service to the club and 16 of them as the most successful manager in Spurs history.

It was not only hooliganism that had robbed Nicholson of his appetite, but also player power and greed. He revealed: "Players have become impossible. They talk all the time about security, but they are not prepared to work for it. I am abused by players when they come to see me. There is no longer respect …"

He dropped a bombshell at a press conference by divulging: "I have recently found it impossible to get the players I want because at Tottenham we pride ourselves in not making under-the-counter payments. It is expected in the London area for players to ask for £7,000 tax free. That's the minimum asking price. I want no part of that world."

Skipper Martin Peters and long-serving defender Phil Beal made a private visit to Nicholson on behalf of the players to ask him to change his mind and stay on, but he said there was no going back. The Tottenham directors wrung their hands, and allowed the Father of Tottenham to leave, when an arm around the shoulders and warm words of encouragement could have made him change his mind.

Eddie Baily, another long-time Spurs servant and a highly regarded and sometimes acid-tongued coach, departed with Nicholson, complaining loudly about what he considered miserly contract-settlement terms. Bill Nick got a 'golden' handshake that he confidentially described to me as "pathetic."

There were strong rumours that Lane icon Danny Blanchflower would take over. This is what Bill Nicholson had advised, but he found the directors deaf to his suggestions. Instead, the Board appointed another Irishman … Terry Neill, a red-blooded former captain at Highbury who had Arsenal written all over him. Many of the Tottenham fans were incredulous. The Board had turned the clock back to the Joe Hulme days. A Gooner in charge at The Lane. It could only end in tears.

Bill Nicholson was incredulous, and told me privately: "I cannot believe that the Tottenham board have preferred Terry Neill to Danny, who is Spurs through and through. No disrespect to Terry, but he is a Highbury man and will find it very difficult to persuade the Tottenham fans to think otherwise."

Neill brought in Scottish strikers John Duncan and Alfie Conn, but it was an 'old hand' who saved Tottenham from what looked certain relegation. Martin Chivers, recalled after two months in the wilderness, scored one of the goals as Spurs just beat the drop with a 4-2 victory over Leeds in a nail-nibbling end of season game at White Hart Lane.

Bill Nicholson and Eddie Baily made quiet returns to football in the summer of 1975, both of them joining West Ham in scouting and consultant roles. Meantime, Terry Neill was fighting an uphill battle to pump confidence and belief into his Tottenham players. He did not mince words after a goalless draw with Arsenal at White Hart Lane: "I apologise to everybody who paid good money to watch this rubbish. It made me feel ashamed. It was the kind of stuff that could kill football."

Terry, whom I have known and liked since his days as a teenager under Billy Wright at Highbury, had a lot of big ideas, but never truly settled at White Hart Lane. Die-hard Tottenham fans could not accept him as "one of us." They might have changed their mind if he had managed to pull off an audacious transfer deal in February 1976. He discovered that Johan Cruyff was unsettled at Barcelona, and moved in with a bid that was turned down.

Johan Cruyff in a Tottenham shirt. Now that would have been something special.

Terry Neill (left) went home to Arsenal and made way for Keith Burkinshaw (below centre), who stunned the football world by bringing Argentinian 1978 World Cup stars Ricardo Villa and Osvaldo Ardiles to Tottenham. Suddenly it was South American fiesta time at The Lane of Dreams.

Three days after he had been rebuffed by the Dutchman, Neill gave a full League debut to a 17-year-old midfield player who would one day become Cruyff class with his passing. Enter Glenn Hoddle, who marked his arrival on the senior stage by firing a spectacular shot past Stoke City and England goalkeeper Peter Shilton.

Terry was not at Spurs to see Hoddle develop into a footballing master. In July 1976 he followed his heart and went home to Highbury as Arsenal manager in succession to Bertie Mee. It is no secret that a lot of Lilywhite supporters said: "Good riddance."

The Spurs directors, now with the enthusiastic Irving Scholar at the helm, promoted coach Keith Burkinshaw to the Tottenham hot seat, and one of the first things that he did – sensibly and fitting – was to invite Lane Legend Bill Nicholson back in an advisory role. It should be placed on record that Irving Scholar played a major part in the return 'home' of Nicholson. He was a chairman who fully appreciated just what Bill Nick had done for the club. And now Burkinshaw was emerging as a manager in the Nicholson mould.

Everybody – fans, players, directors, media circus – liked Keith, an ex-Barnsley miner who came up the hard way and had Nicholson-style principles and work ethic. He had beeen a peripheral defender at Liverpool before giving long service at the football outposts of Workington and Scunthorpe. He learned his coaching trade in Zambia and then with Newcastle, joining Spurs in 1975 – one of Bill Nicholson's final signings for the backroom team. A true student of the game, he used to sit at Bill Nick's feet learning all he could from the great man. Like his mentor, Keith was a dour Yorkshireman who wore blinkers that meant he saw nothing but the world of football.

His first season in full control climaxed with the ultimate humiliation: relegation in bottom place, ending a 27-year unbroken run for Spurs at the top table.

The directors kept faith with Burkinshaw, and he rewarded their confidence by leading Tottenham straight back up again … but not before a transfer in August 1977 that baffled and bewildered just about everybody.

Pat Jennings, arguably the greatest goalkeeper in history, was allowed to join his Northern Ireland buddy Terry Neill at Highbury of all places. Over the next eight years, Pat went on to give Arsenal nearly as good service as he had given to Spurs.

On their way back up to the First Division – magnificently marshalled on the pitch by big-hearted Steve Perryman and steered by the gifted Glenn Hoddle – Tottenham found they had still not rid themselves of the curse of hooliganism. There were 85 people hurt when fighting broke out on the pitch between rival fans when Tottenham were beaten 3-1 by promotion rivals Brighton at the Goldstone Ground on April 15 1978.

With the season into its last embers, Tottenham, Bolton and Southampton were neck and neck at the top of the table, with Brighton just two points behind. Spurs clinched an instant return to the First Division with a tense goalless draw against Southampton, pipping Brighton on goal average for third place. This, of course, was before play-offs were introduced, and it was a finale that tested nerves like never before. Many Spurs fans talked of feeling physically sick during that last game against the Saints.

Speaking on a personal level, I was so pleased for Steve Perryman, who ran himself into the ground to help push Spurs to promotion. I had seen him grow up from the baby of the team to taking on the role of leader, He could not compete with the likes of Glenn Hoddle for skill – who could? – but his effort and energy lifted and inspired those around him. He was devastated when Tottenham were relegated, and secretly vowed that they would bounce back immediately. He kept his target to himself. Like so many of the great players, Steve was a man of action rather than words.

Few will forget the highlight of that promotion season, a 9-0 thrashing of Bristol Rovers at The Lane on October 22 1977. Colin Lee, signed from Torquay just 48 hours earlier for £60,000 to partner bullocking Ian Moores, found the passes from Hoddle and thrusting winger Peter Taylor like a silverplate service after his days down the League. He scored four goals in the humiliation of Rovers. Just a week earlier Spurs had gone down to a 1-4 defeat against Charlton Athletic. What was that Greavsie says about it being 'a funny old game'!

While Colin Lee took all the headlines, a rival to him as the man of the match was the unsung John Pratt, who continually won the ball in midfield and then fed it to Glenn Hoddle, who finished off the banquet with a stunning strike that put a golden seal on Tottenham's record League victory. It was just a glimpse of the Hoddle magic that was waiting to be unwrapped on the return to the First Division stage.

While most managers were sunning themselves on beaches in the close season, Keith Burkinshaw made a top-secret trip to South America and, amazingly, returned with the signatures of two of the heroes of Argentina's 1978 World Cup triumph. It rated as one of the most sensational double transfer coups in football history when Spurs bought Osvaldo Ardiles (from Huracan) and Ricardo Villa (from Racing Club) in a £700,000 investment that staggered everybody.

Spurs were boldly making the most of the Professional Football Association's decision to lift the ban on foreign players, and the newly introduced freedom of contract suddenly made the Football League an attractive proposition for overseas players.

PFA officials Cliff Lloyd and Gordon Taylor expressed their concern over the deal, and were worried about a sudden influx of foreign players. "If the trickle becomes a flow we will take a very serious view of it," said secretary Lloyd, the man who with Jimmy Hill negotiated the lifting of the £20 maximum wage just 17 years earlier. "We are concerned about our members who will not be able to get first-team football because of these newcomers from overseas."

Before the end of the Century, all Cliff Lloyd's fears would be justified. It was a revolution started by Tottenham, and it quickly brought rewards.

Fasten your safety belts as we go into the 'eighties.

AFTER their 'lost' year in the Second Division, Tottenham took a season to find their feet back at the top table and then came into the 1980s with something of a swagger, a lot of style and a hint of a smile. And, of course – almost as footballing folklore demanded – they marked the first year of the decade, 1980-81, with a major trophy.

There are many Spurs supporters who will tell you that the Tottenham team of those early '80s played the best football of any White Hart Lane side. Those of a certain age would continue to champion the Push and Run and/or the Double team as the ideal combination. But there can be no denying that Keith Burkinshaw had inspired his team to touch Everest peaks of perfection in the best traditions of Tottenham.

No dispute as to which player did most to motivate the Spurs revival movement with his skill, perfect balance, passing control and shooting accuracy. Take a bow Glenn Hoddle, who in that first season back in the First Division revealed that he had matured into a midfield master of international class.

In that regrouping campaign of 1978-79 – while bedding in Argentine aces Ardiles and Villa – Hoddle really flourished, scoring 19 goals in 41 League appearances and winning recognition as the PFA Young Player of the Year. He also managed to fit in a debut goal for England against Bulgaria in November 1979. Meantime, Steve Archibald and Garth Crooks had arrived at The Lane as a £1.5 million tandem team to give the attack extra authority and artistry.

Gradually Hoddle and Ardiles got their double act together, perfecting their footballing tango partnership. This was Strictly Come Passing. Alongside them in a magnificent midfield engine room, the perpetual motion man, Stevie Perryman, was more into the hokey-cokey, keeping one foot in defence and one in attack.

Ossie was becoming a White Hart Lane folk hero. A likeable, intelligent man, he happily went along with Cockney singing duo Chas and Dave turning him into a short-term hit-parade star in *Ossie's Dream (Spurs Are On Their Way to Wembley)*. In the recording studio, Ossie turned the endearing ' … in de Cup for Tott-ing-ham' line into a perfectly spoken, '…in the Cup for Tottenham.'

Chas and Dave had based their lyric on an early interview with Ossie. They stopped the recording and pointed out that he needed to stick to the line as written. "But I can say Tottenham properly now," said a bewildered Ardiles.

A key player in Argentina's 1978 World Cup winning team, Ardiles was known in his homeland as Pitón (Python) because of his snake-like, low gravity weaving and dribbling. He settled more quickly to the pace and demands of English football than his bearded, often brooding compatriot Ricardo (Ricky) Villa. It took him a long time to win the hearts of the Tottenham fans, but in the 1981 FA Cup replay against Manchester City he entered the land of soccer legend. He conjured one of the goals of the century to give Tottenham a dramatic 3-2 victory. It deserves a full description:

Tony Galvin, patrolling Tottenham's left wing with imagination and flair, released a seventy-sixth minute pass to Villa on the left hand side of the pitch some fifteen yards outside the heavily populated City penalty area. The score stood at 2-2 in what was the 100th FA Cup final, and the thought of extra-time – as in the first match five days earlier – was beginning to come to mind. The only thing that had distinguished the first drab game was that City's giant-hearted Scot Tommy Hutchison had managed to score for both teams.

But there was nothing drab about the replay, staged on the following Thursday for television scheduling purposes. What followed as Villa took possession of the ball from Galvin was the stuff of which fairytales are made. The player who had sulked off the pitch in tears when substituted in the first deadlocked match switched moods from siesta to fiesta. Where there had been tears in the eyes there was now a twinkle.

He set off on a diagonal run towards the City goal, but as there were five defenders ahead of him it seemed a pretty useless exercise. Those of us who have no grasp or understanding of an artist's invention and intention assumed that he would be passing the ball to a better-positioned colleague. What do we know! We looked on intoxicated as Villa suddenly changed direction and started running across the face of the City goal, side-stepping tackles with the casual grace of a Fred Astaire flying down to Rio, or perhaps Buenos Aires. There was certainly something of a tango rhythm to his movement as he went this way and then that past bemused and confused defenders.

Two City players were so befuddled by his unorthodox progress that they ran into each other as they tried to block his path. The bearded and hefty Argentine, a Wild Bull of the Pampas yet as light on his feet as a spring lamb, had the appearance of his countryman Che Guevara on a revolutionary march. He was creating a goal that launched a million metaphors.

Villa showed strength to go with his skill as he survived buffeting challenges before unbalancing the oncoming City goalkeeper Joe Corrigan with a pretence at a shot, and then sliding the ball right footed into the net from eight yards for a goal that deserved an oil painting rather than a photograph.

It was all over in less than ten blinding seconds, but has remained on the memory

It takes one to tango as Ricky Villa completes his destructive dance through the Manchester City defence

screen of all those who witnessed it live and on television. In a nationwide poll in 1999, it was voted best ever FA Cup final goal. Who's arguing?

Once the ball bulged the back of the City net it became South American carnival time as Villa raced around Wembley on a wild dance of delight, with his diminutive countryman Ossie Ardiles trying to catch him. The celebration was as unique as the goal.

A match that had almost died on its feet on the Saturday had been given the kick of life and it guaranteed that the 100th FA Cup final would be remembered through the following century of matches. Villa, who usually had to operate in the shadow of his more illustrious colleague Ardiles, said in hesitant yet charming English:

> ❛On Saturday I was so unhappy. Now I am the happiest footballer in the world. When I ran towards the goal the ball seemed to stick to my feet. I did not think of passing because I enjoy running with the ball. My big thanks to the manager Mr. Keith Burkinshaw for picking me. I did not think he would ever select me again after the way I left the field when I was substituted. But now I have repaid him with the greatest goal of my life. On Saturday I wanted to cry, today I laugh and laugh!❜

The winning team: **Aleksic, Hughton, Miller, Roberts, Perryman, Villa, Ardiles (Brooke), Archibald, Galvin, Hoddle, Crooks**

While Spurs were purring to the FA Cup, White Hart Lane was being given a face-lift. The old West Stand was demolished to make way for a smart, state-of-the-art new structure that cost £4-million to build. It was officially opened on February 6 1982, with Wolves the visitors in a First Division match. Cup hero Ricky Villa led the celebrations with a hat-trick as Tottenham walloped Wolves 6-1.

Tottenham were tasting heady Nicholson-style success under Keith Burkinshaw. At one stage in the 1981-82 season, 'Burkinshaw's Beauties' had White Hart Lane fans dreaming of not just another Double, more like a a Treble or even a Quadruple! They were in the hunt for the League championship right up until Easter (finally finishing fourth behind winners Liverpool), and went all the way to the European Cup Winners' Cup semi-final – going down 2-1 on aggregate to eventual winners Barcelona, who angered Spurs with their cynical and clinical win-at-all-costs tactics.

Burkinshaw TWICE led out Tottenham at Wembley in that always exciting, often explosive and never less than eventful season, first of all in the League Cup against Liverpool. It was the first League Cup final sponsored by the Milk Marketing Board, and it turned sour for Spurs, even with ex-Anfield goalkeeper Ray Clemence bringing Pat Jennings-type quality to the goal-line. They grabbed the lead through Archibald, but ran out of steam against a mighty Liverpool team powered by the likes of Kenny

Dalglish, Ian Rush and 'the Spur who got away' Graeme Souness. Tottenham conceded a late equaliser to Ronnie Whelan, and were buried in extra-time by a goal from Rush and another from Whelan. For the first time, Spurs had lost a domestic final and this defeat ended an astonishing run of 25 consecutive unbeaten cup games. There was laughter to go with the tears. The TV cameras panning the crowd settled on a waving Tottenham banner, but quickly moved on when the message registered: 'Hold on to your knickers, it's the year of the Cock.'

Two months later Tottenham were back at Wembley to defend the FA Cup, but without Ardiles or Villa. The misfortunes of war meant they had to temporarily leave the country while Britain and Argentina battled over The Falklands – or, if you listened to Ossie and Ricky, the Malvinas Islands.

Waiting for Tottenham in the final were London neighbours Queen's Park Rangers, under the management of former White Hart Lane schemer Terry Venables. Two largely unforgettable games were finally settled in the replay by a Glenn Hoddle strike from the penalty spot. Venables and Hoddle would often find themselves in the headlines together in the coming years.

The FA Cup winning team in 1982:

Clemence, Hughton, Miller, Price, Hazard (Brooke), Perryman, Roberts, Archibald, Galvin, Hoddle, Crooks.

While on the pitch everything looked smooth and well organized, there were the beginnings of upheaval in the boardroom that was to become commonplace. The Wales' had made way for the Richardsons – Arthur and Geoffrey – but the family image that had been so jealously guarded became a thing of the past. Douglas Alexiou took over as the first of a procession of high-powered businessmen filling the prestigious chairman's seat. Pulling the strings were future chairman Irving Scholar and Paul Broboff, who had taken effective control when trend-setters Tottenham became the first football club to float shares on the London Stock Exchange. From now on, profits were as important as points for Tottenham Hotspur PLC. What would those pioneering boys who gathered under the gas-lit lamppost in Tottenham High Road back in 1882 have made of it all?

Burkinshaw was making no secret of the fact that he was unhappy with the high-pressure business approach to the game and was having regular battles in the boardroom. He was further unsettled by a running dispute with Steve Archibald that spilled over into the newspapers. His disillusionment reached new depths as he steered his stylish side to the 1983-84 UEFA Cup, with a dramatic penalty shoot-out victory over Anderlecht.

The teams were deadlocked at 2-2 at the end of extra-time in the second leg at White Hart Lane, and – with young goalkeeper Tony Parks the hero – Spurs won 4-3 on the Russian roulette penalties system. There was general agreement that Tottenham would have lost the final if skipper Graham Roberts had not produced a barnstorming display

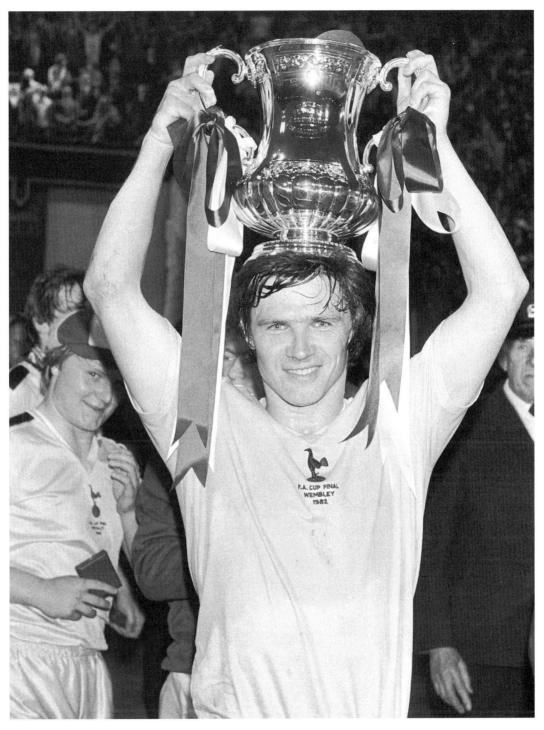

"On me 'ead, son!" Steve Perryman, Spurs skipper, appears to wear the FA Cup

over the two legs that knocked the breath out of a polished Belgian side.

Tottenham captured this latest trophy without their key man Hoddle, who was being continually troubled by niggling injuries. The highlight of the run to the Uefa Cup was a 6-2 aggregate second round victory over Feyenoord, who had the veteran Johan Cruyff controlling their midfield. Hoddle outmastered the master to confirm that he had now established himself as a player of world class. The winning team:

Parks, Hughton, Miller (Ardiles 77), Mabbutt (Dick 73), Thomas, Roberts, Galvin, Hazard, Stevens, Falco, Archibald.

The Uefa Cup triumph marked the end of Burkinshaw's reign that had brought promotion and three trophies, along with stylish football that was easy on the eye in the best traditions of Tottenham. Totally disenchanted with the boardroom situation, he kept to his pledge issued earlier in the season to quit. He made his exit with the sad comment: "There used to be a football club here …"

With Irving Scholar now in the chair, Burkinshaw's assistant Peter Shreeves was promoted to manager. But there was little doubt that Scholar was the man in control. A walking record book on the club history, he stressed that his priority was making Tottenham Hotspur PLC profitable. He introduced the age of the executive boxes that many die-hard Spurs fans felt had the effect of robbing White Hart Lane of its famous atmosphere that 'in the old days' had been considered worth a goal start to the team. The Shelf (but not its spirit) was disappearing into history.

We need to pause and take into context what was happening in football in general to understand some of the reasons for the changes at The Lane. Three appalling disasters plunged the '80s decade into a darkness that continues to haunt those caught up in the terrible aftermath.

I will list the tragedies here, not only out of respect for those whose lives were lost but because they led to a revolution in the game that was to change the face of football forever.

The nation was sent into mourning first of all by the Bradford City fire of 1985 that cost 56 lives when a stand at the antiquated Valley Parade ground went up in flames during a Third Division match against Lincoln City.

This was followed just three weeks later by the horror of Heysel Stadium. Thirty-nine mainly Italian spectators died from crushing and suffocation during the European Cup final between Juventus and Liverpool in Brussels on 29 May 1985, a day that will go down in infamy.

The catastrophe generated an international debate on hooliganism and scarred the reputation of English football supporters. Subsequent investigations into the tragedy laid the blame on the Liverpool fans, and the repercussions were felt throughout the English game.

All League clubs were banned by Uefa from taking part in European competitions, leaving English football to stagnate. By the time the ban was lifted in 1990 English teams were trailing their European rivals both tactically and technically.

Just as the nightmares of Bradford and Heysel were being pushed into the farthest corners of our memories a third devastating tragedy struck. Ninety-five Liverpool supporters were killed and 170 injured on overcrowded, tired terraces during the Liverpool-Nottingham Forest FA Cup semi-final at Hillsborough on April 15 1989. It was a disaster witnessed by millions on television, and led to a whirlwind of change. All-seater stadiums were demanded and it brought an end to the Victorian terrace culture. The game would never be the same again, and all this served to help push Scholar into redeveloping the famous old White Hart Lane ground beyond recognition. Only those of us of a certain age will be able to recall the atmosphere of those fantastic glory-glory nights that made the hair on the back of your neck stand on end … without a ball being kicked.

The point I am making is that all blame for the massive alterations at The Lane should not be loaded on Scholar's shoulders. Changes were forced by the sadness of the times. It signalled the approach of the corporate influence on major clubs, and the emergence of the 'prawn sandwich' supporters.

For Peter Shreeves, 1984-85 became a season of promise that ended in heartache. He got off to a rocketing start and at Christmas Tottenham were top of the table. But they were eventually overtaken by Liverpool and Everton, and the consolation of a place in the Uefa Cup was snatched from Shreeves by the blanket ban on English clubs following the Heysel Stadium tragedy.

Tottenham fans wondered if they were dreaming in January 1986 when world master Maradona appeared in a Spurs shirt. But it was only a one-off appearance for the Ossie Ardiles testimonial match. The supporters were only half joking as they chanted everytime Maradona settled on the ball: "Sign him ... sign him ..."

After a flat and generally undistinguished second season in charge, Peter Shreeves made way for the arrival of David Pleat. In a spectacular first season, the full-of-enthusiasm-and-ideas former Luton Town boss steered Tottenham to third place in the First Division and a third appearance in an FA Cup final in six years.

Pleat's Plan of a five-man midfield fomation (Glenn Hoddle, Ossie Ardiles, Steve Hodge, Paul Allen and the clever Chris Waddle) supporting the razor-sharp lone striker Clive Allen worked almost to perfection. The disappointment of defeat in a three-match League Cup semi-final serial with the dreaded Arsenal was off set by a thumping 4-1 FA Cup semi-final victory over Watford.

Their opponents in the 1987 FA Cup final were Coventry City, a club with a history mainly of taking part rather than winning things. The Sky Blues were at Wembley for the first time in their 104 years, while Spurs were bidding for their eighth victory in eight FA Cup finals.

Glenn Hoddle, supreme as a player at The Lane but mediocre as a manager.

It would have taken a brave or foolish man to bet against Tottenham continuing their winning streak when, in less than two minutes, Clive Allen scored his forty-ninth goal of the season for Spurs. There had not been finishing finesse and consistency like this since the days of Jimmy Greaves, who had pushed Clive's dad, Les, out of the Tottenham team.

In the end, it all came down to glory and grief for Tottenham's marvellous defender Gary Mabbutt, who played at the top level throughout his career despite being a chronic diabetic.

He scored Tottenham's second goal to put them 2-1 in the lead, which was cancelled out on the hour by a diving header from Coventry marksman Keith Houchen.

For the fifth time in seven years an FA Cup final drifted into extra-time, and in what was the 97th minute the unfortunate Mabbutt turned a cross into his own net to give Coventry a victory they thoroughly deserved.

The Tottenham team: Clemence, Hughton (Claesen, 97), Thomas, Hodge, Gough, Mabbutt, Paul Allen, Waddle, Clive Allen, Hoddle, Ardiles (Stevens, 91).

It was the end of an era, with Glenn Hoddle closing his glorious Spurs playing career after contributing 110 goals and a million spot-on passes in 490 first-team matches. He was signed for £750,000 by AS Monaco, and joined forces with their new manager, a scholarly chap called Arsene Wenger. The move broke up the thankfully short-lived double act of Hoddle and Waddle, who had managed to sing their way into the pop charts with the single 'Diamond Lights'.

Let me go on record by saying that Hoddle and Waddle will be much better remembered in White Hart Lane folklore for their footballing rather than singing skills. Both can be mentioned in the same breath as any of the all-time idols. What a pity that a growing financial crisis meant they could not be kept together to please Tottenham fans and tease opposition defences with their glorious talent.

By October 1987 the Tottenham lights went out for David Pleat. He was treated appallingly by the tabloids as he got caught up in a kerb-crawling sex scandal that should have remained a private matter.

His position became untenable at White Hart Lane, and he was shown the door.

I talked a distressed David out of writing a book about the episode, because I knew he had the character and the intelligence to make a comeback. He has since proved himself one of the game's great philosophers, and the stress and strain of those last days in charge at White Hart Lane soon disappeared into a locked memory box. He would return.

As Pleat exited in the autumn of 1987, a Tottenham old boy made his entrance as manager. The fun, the games – and the fury – of the Terry Venables era were about to kick off.

TERRY VENABLES was rarely out of the headlines in the 1990s – come to think of it, he was rarely out of the football news from the 1960s onwards. He and I have known, and largely avoided each other for coming up 50 years, from when he was first starting out as a 17-year-old boy wonder with Chelsea. When we were young married men we lived around the corner to each other in semi-detached houses. How times have changed for footballers! I have followed his career closely every step of the way, and the Tottenham adventure took his ability to surprise to new horizons.

The occasionally swaggering, often amusing and always enterprising Cheeky Chappie of football left QPR in 1984 for a spell in Spain where – after winning La Liga – he became affectionately known as El Tel. While in charge at Loftus Road he supervised and encouraged the laying of the first synthetic pitch – and wrote a novel about it called *They Used to Play on Grass*. But his vision of the future proved blurred. Luton, Oldham and Preston were the only other clubs who followed Rangers into the plastic revolution, and by 1993 they were all back on grass. Football was not in need of plastic surgery – yet. Tottenham, however, WAS a club urgently requiring financial surgery when Venables was tempted back to White Hart Lane in November 1987.

His arrival was a prelude to the best of times and the worst of times, with the club making as many headlines on the news and business pages as on the sports pages. Terry kept the supporters happy by bringing in Geordie entertainer Paul Gascoigne from Newcastle for a then club record £2-million, and he then went back to his old club Barcelona to coax that crisp finisher Gary Lineker home to the British game in the summer of '89 for a fee of £1.2 million. Celebrations over this coup were short-lived when – to try to balance the books – Tottenham had to sell the enormously popular Chris Waddle to Marseille for 'an offer they could not refuse' – £4.25-million.

A third place in the First Division in 1989-90 was proof that Venables was starting to get things right on the pitch, but there was blood on the walls of the boardroom. The 1990 property slump hit chairman Irving Scholar like a wrecking ball to the wallet, and suddenly Tottenham was a club wide open for a take-over.

Scholar had many critics shooting from the lip, but the years of his reign had lots of sunshine before the money-devouring East Stand development brought dark financial

*Terry Venables hand in hand with Cloughie before the 1991 FA Cup final (above) ...
and shoulder-to-shoulder in unison with Alan Sugar (below). It would end in tears.*

storm clouds over The Lane. In his ten-year involvement with the club (not counting his life-long, scarf-waving support) he was at the helm for some eventful times ...

1982 - FA Cup Winners, 3rd in the League
1983 - 4th in the League
1984 - Uefa Cup winners
1985 - 5th in the league
1986 - 10th in the League, David Pleat appointed manager
1987 - 3rd in the League, FA Cup runners up
1988 - 13th in the League, Terry Venables manager, Paul Gascoigne signed
1989 - Gary Linker signed, 6th in the League
1990 - Third in the League
1991 - FA Cup winners

But it was off the pitch where Scholar's Spurs were coming apart at the seams. The *Financial Times* made much more worrying reading than *Shoot Magazine*:

> •Tottenham's losses for the year are £2.6-million. Trading profits of £1.3-million were erased by interest charges. Delays and rising labour and material costs in the rebuilding of the East Stand have sent the debt to Midland Bank spiralling to £12-million ...•

Cries for a saviour just about stopped short of supporters writing 'HELP' in huge letters on the famous White Hart Lane pitch. It was widely reported that sailing to the rescue was 'Captain' Robert Maxwell, nobody – least of all his staff – realizing that he was using *Mirror* Newspaper pension funds to muscle in on all sorts of business deals.

In the autumn of 1990 Tottenham's shares were suspended at 91p by the City watchdogs, and newspaper maggot (sorry, magnate) Maxwell seemingly abandoned takeover plans that always appeared confused and never set in concrete.

If you think I am going over the top with my description of 'Robber' Maxwell, translate it as a few lightweight blows on behalf of my old mates at the *Mirror*, who were criminally cheated out of their pensions.

To get the full inside story of the battle for power at The Lane I recommend you read *Down Memory Lane* (Green Umbrella Publishing) by Harry 'Scoop' Harris. He was a confidant of Maxwell, Scholar, Alan Sugar and just about everybody but Terry Venables, and has written an astonishingly informative book that is about the politics of Spurs, while I prefer mine to be about the passion and the pride. Yes, you can interpret that as meaning I was not as well informed as Harry. I could easily have nicked all the

The sickening moment in the 1991 FA Cup final when Paul Gascoigne's reckless tackle against Nottingham Forest right-back Gary Charles very nearly ended Gazza's career.

facts from his book and said nowt, but a plagiarist I'm not. You would not normally read this sort of thing in a book, because the publishers would have a fit. But as I am self publishing, I see nothing wrong with a little honesty and an admittance that Harry's book gives a better insight into the boardroom shenanigans at The Lane. Uh, can you pay for this book before switching to his :-).

Harry had the inside track on what was happening at The Lane, but what I *did* know is that leading the charge for control of Spurs was a consortium headed by none other than my old mate El Tel! Meantime, Paul Gascoigne had turned himself into one of the world's hottest properties with his talent (and his tears) on the 1990 World Cup stage in Italy. There was talk of him being worth a world record £15 million in the transfer market, which gave a sudden boost to the Tottenham shares.

Gazza, who often seemed from another planet with his audacious play but suspect temperament, was crying again at Wembley in 1991, this time in pain. Playing for Tottenham in the FA Cup final against Brian Clough's Nottingham Forest, he made a crazy, scything tackle on Gary Charles in the fifteenth minute. Gazza injured his knee so badly in the challenge that he was carried off and taken to hospital for an operation that delayed his £8-million transfer to Lazio, money needed desperately by near-bankrupt Spurs. If he had not been stretchered off, the likelihood is that he would have been sent off for his recklessly dangerous play, which – in fairness – was completely out of character. He was daft but never dirty.

A month earlier, in the first semi-final ever played at Wembley, Gazza had helped beat deadly rivals Arsenal with a rifled thirty-five yard free-kick that completely baffled England goalkeeper David Seaman. "One of the best free-kicks I've never seen," Seaman told me later when we worked together on a series of football video productions.

Gazza, the most naturally gifted footballer of his generation, was a player and a person of many different faces and moods, and to a lot of us looking on seemed like somebody almost certainly on a collision course with calamity. Gary Lineker plundered the other two goals in Tottenham's so-satisfying 3-1 victory over Arsenal, the team being master-minded through a glorious run of success by George Graham. Terry Venables had been George's best man when they were close chums back in the mid-sixties. Here he was, more then 20 years later, best man again.

The Tottenham-Forest final went into extra-time. Bizarrely, while El Tel was out on the pitch coaxing and encouraging his players in the short break, Cloughie stood passing the time of day with a policeman. Spurs went on to win 2-1 when Forest defender Des Walker deflected the ball into his own net. It was FA Cup win number eight for Tottenham, and – naturally – with an 01 in the year.

The FA Cup was the one trophy that always eluded Cloughie, who said of the policeman incident: "He was a very nice chap and I was interested in what sort of day he was having. Trying to crowd thoughts into players' minds at that stage is pretty pointless.

If they don't know what to do by then they should not be professional footballers."

There will never be another quite like Brian Clough.

The Spurs team: **Thorstvedt, Edinburgh, Van Den Hauwe, Sedgley, Howells, Mabbutt, Stewart, Gascoigne (Nayim 17), Samways (Walsh 82), Lineker, Paul Allen**

Victorious Venables got his mind back on business rather than football matters, and in June 1991 joined forces with East End tycoon Alan Sugar in a combined bid for the club, as Robert Maxwell – advised by his chief *Mirror* reporter Harry Harris – came back into the frame. Scholar, with anxious bankers breathing down his neck, handed control over to the Venables/Sugar team. I believe that Scholar genuinely always wanted what was right for Spurs, and was one of the few chairmen who could quote chapter and verse on the history of his club. Did Alan Sugar know a Waddle from a Hoddle?

Venables teaming up with Sugar seemed a marriage made in heaven, but the path was to lead to hell. Peter Shreeves was briefly brought back as manager, while chief executive Venables concentrated on running the club in harness with major shareholder Sugar. Very quickly, their honeymoon turned into a headline-hitting divorce. Bill Nicholson, honoured with the club Presidency, looked on with increasing disillusionment. He hated it when the activities of the boardroom overshadowed the football.

Shreeves was dismissed again in 1992 after an indifferent season, with Venables taking on many of the managerial responsibilities, supervising the work of joint coaches Ray Clemence and Doug Livermore.

Sugar was appalled by some of the business transactions that were taken as the norm in football. In 1993 – at the dawn of the Age of the Premiership – he sensationally sacked Venables (I wonder if he actually said, 'You're fired!'). During a vicious bout of legal fisticuffs in the High Court, they did not just wash Tottenham's dirty washing in public; they tumble-dried it, and spun it inside out. Alan Sugar brought a new word into the sporting vocabulary when he talked in court of the 'bung' mentality of football.

Do you remember the first Spurs 'scandal' in the opening chapter – Ernie Payne and the ten-bob boots (page 19)? This was the modern version with bells on. There were astonishing revelations in the courtroom. The graphic picture painted by the legal eagles was of a football world populated by men on the make, meeting in shadowy secret in motorway cafés to swap bags of money. In his sworn statement, Sugar alleged that Venables had told him that Brian Clough, the Forest manager at the time of Teddy Sheringham's move to The Lane, 'likes a bung'. It was claimed by Sugar: "Mr Venables told me that what actually happened was that people would meet Mr Clough in a motorway cafe and hand him a bag of money ... I told Mr Venables it was out of the question. It was not the way I like to conduct business."

You're hired – three Sugar-coated appointments to the White Hart Lane manager's hot seat, Gerry Francis (top left), George Graham (top right) and Christian Gross.

Clough and Venables both strongly denied the allegation "Not a penny was passed between Terry Venables and me,' Clough told me when I contacted him at his Derbyshire home. 'The last time I was in a motorway service station, I went for a wee."

In his affidavit, Venables said: "The allegation that I told Mr Sugar that Brian Clough 'liked a bung' is untrue. I have never used that expression and I have never used those words or words to that effect to Mr Sugar. As to what I am alleged to have said to Mr Sugar about Mr Clough meeting people in motorway cafes to collect bags of money, it really is a lot of nonsense. Mr Sugar is either making it up or is repeating something he heard from another source."

It all eventually led to an FA probe and Tottenham being found guilty of making illegal payments to players. They were given one of the severest punishments in English football history: a crippling 12 point deduction, a one year FA Cup ban, and a £600,000 fine. Sugar protested and the Cup ban was quashed, the fine increased to £1.5-million and the all-important points deduction reduced to six (and later kicked out altogether). Sugar won the court case, and Venables departed to start astonishing new chapters in his career, including becoming one of the finest of all England team managers.

Last time I saw him was at the House of Lords, of all places, where Lord Seb Coe was hosting a 2008 party to mark 50 years of *Telegraph* writing by doyen of sports scribes, David Miller. Venners gave me that cheeky grin that I had first seen on his teenage face back in the '60s. He said in an exaggerated Cockney accent, "Life's fun, ain't it ...!" His squabbles with Sugar left a sour taste. No apprenticeship could have prepared him for the experience, but he came through it all with his humour and swagger intact. Nice one, Tel.

There was general all-round approval when, in the summer of '93, Ossie Ardiles returned to White Hart Lane, this time in the role of manager and with another Lane Legend, Steve Perryman, in harness with him as assistant manager. They boldy flourished the 'Famous Five': Teddy Sheringham and dynamic German import Jürgen Klinsmann up front, Nick Barmby in a support striker role just behind them, with Darren Anderton and Ilie Dumitrescu attacking from the right and left flanks. It was enjoyable to watch, particularly with Klinsmann bombing in for spectactular goals that made him a huge hero at the Lane. But the defence leaked goals like a sabotaged sieve, and by November 1994 dear old Ossie was 'Tangoed' and told to vamoosh.

Steve Perryman had one game in charge as caretaker manager before he, too, was shown the door. "I was very disappointed," said Steve. "Ossie and I were not given a proper chance to get things right because there was so much turmoil affecting the club off the pitch. We were there for football, not politics. I felt very sour about the whole thing. It was not the club I had known and loved as a young player."

Sugar and Klinsmann, who had two spells at The Lane, had an acrimonious spat that led to the Spurs owner saying on television: "I would not wash my car with Klinsmann's shirt." Hands up all those who truly believe that Sir Alan gives himself the task of washing his own car.

Next to try to take the heat out of the Tottenham hot seat was Gerry Francis, the ex-England captain who had made his name as a buccaneering midfield player with Queen's Park Rangers. A satisfactory first season – seventh in the Premiership and eliminated in the FA Cup semi-finals by Everton – were followed by two flat years, and in November 1997 Francis sadly walked away, with Spurs battling against the threat of relegation. He had not been helped by the forced sale of team motivator Teddy Sheringham to Man United after a breakdown in contract negotiations. There was no talk of bungs.

Spurs fans could now watch the suffering of their side on the first giant Sony Jumbotron TV screen installed at The Lane in 1995. The capacity of the stadium was an all-seater 33,000. Following a rights issue in 1996, capital was raised to build a new upper tier on the Paxton Road Members Stand that was completed in 1998. This also incorporated the second Jumbotron screen and increased ground capacity to just over 36,000. Yes, there was comfort and mod-cons, but you could find few supporters above thirty who considered the atmosphere of the ground close to matching that of the 'old days.'

The joke doing the rounds was that while rebuilding the ground they had fitted a revolving door on the manager's office at White Hart Lane. Next up Christian Gross, who was coach of Swiss champions Grasshoppers. He wanted to show that he was a peoples' manager, and arrived at the ground at the start of his reign by tube train. Somebody cynically and unkindly asked at his welcoming press conference if he had bought a return ticket.

Gross lasted just nine months, despite saving the club from relegation with only one defeat in the last nine games of the 1997-98 season. The performance that virtually clinched safety was a 6-2 victory at Selhurst Park over Wimbledon, with Klinsmann – back at the club on loan – scoring four of the goals.

Three matches into the following season Tottenham went down to a 3-0 home defeat against Sheffield Wednesday. It was a taxi rather than a tube train for Gross.

Let's take another breather away from The Lane to see what was happening in the rest of the football world, which will help show the competitive arena in which the procession of Tottenham managers were being mauled.

Groundbreaking would be an accurate way to describe that decade. There was not so much a wind of change as a hurricane, and it brought with it some unsavoury business. They were the naughty nineties. The word "sleaze" became part not only of the political vocabulary but also of soccer speak. The triple tragedy of the Bradford fire and the horrors of Heysel and Hillsborough provided a springboard for a football revolution.

If you have been paying attention at the back there you will recall that in the immediate post-war years there was standing room only at the Football League's packed grounds, particularly White Hart Lane, which was always bulging with excited, expectant Lilywhite fans. Now there was to be no standing room at all.

All-seater stadia gradually replaced the Victorian mausoleums that had become a blot on the football landscape. More than metaphorically, a huge demolition ball was swinging through the game, and with the new look came a brand new competition: the FA Premier League; actually the old First Division dressed up in bright new clothes, disguising familiar faces but not managing to hide all the old faults and warts.

"Loadsamoney" – a catchphrase from Thatcher's eighties – travelled first-class into the nineties on the football gravy train. Millions were poured into what was then the FA Carling Premiership by the satellite television company BskyB in return for wall-to-wall coverage dished up for their growing army of subscribers. Suddenly clubs did not have to rely on bums-on-seats at their grounds to keep them afloat. Couch potatoes were important new customers. But it was a revolution with a price to pay. It brought mixed fortunes as the lower division clubs of the old Football League scratched a living, while the Premiership fat cats made money (and in many cases ran up debts) like never before. Suddenly it was a game of the haves and the have-nots, and many of the 'haves' were only staying in the race by mortgaging themselves up to the hilt.

Football had stopped being a sport. It was big, big business. Mega-rich owners like Jack Walker (Blackburn) virtually bought success, and tycoons such as Sir John Hall (Newcastle United) floated their clubs on the Stock Exchange. Shareholders now had to be satisfied along with the supporters. Chelsea was not yet even a glint in the eye of Roman Abramovich, but Ken Bates was digging deep to lay the foundations to a new-style Stamford Bridge. Alan Sugar often gave the impression of being a reluctant force in football as he struggled to find success at White Hart Lane.

The Bouncing Czech Robert Maxwell had fun in football, secretly using his employees pension money to first fund Oxford United and then Derby County. But the "Swindler of the Century" became part of a different sort of floatation when – not long after trying to buy a controlling interest in Spurs – he slipped off his yacht and died in the warm waters off the Canaries in 1991. Goodness knows what he would have got up to with football club accounts had he been around when the Sky money came pouring in.

They said in 1947 when Tommy Lawton moved from Chelsea to Notts County for £20,000 that the game was going crazy. Fifty-one years later Alan Shearer, the Lawton of his time, was sold by Blackburn to Newcastle for what was then a world record £15 million. Players earning £10,000 a week was suddenly commonplace, and the "superstars" were gathering in more than £40,000 a week as clubs competed to attract the best talent. England had almost overnight become a gold mine for overseas stars, attracting prospectors of the quality of Klinsmann, Bergkamp, Cantona, Gullit, Juninho,

French artist David Ginola, a proud member of the Tottenham Hall of Fame, is flanked by two other White Hart Lane favourites – Les Ferdinand and Gary Mabbutt.

Zola, Ravanelli and Asprilla. And let it be noted that it had all started with the arrival at The Lane of Ardiles and Villa. Si, viva la revolución.

Those of my generation, who had grown up with the mentality of the maximum wage of £20 a week, watched with open mouths. The phrase "It can only end in tears" was often heard, but the footballers – and a contagious rash of agents – were laughing all the way to the bank. With the money came controversy, and stories of betting and bung scandals dominated the headlines, with the Sugar v. Venables courtroom battle topping the bill. Liverpool goalkeeper Bruce Grobbelaar had the highest profile of players accused in court of throwing games for money. It gave a whole new meaning to a fistful of dollars.

The biggest managerial casualty was phenomenally successful Arsenal manager George Graham, who was dismissed by the Highbury hierarchy for taking what was euphemistically described as "a bung." That was a Sugar-coated phrase.

In eight electrifying years in charge at Highbury, a ground he graced as a player in Arsenal's 1970-71 Double side, Graham had claimed six trophies. It was Graham who pieced together, coached and cajoled one of the finest club defensive combinations of any time. I know there will be Tottenham die-hards who will object to too much emphasis here on "that other lot" from North London (via South-East London), but I need to capture the era when George Graham was, so to speak, caught red handed. There was no way in a million years that he could be considered Spurs material. Could there?

Spurs fans looked on enviously at their success, hiding behind the consoling chants of 'Boring, boring Arsenal' as the Gunners ground out a succession of grim 1-0 victories. But at this time victories were becoming few and far between for Tottenham.

Then, in his 1995 winter of malcontent, came an explosion in George Graham's football world that reverberated throughout the game. He was investigated for allegedly taking kick-back money from transfer deals. Arsenal sacked him, and he was banished from all football for a year. I collaborated with George on his inside story of the scandal: *The Glory and the Grief.* He went up rather than down in my estimation as I got close to him during the toughest moments of his life. Lesser men would have crumbled under the pressure, much of it self-inflicted. But George was determined to come through his ordeal a stronger and better person. He did not try to protest his innocence, and was prepared to own up to naivety. He told me:

> **'**If I could turn back the clock, there is little that I would do differently in my eight years as Arsenal manager. I have never claimed to be some sort of shining knight, and I am as weak as the next man when it comes to life's temptations. I concede that greed got the better of me, but only temporarily.**'**

George eventually handed the money – the little matter of £425,000 – to Arsenal. He came out of it all empty handed, and without a job, his career in ruins. As I write, he remains the only manager to have been caught and punished for what we close to the game know is a common occurrence in football. George Graham, scapegoat.

Guided by legal eagles, George and I went out of our way in his book not to use the word "bung" to describe the money he had received. We were instructed to call it "an unsolicited gift." I passed this message on to the then Editor of *The Sun*, Stuart Higgins, a good old friend of mine, who assured George he was in the best possible hands when *The Sun* bought the serialisation to the book.

So you can imagine how George and I felt when, on the first day of the book's launch, *The Sun* ran a monster headline that filled the front page with the words, "George Graham confesses: 'I took £425,000 bung!'"

When I telephoned Stuart to complain on George's behalf, he told me with a tongue buried deep in his cheek: "'Uh, well, you see 'unsolicited gift' wouldn't fit."

He had got us by the tabloids.

George served his suspension with dignity, and then bounced back as Leeds manager in 1996. He took over from Howard Wilkinson, who in 1991-92 had guided Leeds to the final First Division championship before it morphed into the Premiership.

In 1998, Graham surprised everybody – probably even himself – by leaving Elland Road to take charge of Tottenham, the club he had dwarfed while winning everything in sight down the road at Highbury. After just four months in the job he lifted the League Cup, but he was never allowed to feel at home at White Hart Lane by a faction of the crowd who saw Arsenal red every time they looked at him. It was the third time Spurs had regretted putting a Gooner in charge. Like Joe Hulme and Terry Neill before him, George was always made to feel a passing stranger.

He had the satisfaction in his first season of giving Tottenham their best spell on the pitch for several years. They secured a mid-table finish, captured the League Cup and were robbed in an FA Cup semi-final against Newcastle when a definite penalty was turned down with the score deadlocked at 0-0. The Geordies won with two extra-time goals, and went down 2-0 in the final against Manchester United.

The League Cup victory was carved out with courage after Tottenham had been reduced to ten men on the hour, when Justin Edinburgh was sent off after a clash with that annoying wasp of a player, Robbie Savage. The game was into its 90th minute when Allan Nielsen scored the winner for Spurs with a dramatic diving header.

Tottenham's winning team:

Walker, Carr, Edinburgh, Freund, Vega, Campbell, Anderton, Nielsen, Iversen, Ferdinand, Ginola (Sinton).

The icing on the cake of an agreeable season came with idolized French flier David

Ginola collecting both the PFA and Football Writers' Association Footballer of the Year awards. Cross-Channel charmer David has these recollections:

'My days at White Hart Lane were among the happiest of my career., and I was always made to feel at home by the amazing Tottenham fans. My outstanding memory is of a goal I scored against Manchester United from long range in a League Cup tie. I caught the ball perfectly with my left foot and knew from the moment it left me that it would find the net.

That was my most memorable season because the players and football writers voted me their footballer of the year. It was very special to me, but as I said when receiving my trophies I could not have achieved so much without some great players around me at Spurs.

I became emotional when told I was being inducted into the Tottenham Hall of Fame. It was very special when the award was handed over by Gary Mabbutt, a player and a man for whom I have tremendous respect. He was an example for any youngsters coming into this great game.

Believe me, I will always have a little bit of Tottenham in my heart. It is a fantastic club and I am so proud and privileged to have worn the Spurs shirt. When I am an old man I will tell my grand-children how I played football for one of the greatest clubs on earth. And I might have a film or two of my goals to show them, just to prove I was not dreaming. One day, who knows, I may come back to a role at White Hart Lane. I will always have the Spurs spirit burning inside me...'

Ginola was, of course, a huge favourite with the White Hart Lane faithful, and Graham's popularity hit freezing-point when he sold the entertaining but enigmatic Frenchman to Aston Villa. It has to be said that there was huge surprise but no mass mourning when George was dismissed in March 2001 for allegedly being too open with the media about his budget restrictions at Tottenham.

But the timing of his dismissal was strange, to say the least. He had steered the club to the FA Cup semi-final (against Arsenal, of all teams), and he described his sacking as "bizarre and inexplicable."

I know for a fact that George had big, ambitious plans for Tottenham that he was going to put into operation in the following close season, but they were ideas that never got beyond paper. His dismissal was handled by vice-chairman David Buchler, who commented: "We cannot conduct the affairs of Tottenham in the press, and I have summarily dismissed George Graham for breach of contract."

The White Hart Lane musical chairs continued. Welcome back, Glenn Hoddle!

TOTTENHAM tottered into the New Millennium with a crisis of confidence eating into the club. Alan Sugar's appetite for any long-term association with football in general and Spurs in particular had disappeared without trace during the High Court trial, when he continually had to run a gauntlet of hate spilling from an angry gathering of pro-Venables supporters. It was not a pretty sight.

Rumours that he wanted to relinquish his ownership of the club gathered pace as the 20th Century slipped away into the history books, and by 2001 there was a shift of power to ENIC Limited, an investment company established by Bahamas-based British billionaire Joe Lewis.

ENIC (an acronym for English National Investment Company) gradually built up an 82% stranglehold on the Tottenham shares, 57.89% held by Lewis and 24.1% by ENIC senior executive Daniel Levy, who was installed as club chairman with responsibility not only for the day-to-day running of the club but also for its future direction.

There was just shared enthusiasm when the founders started the club under that Victorian lamppost in 1882.

Levy had graduated from Cambridge University with a first class honours degree in Land Economy, but from the moment he sat in the sizzling chairman's seat at Tottenham it was just the patch of green and the surrounding ground at White Hart Lane that dominated his thinking.

To say that Levy has had it easy is akin to saying that Hillary's climb up Mount Everest was a doddle. There was no Sherpa Tenzing to guide him. He has had to face fierce criticism from some quarters but every decision he has made has, in fairness, been with the best interests of Tottenham at heart. A queue of managers have come and gone in his quest for the right man for the job, and the dedicated David Pleat – restored at the club as Director of Football – was often on call for caretaker duty.

Levy has not always found it easy to satisfy the success-hungry Spurs supporters. These fans – even though they have not a share between them – think they 'own' the club, rather than the businessmen in charge in the boardroom. Spiritually, it IS their club … and, symbolically, the light from that Victorian lamppost continues to shine at The Lane

First to come and go under the new regime was Glenn Hoddle, who had been idolized

Look who's back. Glenn Hoddle, one of the great Lane legends, was the man chosen to take over from George Graham as The Boss. As a player he could do no wrong, but he had to withstand a barrage of criticism of his managing abilities. He promised much when returning to Tottenham, but ultimately produced little and was dismissed. Unsympathetic critics suggested he was being punished for sins in a previous life.

as one of the finest players ever to pull on the Tottenham shirt. He upset Southampton with the manner of his leaving to return to the club where he had started his career, but on his reappearance at The Lane he received a warm welcome 'home'.

Hoddle made a promising start, with the highlight of his first season a 2001-02 League Cup final appearance against Blackburn Rovers at Cardiff's Millennium Stadium. Christian Ziege cancelled out a Matt Jansen goal to make it 1-1 at half-time, and goal-machine Andy Cole snatched the winner for Rovers in the 69th minute. Les Ferdinand missed a sitter, and Teddy Sheringham fumed when referee Graham Poll turned down a last-minute penalty appeal. Spurs finished feeling frustrated, furious and potless.

Hoddle was named Premiership Manager of the Month the following August as Tottenham roared to the top of the table. But it was a false dawn, and there were mutterings of discontent when the team dropped away to a disappointing tenth place. It was not a happy camp, and stories leaked out from senior players complaining about Hoddle's alleged lack of management and communication skills.

Just four points from the opening six games of the following season confirmed Hoddle's fate, and in September he was politely invited to pack his bags. Perhaps he

Daniel Levy and the leaving managers ... Juande Ramos (above, right), who followed Jacques Santini (bottom left) and Martin Jol through the White Hart Lane exit door.

was being punished for sins perpetrated in a previous life.

In the last ten games that Tottenham played under one of the great attacking architects they scored just six goals and conceded 25 – this, despite having brought in £7-million goal gourmet Robbie Keane from Leeds. In fairness to Hoddle, maybe the defensive record would have made better reading had he not lost the rock-solid Sol Campbell to, of all clubs, Arsenal under the Bosman free transfer ruling. To many Tottenham fans, that was a deal of the devil that they would never ever forgive.

David Pleat, who had briefly held the fort before Hoddle took over, was back in temporary charge until the appointment at the start of the 2004-05 season of Jacques Santini, a highly regarded coach who had led France to the Euro 2004 finals. At the same time, Denmark's Frank Arnesen was brought in to take Pleat's old job of Director of Football. The lines of duty were clearly drawn: Santini to handle the daily training and tactical sessions and to select the team; Arnesen to scout for new talent and to be in charge of transfer dealings.

The football world was stunned when Santini announced after just 13 games (five wins, four defeats, four draws) that he was quitting, citing personal reasons. The rumour mill was spinning with stories that Santini and Arnesen were incompatible and continually arguing over responsibilities.

To add to the gloom, Bill Nicholson – Mr Tottenham – passed on in the autumn of 2004 at the age of 85. There is a bust of him at White Hart Lane and the approach road to the ground was renamed Bill Nicholson Way, reminders of the days when Tottenham was a byword for stability rather than turmoil. Goodness knows what Bill Nick would have made of the comings and goings at his glorious old hunting ground.

Martin Jol, who had been appointed assistant coach to Santini by Arnesen, took over first as caretaker boss and then on a permanent basis. Meantime, Arnesen got caught up in an episode that could have come from a John Le Carré thriller. He was photographed on board one of the luxury yachts belonging to Chelsea's Russian owner Roman Abramovich, and Chelsea and Spurs got involved in a verbal and legal punch-up. It finished with the Chelsea side having to cough up £5-million compensation when the Dane, metaphorically, jumped ship and joined Chelsea.

Jol's three years in charge brought smiles and the promise of success back to The Lane. He guided the club to two successive fifth place finishes in the Premier League, and encouraged an old-style attacking attitude that cheered up fans fed for too long on a diet of dull defensive football. They looked booked for a Champions League place, but in the final game of the 2005-06 season were forced to field a team at West Ham that was savagely weakened by the outbreak of a stomach virus. They tried to get the game postponed, but were ordered to go through with it. A defeat by the Hammers meant they lost their Champions League spot to Arsenal. Tottenham were sick as, uh, parrots.

Ledley King, versatile defender who has earned Lane Legend status on the pitch and some notoriety off it. Hary Redknapp came down on him like a ton of bricks after he got involved in a headline-hitting, drink-fuelled incident outside a Soho nightclub.

Everybody liked the always cheerful Jol, but having recruited the likes of Darren Bent – at a club record £16.5m – Gareth Bale and French defender Younes Kaboul during the summer, Spurs suffered a stuttering start to the 2006-07 season, recording just one victory in 10 league games. Jol may have been jolly but the results were evidence that he was struggling to get things right on the pitch, and Levy – "regretfully" – fired him and assistant Chris Hughton.

Next to get a seat in what seemed to onlookers like a crazy game of managerial musical chairs was Juande Ramos, a Spaniard who had turned down the chance to take over at Tottenham in the summer of 2007. He justified his appointment by collecting long-awaited silverware in his first season. Tottenham fans were overjoyed to roar their appreciation of Ramos when Spurs hammered Arsenal 5-1 in the second leg of the League Cup semi-final at The Lane. It was their first victory over the old enemy since 1999, and it clinched a place in the final against Chelsea at the new Wembley.

Spurs went behind to a Didier Drogba free-kick, but a Dimitar Berbatov penalty took the game into extra-time. Jonathan Woodgate snatched the winning goal to give Tottenham their first major trophy for eight years, and it earned them qualification for the 2008-09 UEFA Cup. Tottenham's team:

Robinson, Hutton, Woodgate, King, Chimbonda (Huddlestone), Lennon, Jenas, Zokora, Malbranque (Tainio), Berbatov, Keane (Kaboul).

Spurs had become the only club apart from Man United to win a trophy in each of the last six decades. At last, so the fans thought, a settled side and an inspired and rewarding period to look forward to. Wrong!

Hopes and dreams came tumbling down again as Spurs made their worst Premier League start ever the next season. It added to the depression caused by the failure to hold on to their star strikers Berbatov and Robbie Keane. The fans saw red as born predator Keane went to Anfield and the gifted yet maverick Berbatov to Old Trafford.

With only two points collected from their first eight matches, Tottenham were in free-fall by October 2008. Levy did not mess around in trying to get things sorted to the satisfaction of the demanding supporters. Acting with an executioner's alacrity, he dismissed Ramos, first team coach Marcos Alvarez, assistant manager Gus Poyet and Director of Football Damien Comolli.

Within eight weeks, Ramos – who could barely speak understandable English – was happily counting his compensating money while accepting one of the top jobs in Europe: manager of Real Madrid.

Where oh where would Daniel turn next? Portugal? Spain? France? Germany? Holland? Outer Mongolia?

Surprise, surprise, he turned to a man from the East – born in East London within bell ringing distance of The Lane (provided it was a quiet Sunday morning and there was a strong North-Easterly wind). Enter Harry Hotspur.

IT is difficult to imagine anybody better suited to managing Tottenham than Harry Redknapp. In personality, purpose, pride and pedigree, he looked perfect for the job. Chairman Daniel Levy has had to take a lot of stick for what his critics consider a procession of wrong decisions, so let's have a Lane of Dreams fanfare in recognition of the fact that he got this appointment right. Well done, Danny Boy.

It took 'Harry Hotspur' a long time to return home to White Hart Lane. In his early teens he was on Tottenham's books, training at the club regularly in the great era of the Double side. The team – the football they played and the confident, composed way they carried themselves – made a lasting impression on Harry, a knowledgeable football historian.

He eventually started his playing career at West Ham, where he came under the influence of a professor of football in Upton Park manager Ron Greenwood, who also believed in the Spurs creed of putting skill and method before might and muscle. Wherever he has gone on the managerial roundabout, Harry has been a purist. Yes, perfect for Tottenham. And he speaks understandable English, provided you don't mind a sprinkling of dropped aitches, some strangled English grammar and an occasional reacquaintance with the Anglo Saxon tongue.

Let's quickly get rid of the skeleton in his cupboard. His first allegiance as a boy (born down the road to me in Poplar, in the heart of London's East End) was — brace yourself — to Arsenal. But this was before he could think for himself. Harry's Dad was a Gooner, and used to take his young son to Highbury.

But as soon as he could appreciate the finer points of the game, he realised that Spurs were playing the best football in town. The manager he rated above all others was 'Mr Tottenham,' Bill Nicholson.

"I would not be fit to lace Bill Nicholson's boots," is Harry's as-ever totally frank assessment of Bill Nick's stature in the game.

But of all the managers Tottenham have had since Nicholson let go of the reins – sixteen of them – Harry seems to be the best suited to carry on the Nicholson and Tottenham tradition of winning with style and guile.

If Levy had got his way, the Redknapp reign would have started eighteen months earlier but he finally hooked his man in return for a whopping £5-million compensation fee to Portsmouth, the club Harry had, against all odds, steered to the FA Cup six months earlier.

Harry and I are fellow East Enders who have chosen dozy, delightful Dorset as our adopted county. We often bump into each other and discuss the old days when he and I were members of Bobby Moore's Black Lion drinking school back when Mooro was the undisputed king of the Hammers. Harry was a skilful and very quick right winger who was unlucky to establish himself as a touchline-hugging express just about the time Alf Ramsey was making wingers redundant. He was as fast as Lennon, but crossed the ball more like McCartney (excuse the pun, Aitch). I reported on his debut for the Hammers in the *Daily Express*, and nicknamed him the Boleyn Greyhound. He was a slim-line, thoroughbred of a player, all nervous energy and wanting to be involved in everything; just like he is as a manager. Harry taught his son Jamie how to make the ball do the work with passes of Hoddle-class, but as a player he liked to run with the ball as if it was tied to his flying boots.

He was always inquisitive about tactics, and used to pick the brains of everybody who knew the difference between an overlap and an underpass. It came as no surprise when he switched to coaching and managing at the end of his playing career.

I knew that he would not be able to resist the Spurs stage when it was offered to him. Tottenham is the big club he deserves. It is something of a sleeping giant, and if anybody can give it the kick of life it's 'Harry Hotspur'. The wake-up call has started.

He is a wheeler-dealer like none other in the transfer market, and is such a good judge of players that he rarely makes a mistake. The few times he does get it wrong, he is man enough to admit it and rectifies it with another lightning buy-and-sell market raid. As I write this chapter, a rollercoaster of a season is coming to its final shots, and Harry has performed wonders to put the confidence and bounce back into both his players and the long-suffering club supporters.

When I started writing the book Tottenham were bang at the bottom of the Premier League, and there was a smell of relegation fear permeating deep into the nostrils of Tottenham players and supporters.

Within a few weeks of taking charge, there were smiles where there had been scowls and hope where there had been despair. Harry was not waving a magic wand. He was simply doing what he has done throughout his managerial career, quietly motivating players with commonsense advice, rollocking when necessary and always spreading an air of self belief that is contagious.

Unforgiving when any player gives less than his best, Harry sets high standards of skill, dedication and sportsmanship. He does not want his players cheating, but he does want them competing at all times. Harry does it the Spurs way. The Bill Nicholson way. Is there a better way?

He pulls no punches when talking about life in general and football in particular, as

Harry Redknapp, dedicated to spurring Tottenham to Glory-Glory heights

the directors and shareholders discovered when he addressed the Tottenham annual meeting two months after taking over, making it crystal clear that he means business. There was a sharp intake of breath as he said about the club's playing ambitions:

> ❛It depends where you want to finish. If you are talking about getting into the top five or the top four, the squad is well, well short of that. There is a lot of work to be done to become a top team. I cannot tell lies. The squad is still well short of challenging for a place in the top four.
>
> We are not as good as Aston Villa or one or two other teams, so there is a lot of work to be done to get where we should be. I have probably upset the chairman now!
>
> I have got a good group of lads and they are a very good squad. They come and work hard on the training ground.
>
> This is a proper football club, and we need proper players and a proper team that this club deserves. I want to bail out in a few years time and leave this club in the top four.❜

When he arrived at The Lane, Tottenham were a club in intensive care. They were four points adrift at the bottom of the Premier League after taking just two points from eight matches. Harry Hotspur quickly proved himself Harry Houdini, motivating the players into producing a run of five wins and one draw in six games. It was one of the greatest starts to the reign of any Tottenham manager in history. There was a new bounce and buoyancy on and off the pitch, and he inspired the likes of Pavlyuchenko, Bent and Campbell to recover their confidence in the penalty area.

He showed his typical boldness in the transfer market by bringing back master marksmen Jermain Defoe and Robbie Keane, stiffened the backbone of the team with the purchase of Wilson Palacios from Wigan, motivated jet-paced Aaron Lennon (a winger in the young Redknapp style) and nursed Ledley 'The Legend' King so that he could continue playing despite recurring injuries. He gave Tom Huddlestone the encouragement to show his wares, and supporters started to rub their eyes. Were they really seeing a player who could strike a ball as well as Glenn Hoddle?

Even Harry had to admit he was astounded by the performance of the reborn Spurs side when they clawed their way back to an amazing 4-4 draw against Arsenal when two goals down with just minutes left to the final whistle. Suddenly the description 'Miracle Man' was tumbling from the lips of Tottenham supporters aching for the return of the Glory-Glory years.

The players revealed there was a new spirit blowing through the club from the moment of Harry's arrival ... the fans (their nails chewed to the bone) were for the first time in months becoming relaxed .. and the media were reporting events at The Lane without having to resort to words like 'crisis' and 'shambles.'

Harry surrounded himself with a backroom team of people he knew he could trust, the likes of Clive Allen, Tim Sherwood, Kevin Bond and his former Portsmouth righthand man Joe Jordan. For Harry, familiarity breeds content.

Spurs very nearly retained the League Cup just weeks after his arrival, eventually going down on penalties to Manchester United at the new Wembley.

Tottenham might have won in normal time, but for United's second string goalkeeper Ben Foster making a stunning save from Aaron Lennon when a goal looked inevitable.

Ryan Giggs, Carlos Tevez, Ronaldo and Anderson found the net for United from the spot in the Russian Roulette shoot-out, but only Vedran Corluka scored for Spurs.

The Tottenham team:

Gomes, Corluka, Dawson, King, Assou-Ekotto, Lennon (Bentley 102), Jenas (Bale 98), Zokora, Modric, Bent, Pavlyuchenko (O'Hara 65).

Late in the nerve-jangling, rollercoaster season, Spurs looked on course to end a 20-year drought at Old Trafford when leading 2-0 at half-time. But they came apart at the seams after an appalling penalty decision pumped new life into United.

But the only thing that mattered to Harry as the curtain came down on his first season was Premier League survival. He virtually gave up on the Uefa Cup challenge as he concentrated on his one priority of beating the threat of a relegation that would have been disastrous so soon after the unveiling of plans for the new multi-million pound Northumberland Park Development project. Chairman Daniel Levy, announced:

> 'The Northumberland Development Project will deliver a world class scheme and substantial new investment for Haringey and our supporters. It represents a significant step in the growth of the Club, with a proposed stadium capacity of 60,000 and will provide state-of-the-art facilities, important public space, new jobs and homes and a significant boost for the local economy. It will also enable us to provide a new base for the Tottenham Hotspur Foundation, so that its award-winning programmes can continue and have an even greater impact in the local community.
>
> Tottenham Hotspur is proud of its roots in Haringey. We have been in the Borough for 126 years and the Club is inextricably linked with this part of London. We believe that this scheme has the potential to create a truly inspirational environment for the Club and the community as well as acting as the catalyst for the uplift of the wider area.
>
> We are at an early stage of what is part of our long term plans for the Club and now we want the views of local people and our fans. I hope people will take the time to look at our plans and let us have their comments.'

A glimpse into the future, and the spaceage new stadium. Chairman Daniel Levy's brief to the architects KSS was that they design an iconic stadium that would rival the best in Europe, while recreating the atmosphere of 'the old' Lane. What would the Spurs founders who started out on Tottenham marshes think?

The existing 36,000 capacity stadium has remained largely the same for over a decade, but ambitious plans for change have been on the table for several years. As I write, Spurs are in the position of having 70,000 registered club members and a waiting list for season tickets of around 22,000 people.

There is an army of Spurs fans who would like to continue with the name White Hart Lane, and there is a lot of support for The Bill Nicholson Stadium. But commercial demands will dictate that the ground will carry a sponsors' name.

In all models of the Spurs-home-to-be there is a huge 'Naming Rights' title either side of the Tottenham cockerel emblem, hoping to attract the interest and purse of a major sponsor.

What odds Lilywhite fans will still say on match days: "We're going down The Lane"?

As much as we do not want to say goodbye to the old White Hart Lane, a new stadium will usher in an exciting era. It will be born-again Tottenham, with the facilities, the financial clout, and – above all – the fan base to challenge for a consistent place at the top where they belong.

In Harry Redknapp, they have the right manager to lead them into the new world.

And they can call on the best supporters, who live, breathe and dream Tottenham Hotspur – as the memories on the following pages will reveal.

WHAT I hope makes this book different is that as author and publisher, I have involved YOU, the Tottenham fans. Let's be honest, it is the supporters who have done as much as the teams to give The Lane its legendary status. Before all-seater stadiums were forced on fans for safety reasons, there was nothing quite like the atmosphere generated at White Hart Lane by a crowd that has always been worth a goal start to the Tottenham team. And even since the sitting rule (often ignored!), there remains a passion in the ground that is special to Spurs.

Let's hope that once the ground is bulldozed into history, the spirit and the soul of The Shelf lives on in the new home.

Now I invite you to sit back and wallow in the memories of a queue of Tottenham supporters who kindly shared their recollections of great Lane experiences on line at our website http://www.thelaneofdreams.co.uk.

We kick off, fittingly, with family recollections because Tottenham is very much a family-oriented club:

A FREE VIEW AT THE LANE *MAUREEN CARPENTER, Hayle, Cornwall*

My grandparents, my parents, my husband and all his family, my children and now my grandchildren, were and still are Spurs fans. My husband was born in Whitehall Street opposite the ground, and for more than three decades his grandfather Archibald Chase was the programme seller at the main entrance to the ground. Going to The Lane – in the late 50's, early 60's – meant being in the Paxton Road end with both sets of supporters.

I remember being there when Spurs played Glasgow Rangers in the European Cup Winners' Cup, and being offered some haggis and a glass of whisky by the Scottish supporters.

On other occasions when we had two children and my husband had gone to the Saturday match, I would do the shopping in time to make sure I was at the Park Lane entrance at half-time, because they used to open the gates and you could go in for free.

I used to wheel my pram in so my eldest son could watch Jimmy Greaves. Those were the days when they still used to sing MacNamara's band. When they won the double in 1961, we celebrated for over a week. Happy days.

OF BIKES, MINI-VANS & BOMB SCARES *MAUREEN TURNER, Chingford*

I am Maureen Carpenter's cousin, and something she may have forgotten to mention is how our Nan and Granddad used to look after the bikes of the Tottenham fans in their front garden in the days when few people had motor cars. They would put a raffle ticket in the brake, and give the other part to the fan. They must have had about 50 or 60 bikes in their Whitehall Street garden, and for a penny extra the bike was put in the passage or their bedroom to keep it dry.

And now for a confession. It was our family business mini-van that caused the long delay to the derby with Chelsea in March 2009. Our driver had broken down outside the ground, and the police – just a few days before the G20 summit – were so nervous that they were on the point of blowing it up until I arrived with the keys.

Sorry for the inconvenience everyone. COYS!

THE 50-YEAR WAIT *HENK ZANBERGEN, Leiden, Holland*

Back in 1962 at the age of six I bought a pack of chewing gum knowing there were football cards inside. The first one I got hold of was a picture of the Double winning side of Tottenham Hotspur. The club name really impressed me and from that time on I was a fan. For a Dutch boy it isn't common to support a team like Tottenham, but I kept following them as much as possible by newspaper or television.

Still it took me almost 50 (!) years before I went over to watch my favourites. All my friends knew about my love for Spurs and for my 50th birthday in 2006 they bought me a ticket for Spurs vs. Manchester City.

Saturday April 8 I was on the train from Liverpool Street very nervous. Almost sprained my neck looking for the first glimpse of the stadium. I felt excited but also ashamed for being so remiss in not going years earlier. Because this was what I always wanted to do – see my beloved Spurs playing at The Lane.

Coming off the train walking towards the stadium it felt very familiar. Here, at last, I was surrounded by people with the same passion as me. I've been to many clubs and stadiums in Holland, but it never gave me goosebumps like this day. It stayed for the next several hours.

Before entering White Hart Lane I walked round the stadium, had a few beers in the pub and tried to buy not too many things from the club store. I had a ticket for the Upper West Stand. It seemed like the climb upstairs took me hours, but then all at once I was standing in the Lane of my Dreams.

What a view, what a noise and what a pitch ... the place where my heroes like Dave Mackay, Glenn Hoddle and Robbie Keane have their footsteps!

And what a regret it took me almost 50 years to get here!

Walking down after the match I made a promise to myself: Come back and enjoy the unique atmosphere and don't wait another 50 years. So now you can walk into a grey haired boy from Holland once or twice a year at White Hart Lane, still excited when he steps from the train towards that great stadium hosting a wonderful football club.

OH DANNY BOY *RICHARD EARLY, Sussex*

Ten to three on a Saturday afternoon, my friend Nicky Halligan and I standing so close to the White Hart Lane pitch that we could count the blades of grass. Suddenly, to the rousing sound of McNamara's Band and the roar of the crowd, the team ran out. I furtively put on my cringing National Health specs and everything was brought sharply into focus – 11 heroes in white led out by Danny Blanchflower. This is what mattered. In crowds regularly of 50,000 and 60,000 the hearts of two young boys leapt.

Just one story from those 1960s I would like to share with you now because it speaks directly of my hero Blanchflower. The season after winning the Double Spurs were progressing well in the European Cup. However, in the first leg of the semi final the Portugese champions Benfica had beaten Spurs at home. Nick and I went to the second leg a couple of weeks later at White Hart Lane. The crowd was huge, the occasion dramatic, the action pulsating. We had to reverse a 3-1 score from the first leg.

It was 1-1 when Spurs were awarded a penalty. Danny placed the ball on the spot and the crowd of 60,000-plus fell silent – held its breath. Utter silence. Palpable, all embracing, oppressive silence. All those souls and not a murmur. No movement. Even the heartbeats seized. But in that cauldron of tension a man shouldered the pressure and stepped up to do his duty. How I marvelled at his composure. The resulting roar reverberated around North London.

Devastatingly it wasn't enough and although Spurs threw everything at the Benfica goal they were not able to breach it again. On the trip back to Liverpool Street the train was an eerie ride. Each man and boy stood silently inside his own despair, bereft and exhausted. Not a word was being spoken the length and breadth of the carriage apart from a muted conversation in an alien tongue among a small group of Benfica supporters in the corner. So near, so far.

Danny, if you are in that great football ground in the sky, and you can hear me, I want to say that you are in your rightful place now: in the company of gods.

MAGNIFICENT SEVEN *MICHAEL KLINGER, Radlett, Herts*

November 18th 1950 – this 14-old-schoolboy in packed crowd on "The Shelf"... 70,000 in the ground for visit of Newcastle United. Four minutes gone, Les Bennet stoops low to head in left wing cross. What a roar from crowd. Final score 7-0. The previous two home matches had all been won by Spurs – Stoke 6-1, the reigning champions Portsmouth 5-1. What a season, what memories.

Same boy, same position on The Shelf – December 23rd 1950 vs. Arsenal. This was the one we had all been waiting for since promotion from the old Second Division. I can see it now, Eddie Baily's left foot shot from left edge of the penalty area, Len Duquemin flinches as ball passes him and crashes past George Swindin the Arsenal goalkeeper into bottom left hand corner of the net. Ecstatic reaction from Spurs supporters. We won, of course 1-0, and skipper Ronnie Burgess lifted the Championship trophy at the end of the unforgettable season.

THIS IS WHAT IT'S ALL ABOUT, ALFIE *BILL FITZGERALD, Walthamstow*
I have just turned 50 and have been a Tottenham supporter since I was ten. My earliest memories of going to the Lane were getting to the ground at about 11am, and sitting against the wall of the Park Lane end reading my programme with my friend. No all-ticket games in the early 70s. I would arrive early in all weathers, and try to get in the front row of the top tier as close to the centre as possible.

Players at the time were some of the greats like Pat Jennings, 'Nice One' Cyril Knowles, Alan Mullery, Mike England, Martin Chivers, and Alan Gilzean. We had a pretty good side then, but my fondest memory of any home game, and one which remains amazingly clear to this day, is the match against Chelsea in 1975. The losing team was doomed to almost certain relegation.

There was bedlam inside the ground with supporters fighting on the pitch, and a noise I had never experienced before all around the terraces. There were fifty thousand people inside The Lane, and the tension was almost unbearable.

We had real fears the game would be delayed or even abandoned altogether because of the fighting, when the referee, the great 1974 World Cup final ref Jack Taylor, majestically walked out to the centre spot, calmly put the ball down and blew the whistle.

The pitch cleared almost immediately. It was a brave thing to do, and Mr Taylor got a big round of applause from the crowd. I remember being relieved and pleased in equal measure. It was an outstanding performance from the Spurs team, and we won 2-0 with goals from our captain Steve Perryman and Alfie Conn, who was a brilliant player during his brief time at Tottenham.

It wasn't so much the actual game that sticks in my mind, but the atmosphere in the stadium. On our way out after the game, the tannoy played a Bay City Rollers song, Bye Bye Baby. We turned it into Bye bye Chelsea!

The scene was duplicated during the final game of the season, at home to a really strong Leeds team, in which a win would seal our top flight status. We thumped them 4-2 and Alfie Conn was outstanding. If ever one player saved us during the course of a season it was Alfie in 74-75.

FAMINE and FEAST *TIM HART, Wakefield*

I'm a 'young' 54 year-old who now lives in West Yorkshire, but have never lost my allegiance to and affection for Tottenham Hotspur. I first went to White Hart Lane when I was twelve or so, so I endured the 'famine' years between 1966 and 1977 (apart from the 1967 FA Cup win). I can still remember stepping up onto the Paxton terraces for the first time, looking at that pitch bathed in bright sunshine and imaging the Double heroes playing every other team off the park.

Along with about twenty loosely-associated mates and acquaintances, I used to stand at the Paxton end of The Shelf. The best view of a football pitch anywhere, full stop. Travelling down from Enfield Town on the Liverpool Street line, I'd often be at the ground by 1.00pm. Two hours, two whole hours before kick-off!

When the teams in front of us weren't doing it, the resident comedians kept everybody entertained. Ralph 'Chugger' Coates and Cyril 'Nice One' Knowles were particular favourites; the former because he never stopped, always gave 110% and linked play well; the latter because of that languid left foot, and the assassin's smile. Cyril would scythe some unfortunate into Row Q and then placate the ref with a look of innocence completely divorced from the brutality of the tackle.

As an aspiring psychologist, I found the venue and its contents as entertaining as the football at times. The famine years, and the decline towards relegation from the old First Division, bred a sterling endurance and stoicism. We made our own entertainment. The Shelf inviting the Park Lane end to 'sing us a song' when there was a lapse in play (still goes on today, I'm glad to say).

Let's celebrate the players. The G-Men: the sublime sophistication of Alan Gilzean's heading allied to Greavesie's unerring finishing. The years when the great Pat Jennings WAS the Tottenham defence. Steve Perryman – commitment (and skill) incarnate.

I could go on: Gerry 'The General' Armstrong, John Pratt (who won the crowd over through sheer effort), Alfie Conn (such talent, such potential), Martin Peters (sublime vision, classy touch), Mike England (resolute, combative), Peter Collins (an unsung hero, along with Mark Falco, Phil Beal, Peter Taylor, John Gorman, Tony Galvin and others).

Glenn Hoddle: either foot, drop it on a sixpence, and could shoot (accurately) with either foot too. The grit and style of Gary Mabbutt. The arrival and success of a black football icon in Garth Crooks – his importance to black supporters in the locality should not be underestimated. Graham Roberts – a much better footballer than the 'hard man' image might suggest. Clive Allen – one truly unbelievable season. I could go on, as I say.

Whether it's White, Mackay and Blanchflower, or Ardiles, Villa and Hoddle, or Gascoigne, Waddle, and Lineker, they're all sprayed with that N.17 gold dust.

CHEERS CHRIS HUGHTON *CHRIS STREET, Muswell Hill, London N10*
Fifteen years after my first WHL game, I was wont to bet perennially with an Arsenal fan on the outcome of the North London derbies – loser buys the drinks after the game, draw means the home fan pays. I recall with relish buying that Arsenal mate a double brandy and pep in the Rising Sun, Whetstone, after a 2-2 draw. He left when Arsenal were two-nil up and didn't know the final score.

I stayed to the end as always. Chris Hughton scored twice and hit the bar at 2-2. When the mate demanded a double for "such an easy victory", I graciously bought it and then delivered the news which made him choke on it. The record book shows that sixteen days' later we won 3-1 at Highbury and would go on not only to retain the FA Cup, but to finish above Arsenal in the League, too – on goals not points!

A GLORIOUS UNITED SERIAL *JOHN MacCABE Poplar, London E14*
Probably my most cherished memories concern games where we didn't even win a trophy and the real highlights are five games I was at, all from the same season of 1967/1968. Two in eight days pre-season and three in eight days at the end of January.

5 August 1967 Hampden Park – Celtic 3, Spurs 3: We were fresh from our FA Cup final win over Chelsea and the all-Scottish Glasgow Celtic were the newly crowned champions of Europe. A hugely partisan crowd in warm sunshine saw us play Celtic off the park in the first-half but an inspired performance by Bertie Auld enabled Celtic to come back to draw the match.

12 August 1967 Old Trafford, Charity Shield, Manchester United 3, Spurs 3: In pouring rain Pat Jennings put us ahead with a long kick which looped over Alex Stepney. We dominated the game but two glorious bombshells from Bobby Charlton denied us victory. In the space of eight days we had been involved in two outstanding 3-3 draws against the Champions of Europe and the Champions of England .

27 January 1968 Old Trafford – Man United 2, Spurs 2: Martin Chivers had made his home debut for us the previous Saturday in a 1-0 win over Arsenal and in this third round Cup match he scored both our goals, the second being a last minute equaliser.

31 January 1968 White Hart Lane – Spurs 1, Manchester United 0: A Jimmy Robertson header midway through the second-half gave us a deserved replay victory.

3 February 1968 – Spurs 1, Manchester United 2: A virtuoso performance by George Best enabled United to gain revenge for their midweek defeat in the Cup. So after three games in eight days we were honours.

This was quite an amazing period, and myself and many others had the incredible good fortune to see such magnificent players as Jennings, England, Mackay, Mullery, Greaves, Gilzean, Chivers, Best, Law, Charlton and Crerand all on the same pitch, not just once but THREE times in just EIGHT days.

CHEERS FOR THE BLUE AND WHITE ARMY *BEN McALEER, North London*
It was the UEFA Cup 2nd Leg at home to Sevilla. After the first leg, where we cruelly lost 2-1 due to some dodgy referee decisions, I was confident that we could overturn the deficit. Alas, within the first 15 minutes we went 2-0 down and 4-1 on aggregate. This led to the Spurs Faithful feeling rather subdued as the first-half drew to a close.

What happened during half-time really was something special, however. Instead of the fans disappearing to gather half-time snacks and drinks, every supporter stayed at their seat, stood up and chanted the familiar chorus, 'Martin Jol's Blue and White Army!' louder and better then ever!

All that could be heard during the whole of half-time and a majority of the second-half was this continual chant, and it was enough to boost the morale of any team.

I still have clear memories of Robbie Keane leaving the dressing-room and roaring on the crowd to make more noise and gee the lads up!

We cheered all we could but the team couldn't break down Sevilla, eventually crashing out 4-3 on aggregate. But the atmosphere alone was loud enough and moving enough to have seen us right to the final!

So, even though we lost, I still remember every minute of that game due to the chanting from the Spurs faithful and will never, ever forget it. Just thinking about it still sends shivers down my spine!

A KEANE GOAL TO REMEMBER *DAN FIELDING, Chigwell, Essex*
My fondest memory is sitting with the West Ham fans, right next to the Spurs away support at Upton Park three seasons ago in that epic 3-4 victory. I couldn't jump up and down obviously, among a sea of claret and blue ... but I've never felt so satisfied, especially as it was a crucial derby. We were two down at half-time and West Ham had beaten us there on the last day of the previous season to cost us that Champions League place. This was some consolation!

I also have great memories of Robbie Keane's effort against Blackburn at home about three seasons ago. Best goal I've ever seen. Welcome home, Robbie!

A GLIMPSE OF GREAVSIE *DONALD BARKER, Waltham Cross*
I am a third generation Spurs fan. My grandfather, Samuel South, was a friend of the first ever Spurs captain, Bobby Buckle. My mother went to school with Les Bennett and considered herself his first girlfriend! This is my memory:

August 1970, and my friend Ralph and me joined the long queue for the opening game of the season, full of anticipation and expecting to see our boyhood hero Jimmy Greaves in action. The big difference today was that he would be playing for our opponents, West Ham. In March the previous season Bill Nicholson had done the unthinkable and sold our idol. This was especially painful for Ralph, who shortly before that had invested in a large poster of Jimmy to decorate his bedroom wall – a big decision, when like me, he was a fifteen-year-old existing on pocket money.

We normally stood right down the front of the Park Lane End, but on this day had got delayed and turned up much later than normal, so we were happy just to get in. This was my first experience of 'am I going to get in?'– anxiety which I was going to experience many times again as I got older. We got in after the game had started, and immediately began exploring the East Stand for a vantage point. The crowd was big and tightly packed. You would have needed a crowbar to get into it, and for two slightly-built lads the situation was starting to look serious.

We made our way along the East Stand and round to the Paxton End, searching out nooks and crannies from where we could see a bit of the pitch. I remember there used to be a section of railing on the corner of the Paxton End and West Stand, which usually gave a partial view of the pitch, and now it was covered with people trying to see a bit of the action. I eventually managed to balance on a concrete ledge at the back of the Paxton End terrace, and by doing an impression of a giraffe on a pogo-stick I glimpsed Greavsie sliding the ball home at the Park Lane End, as he had done many times before. He wasn't wearing the familiar Lilywhite top, however, but claret and blue.

I agreed with Ralph that it was pointless staying when we couldn't see what was going on, and for the first time in our lives we left before the end of the game. It was strange walking along a quiet Worcesters Avenue hearing the sound of the crowd inside. We reflected that we might not have seen the game, but we finally had to accept that Greavsie had gone. Nothing would ever be quite the same again.

BLACKPOOL ROCKED BY GREAVSIE *MICHAEL GREYEFF, Harrow*

I could fill the book with special memories, but I shall restrict myself to just one: The debut of Jimmy Greaves. It was the last Saturday before Christmas, December 1961. His debut had been held up by registration bueaucracy and he'd scored for the reserves at Plymouth the previous week, when 10,000 fans gathered for a reserve game! Now here he was, trotting out in those long baggy shorts – not fashionable in those days. We had our usual spot "Behind the Boards" (better known as the Shelf), level with the Park Lane penalty area. For 30 minutes, Greaves ambled around, contributing little to the match against Blackpool.

Then: a throw-in from the right, helped on and Greaves with an overhead scissor kick into the back of the net! Moments later, a second goal. We screamed ourselves hoarse, banging the wooden planking with our hands, delirious with excitement.

In the second half, Greaves did a Roy-of-the-Rovers run down the length of the middle of the field, leaving Blackpool defenders spreadeagled in his wake. His shot hit the base of the right-hand post and Les Allen knocked in the rebound. Those moments remain fixed in my mind's eye to this day.

For us supporters, the one word "Lane" carries so much resonance that it has just a single connotation. Whatever else they do when they build the new stadium – they HAVE to keep the name "White Hart Lane". Let's not have an abortion like they have down the road, "The Virgin Atlantic Stadium" or some such nonsense.

RICKY VILLA AND THE SEA CHANGE *GARY SKIDMORE, Wiltshire*

I have an extra-special memory of Ricky Villa's FA Cup final winning goal in '81. At the time I was serving in the Royal Navy and somehow I had managed to get to most of the FA cup matches that season, including the cracking 3-0 semi-final victory over Wolves at Highbury; Ricky scored a blinder that day as well.

Unfortunately, my ship went on deployment leading up to the final at the old Wembley, so I braced myself for even missing it on TV, as ships lose reception as soon as you go to sea.

So there I am the day before Cup Final day stuck at sea with my mood steadily deepening when our skipper decides to call into Copenhagen for a day or so. Seizing our chance, a friend and I caught a plane to London, reasoning we may just get lucky and snag a couple of tickets, and if not we could still find a pub and sample the atmosphere.

Luckily for me I bought a ticket off some Army guys whose friend had let them down. The only problem was that I had to go in with them as it was Army issue, and it was in the Man City end!! I only paid £10 for it when the cheapest we had heard the touts selling them was £60 or more.

That game was by no means a classic and my memory of the day was of Ricky Villa having a nightmare match where the harder he tried the worse he got. He had to be taken off and he walked tearfully to the tunnel. City fans were based at that end and to their immense credit they gave him an ovation, as they could see how distraught he was.

Later that evening found my friend and I in a Copenhagen bar teaching some American sailors a few Tottenham songs; a great night. All this added to the occasion for me, so when Ricky not only scored one in the final replay but capped it off with a mazy dribble that won the Cup for us I went crazy and did not stop shaking for ages after. Who says the FA cup doesn't matter? Hah!

THE DOUBLE AND BEYOND *DAVE GURNEY, Stanstead Abbotts, Herts*

Memories that spring immediately to mind: Standing on a wooden footstool behind the goal at Wembley to see Smithie and Dyson score the goals to win the Double in 1961 as a twelve year old.

Jimmy Greaves, with lots of support behind him at The Lane

*Bill Nicholson,
Mr Tottenham,
with Spurs
Legend, Martin
Chivers, at
the master
manager's
testimonial at
The Lane in
August 2001*

Steve Perryman, always at his post

Ossie Ardiles ... 'is going to Wembley, his knees have gone all trembly ...'

Standing on the same footstool high up on the Holte end at Villa Park on a couple of occasions during that Cup run. It was so high up, I had never seen anything like it. Each time we scored the crowd surged forward and I was carried what seemed like almost to the front, but I was always returned safely to my parents and footstool in no time at all. It was during those away trips that year that I first heard those immortal words 'Glory Glory Hallelujah, the Spurs go marching on'. Magic!

The 13-2 carnival against Crewe after a humiliating draw at their place ... 10-4 against Everton in Billy Nick's first game, a great omen for things to come ... Jimmy G's debut hat-trick ... Great European nights against Gornik, Dukla, Benfica etc. White hot atmosphere thanks in no small part to the 'Angels' of WHL. More Magic!

Queuing for miles around the streets of Tottenham, almost every Sunday morning it seemed, for Cup-tie tickets.

My Mum breaking her ankle as we climbed the perimeter wall to get onto the pitch to celebrate (along with thousands of others) on the night we clinched the League in the double season. Magic, in a strange sort of way.

But my most abiding memory of those days is the sight of the greatest player ever to wear a Spurs shirt, Dave Mackay, striding proudly across every blade of grass on the WHL pitch. What a colossus of a man.

ACROSS THE IRISH SEA *Brian McLaughlin, Letterkenny, Co. Donegal*

I'm going to be honest and say, as an 18-year-old supporter living in Ireland, I have only been at the Lane twice, but the most recent time was very memorable for me. It was the Spurs v Bolton game in the 2008-09 season. We'd just found out that Ramos had been sacked and that Mr. Redknapp would be at the game.

We were all very down and not expecting much. It was a fantastic atmosphere, as with my previous game, also against Bolton [4-1 to the Spurs]. The crowd were well up for getting behind the team and before Harry was introduced to the crowd.

There were huge cheers and chants of "Jermain Defoe's a Yiddo", and when Pavyluchenko's goal hit the net, the crowd went beserk. We might actually win this thing! We were playing some excellent stuff, and were always looking likely to grab a second. It didn't come until the second-half and it was a penalty. But we didn't care – we were winning and were going to win for the first time this season!

It was an amazing game for us, and we headed to one of the local pubs after the victory with the other fans. The banter was top notch and we stayed talking for hours – so happy to finally have some points on the board! Finally we had "more points than a triangle" as the joke went! The next few games were crucial too! Away to Arsenal, home to Liverpool and away to Manchester City but we got seven points and Harry had well and truly arrived.

Another memory: One year my dad and his brother were at the Spurs training ground and were waiting outside the door for the players. Sure enough, they soon came out one by one and they were all very obliging, Sheringham, Campbell etc.

Then Klinsmann came out, but he took off running and dad and his brother chased him. Suddenly, my dad's brother started shouting after him: "For feck sake, would you ever come back here and take a fecking photograph with your fans?!?!" Dad was mortified and was saying, "What are you doing? You can't be shouting after him like that!!"

My uncle wouldn't be stopped though, and he kept shouting until Klinsmann finally posed for the photo! The picture has become part of our family folklore.

BOTTOM BUT ON TOP *JON GODDARD, Kettering*

I have many outstanding memories over the years since coming down to the Lane from the early 70s; glories of cups being lifted, many great individual players and wonderful goals that have been scored which are too numerous to mention. But one memory – although a strange one – sticks out of the last game of the season in 1976-77.

Spurs were playing Leicester City and were already relegated, and for that time the game attracted quite a large turnout of around 28,000 – not bad for a team that had finished bottom. Yes, Spurs won the game, and at the final whistle what seemed like thousands of fans poured on to the pitch to congratulate the team and pledge their support the following season in the old Second Division.

As we left The Lane, it was like coming out of the ground thinking we had just won something rather than having made the dreaded drop. I remember thinking what would this place be like if we DID win something after all this … and just a few years later I found out – thanks to that famous Ricky Villa goal in the '81 Cup final replay and the celebrations in the High Road the following Sunday. Happy days.

GINOLA'S THIGHS AND THE SKINHEAD *PAUL JARVIS, Acton*

So many memories over the years from my first visit to The Lane at the age of eight in 1969, taken by my Arsenal-loving Dad because I wanted to see my hero Jimmy Greaves ... Gazza's elastic face (and rubber tongue) ... Jurgen The German Destroyer ... the hilariously overzealous tickertape reception we gave Ardiles and Villa ... Chris Waddle's ever-tragic haircuts ... 'Ooh'-ing and 'Aah'-ing Hoddle during the warm ups as he would run through his repertoire of tricks ... being right by the corner flag once watching Ralph Coates huffing and puffing trying to skin a defender for pace and thinking, 'Christ, he looks older than my Dad!' ... being mortally embarrassed by my sister, again sitting by a corner flag, as Ginola came over waving and preening to take a corner. The cry of, 'Cor, look at those thighs!' still haunts me.

The game I'll always remember more than any other was the 1984 Uefa Cup Final second leg v Anderlecht . It was the tensest match I've ever been to. The ground was jumping, and you could smell the fear whenever Anderlecht put a decent move together. Directly in front of me was this massive 6'6" skinhead, who lived every second of the game in such an emotional state it was as if he was watching his loved ones dying. Every time we lost the ball he would practically weep, and time after time he had to turn away from the unfolding agony as Spurs didn't look like they would ever score. Each time he did, he caught my eye – rather ominously I felt. When Ossie Ardiles hit the bar, he bent over double and rocked back and forwards as if auditoning for Bedlam. When Graham Roberts equalised he was like an earthquake going off in all directions.

Then came penalties, and by now I'd seen enough of this nutcase to dread ANY outcome, be it tragic defeat or glorious victory. It seemed to me the guy was going to have a stroke of some kind. And he was so big. If he was going down, he was going to take 50 of us with him .

Come the Tony Parks penalty save and all that eye contact with me exploded into direct contact. He picked me up under the armpits and threw me up in the air over and over again as if I was his little puppet as he unleashed the most unearthly primal scream.

After what seemed about two hours of this he eventually got tired, smiled at me as if he'd just seen a puppy for the first time, let me go, and started wading through the crowd on the way out in search of other kicks. I left White Hart Lane elated by our famous victory, and also badly shaken up as I felt I'd just spent the last few hours watching someone have a nervous breakdown right in front of me.

Still, we won, and what harm did he really do I genially pondered. Then, as I reached the ticket barrier at Seven Sisters station, I realised that my pockets had been emptied of cash, along with my train ticket, by the bouncing up and down I'd so enjoyed from the deranged skinhead. I managed to bunk the train fare home, but if anyone ever comes across a return ticket to Haslemere on the floor of the Park Lane end, I'd quite like it back as a souvenir.

'SPURS BOY' WILLIAM SMITH, Wood Green

One cold winter's evening my Dad returned from work with two tickets to attend an evening with Bobby Moore, Steve Perryman and Kenny Lynch at a dingy sports hall somewhere in London's East End. At the time I had no idea who Bobby Moore was, but my Dad told me he was the only Englishman to lift the World Cup and in later years I would look back upon being in the same room as him with great pride.

I must admit I thought nothing of meeting the late great 'Sir Bobby' and just imagined seeing my own hero, the one and only Steve Perryman. I had watched him at the Lane for almost two seasons and – as a captain and player – in my opinion there was no contest as to who I would rather meet. As we left our home in Hackney I felt a twinge of butterflies in my tummy. Would I get his autograph? Would I shake his hand?

Most of the evening now seems a blur. I remember Kenny Lynch doing a stand-up which everyone seemed to find very funny, but it went over my young head. He then introduced 'Sir' Bobby and Steve to the crowd to a very loud reception. The slides slid and the videos reeled but I understood little of the comment and analysis. I sat gob smacked about 10 rows from the front staring at my hero Steve.

Then questions were put to the panel who sat answering them very politely and with a smile. Once everyone had asked what seemed like 10,000 questions Kenny stood up and asked if anyone who wanted an autograph could make their way forward.

My heart leapt and, with my Dad at my side, we rushed forward. As we approached Steve he had autograph books, paper and pens being thrust at him from all directions. He stood up and roared, "One at a time please!". I meekly stepped back barely able to see my hero through the thrashing scrum in front of me, but my Dad – without a word – hoisted me onto his shoulders so I could see Steve. All of a sudden my eyes caught Steve's and he shouted above the din towards me, "You first ... Spurs Boy!".

I'm not sure why he did this. Maybe it was my crisp Spurs replica shirt and early 80's track suit bottoms with Spurs socks pulled over the bottom of them; or maybe it was just that my Dad shouted louder than others. In any case I was hoisted over to Steve with him, my hero, hauling me over the last few people.

By now my heart was racing and before he signed my sweaty scrappy programme of proceedings he asked me my name. My tongue had gone limp and my mouth tensed. My Dad rescued me again, shouting: "His name is William". I heard my Dad as any son would but Steve didn't and just said: "I'll call you Spurs Boy". My heart leapt and then I was whisked away by my Dad.

I did get Bobby Moore's autograph as well moments later, but I thought little of it. With all due respect to the great man, I was only seven or so. Weeks later we placed ourselves on our regular spot in the East Stand. I stood on my wooden step made for me by my Dad, watching the action unfold through the metal fencing of that era.

As we watched, the ball broke loose, bounced and then hit the metal grill directly in front of my face. I pulled away slightly and watched as Steve ran up to collect the ball for a throw in. My hero looked so different. He was intense and immersed in the game, but just before he turned to take the throw-in he caught my eye again and said: "You all right Spurs Boy?"

My inhibitions gone I shouted: "Come on you Spurs!". He smiled again at me, then returned to the maelstrom, and again my heart raced as dozens of hands patted my back. I will never forget the events. and I did meet Steve on two further occasions at Junior Spurs events when he continued to call me Spurs Boy. Yes, I am grown up now, but that Spurs Boy memory will stay with me forever.

A TAYLOR-MADE MEMORY *CHRIS ATKINS, Hornsey*

My earliest and fondest memory of going to WHL was in 1977 when Spurs were in the old Second Division. My Dad took me to see Spurs vs. Mansfield and we stood in the Paxton end. I say I stood but I actually sat on a barrier with the assistance of my Dad, propping me up on his arm from behind.

It was the day after Boxing Day, and I have that everlasting memory of seeing that green velvet pitch highlighted under floodlights as I walked into the ground for the very first time. I seem to remember there being room around us in the Paxton end, with the shallow concrete steps being visible despite there being a crowd of around 36000.

Peter Taylor, my hero of the day, hit a shot about five metres wide of the goal. He struck so hard that I didn't have time to get out of the way as the ball hit me on my cheek and knocked me off the barrier onto the terraces.

I remember being a little dazed as my Dad picked me up and then feeling so happy that Peter Taylor had hit a ball into my face.

My Mum told me to wash my face when I got home but I would have none of it and left that dried mud on my face for a week.

I also remember that my Dad couldn't get a programme on the day as he told me that they had all sold out. However, he did very kindly buy me a badge which I still have to this day. It is a metal hand with two figure sticking up and there is an inscription that says "Victory Spurs" on the base of the hand.

I believe Barry Daines saved a penalty and John Duncan scored for Spurs in a 1 – 1 draw. Dizzy heights: a 1–1 draw against Mansfield in the Second Division and I'm fixed for life.

I drew some pictures of Peter Taylor after the game and wrote to him. He wrote back with an autograph. Life's joys were so much less materialistic then. In a nice twist I had time to kill before the Spurs-Villa game early this year and managed to pick up the programme of the Mansfield game for £1 from a vendor outside the ground.

With all of this in mind, however, I would give Spurs up tomorrow if I could. Let's face it, being a Spurs fan is a real vice.

MY FIRST MATCH AT THE LANE *MICHAEL HODGSON, Peterborough*

It was five years ago – February 7 2004 – that I saw Gus Poyet claim a late dramatic winner for Spurs as they came out on the right side of a seven-goal thriller against Portsmouth (who were managed by Harry Redknapp). Spurs had taken the lead three times through Jermain Defoe on his debut and Robbie Keane (2).
But each time Pompey came back with Eyal Berkovic, Lomana LuaLua and Ivica Mornar on target. But Poyet's shot from Dean Richards' header gave Spurs victory and eased the pressure on manager David Pleat.

These were the main moments of the first ever match I ever saw at White Hart Lane. I was then 14 and went with my dad, Philip, and the atmosphere was 'the most beautifullest sound' I have ever heard. There is a strong Tottenham heartbeat in my family. When we took my Mum to her first game to watch the match against Everton she described the experience as "magical." And how about this – my Dad's Dad – my Granddad – served aboard HMS Hotspur!

I can't believe White Hart Lane is getting demolished. If only the new stadium can be called White Hart Lane, a ground that has given Spurs supporters a journey of a life time. As the new ground is going to be so close, I will think of it as Son of White Hart Lane.

Going back to that first match I watched, it gave me a feeling of better things to come. For me, it was the first step of MY journey of a life time. As my Mum said, "magical!"

CATCHING THE GUNNERS NAPPING *PHILIP LESTER, South Woodford*

Two Lane memories stand out for me above all others ... an unforgettable European night when we defeated Anderlecht on penalties in the 1984 UEFA Cup final second leg, with goalkeeper Tony Parks our hero ... and, the best of all, beating Arsenal 5-1.

Other recent matches standing tall in my memory: last season's remarkable 4-4 games against Chelsea and Aston Villa in the 125th Aniversary. The 6-4 thriller with Reading wasnt bad either!

Oh yes, and then there was the 5-1 v Chelsea Worthington cup semi final second leg January 2002 ... beating a Feyenoord side here in 1983 4-2, containing a certain Johan Cruyff eclipsed by Glenn Hoddle on the night.

Oh yes, and another Glenn Hoddle performance Sept 1982 against Southampton resulting in a 6-0 win ... 9-0 against a hapless Bristol Rovers side in Oct 1977 ... and of course 7-2 against the Saints in March 2000. which is our biggest Premiership win thus far! I could go on and on.

THAT MAGIC MOMENT *BRIAN JOHNSON, Gravesend, Kent*

As a Spurs fan of more than 40 years I remember when my young daughter Jodie, despite my efforts to sway her in the direction of my beloved Tottenham, couldn't make up her mind as to whether her loyalties would lie with Spurs, Newcastle or Liverpool.

It was only when I took her to The Lane for the very first time that we walked up the steps hand in hand to the point where the famous turf came into view. Her face absolutely lit up on seeing the floodlit vision of Magic and she whispered: "I belong here".

Since that day both Jodie and now her younger brother Daniel will not have a word said against the Mighty Spurs.

COME ON YOU SPURS *TIM DRAAIJER, Nijmegen, The Netherlands*
I am a Dutch Spurs fan and try to see as many matches as possible. So far in the 2008-09 season I have visited The Lane four times. My most impressive Lane memory is when the crowd is singing all together: "COME ON YOU SPURS..... COME ON YOU SPURS....." It gives me a wonderful feeling and the sound goes all the way through my body. Unfortunately I have yet to attend a big Tottenahm celebration match, although the 5-0 friendly against AS Roma was nice. Come on you Spurs!

A VIEW FROM THE PRESS BOX *JOHN JENKINS, Verwood, Dorset*
Choosing the best Tottenham players since 1945 - when I first began watching football – is virtually impossible. But here goes:

1. Danny Blanchflower – personally a mixed-up character but a wonderful footballer and inspirational captain. At one time we both reported on football for the *Sunday Express* and through a sports desk mix-up both went to Highbury to cover Arsenal and Spurs. I learned more about football in 90 minutes sitting next to Danny than I had in 10 years of playing the game and 20 years reporting it.

2. It has to be Jimmy Greaves but Klinsmann runs him close. I remember wishing Jimmy a "Happy Easter," in the old Spurs car park. Reporters had to use the tradesman's entrance in those days.

"Happy Easter!" scoffed Jim. "Andy Malcolm at West Ham on Friday, Billy Bremner at Leeds on Saturday and Chopper Harris at Chelsea on Monday.

"I'll have no * * * * * * legs left." He only scored three goals that weekend.

3. The best manager? Bill Nicholson by miles. Totally honest. Totally dedicated to the club, to his players and to the game.

PUSH, RUN AND PNEUMONIA *BOB REILLY, Ware, Herts*
Being a lifelong supporter now nearing retirement age I have many memories of my second religion, Tottenham Hotspur. I was indoctrinated as a Spurs fan before I could walk or talk by my family (all Spurs supporters). I went to my first match at four years old. I was privileged at the age of six to see all the home games during the unforgettable Push and Run 1950-51 season, except the final game when skipper Ron Burgess collected the First Division championship trophy. The reason I was absent is because I had been taken into hospital suffering from pneumonia.

You can imagine what a blow this was to me. However, an uncle of mine, a police sergeant who always managed to be detailed for duty at the Lane, knew of my situation and took my autograph book with him. He went into both dressing rooms and got every player to sign it. The opposition that day were Liverpool and included in their team was a player by the name of Bob Paisley. I still have the autograph book to this day.

THE FAMILY BOND *STEVEN BASING, Harlow, Essex*

Being a fan of Tottenham Hotspur Football Club was not something I chose, but rather something that was thrust upon me. From the moment I was born it was inevitable that I would follow in a long line of Tottenham fans, and as well as inheriting the passion, I would also acquire the agony, despair, and ecstasy that being a Spurs fan brings.

I was raised on a diet of stories of Jennings, Hoddle and Gascoigne from my father, of Bill Nicholson and Danny Blanchflower from my Grandfathers. Inspired by these stories my love affair with Tottenham grew, and the club became a part of me, almost like an extension of my family.

This bond has never ceased or weakened. Even as my father observed a self-imposed exile from the Lane, in protest against Alan Sugar in the early 1990's, his passion never dispelled or wavered, and feeding off this and his stories of the glory nights, of the Tony Parks penalty saves in 1984, or Ricki Villa's wonder goal in 1981 and of Gascoigne's free kick in 1991, my passion grew as well. Tottenham were always with me as I grew older, be it in the hours I spent outside kicking a ball around pretending to be Teddy, or the 'THFC' that was blazoned across all my school books.

Eventually in 2001, my father relented and we returned to White Hart Lane. Since then I have been fortunate to take in many a great moment at the Lane, and gathered experiences and stories that I will one day be able to share with a future generation, just as my grandfathers and father have shared theirs with me.

My single greatest memory is one still fresh in my mind, and one I shall take to the grave ... February 24th 2008 – The day we beat Chelsea at Wembley. The game is much of a blur in my mind. A blur of stress, anxiety, fear, hope and finally exhilaration. But I vividly remember leaving the new stadium. Trudging down the concourses and at a snail's pace, but no-one caring in the slightest. The shouting, the laughing, the excited phone calls. Out onto Wembley Way, I craned my neck for my dad and sister. They had been sitting elsewhere in the stadium. Finally seeing them, the absolute joy as we hugged and celebrated our victory. And that's what Spurs means to me. The dizzying highs and devastating lows. But a lasting passion, made all the more intense and meaningful for being able to share it with my family.

THE ZUMMERZET CLAN *GEORGE KYRIACOU, Weston-super-Mare*

I was born in 1973 and the 80's were a great time to be a Spurs fan. My dad Andrew and my Uncle Perry were Tottenham supporters along with 90% of my mates, which was pretty good considering we live in Somerset! I remember proudly walking down the sea-front in '81 with my Spurs scarf on just after we'd beaten Man City 3-2 in the Cup final, and a Brummie tourist said, 'You only support them cos they won the Cup!' Wrong! The love affair has now lasted nearly 30 years, and it will continue forever.

UNBOTTLED MEMORIES *PETER GRAHAM, South Australia*

I am now 67 year old and living here in South Australia after emigrating in 1969. I was born and bred in Broad Lane, and have been a Tottenham supporter for most if not all of my life. I can remember some of my earliest excursions when Dad would take me to the ground, and the blokes would put me up in the air and pass me hand over hand down to the front just behind the fence. I can remember the lights as I floated above the crowd. I can remember the day when goalkeeper Ted Ditchburn passed the ball out to Alf Ramsey and then turned his back on the game. Meanwhile Alf decided to play it back to the goalkeeper, but as I said he had his back turned and it slowly went over the line for a goal. The crowd were absolutely silenced; no-one could believe it.

The funniest and most awesome thing I recall is when my friends and I travelled on a bus from Tottenham to Sunderland for the FA Cup sixth round tie in the Double year of 1961. Spurs were absolutely brilliant in the first 45 minutes, outplaying Sunderland but the scoreline did not reflect their supremacy. We were only one goal up at half-time.

During the half-time period someone got the crowd going and they started to sing their anthem (The Blayden Races). By the time the teams had returned to restart the game the crowd were now singing this song as one, it was so loud and passionate that it was quite scary. It was my first experience of the famous Roker Roa

What happened was a complete form reversal, with the Tottenham players seeming to be unbalanced by this awesome singing and support. The effect on the Sunderland players was that they were turned into superstars. They scored a well-deserved equaliser and really should have won through, such was their passion and desire.

After the game we all went to the nearest pub and enjoyed a few ales, but then had the marathon bus trip home; so we clubbed together and bought some Newcastle Brown ale. Because it was a dry coach we had to hide the bottles between the back seat and the back window. Fortunately we had consumed most of this brew before we fell off to sleep, for after several hours of travelling we started to hear these wild explosions.

It was the bloody beer exploding because of the bumps in the road, and the tops were bursting off and the coach was full of foaming beer. Needless to say the driver was furious and threatened to throw off the guilty persons if he could find them but we would not own up. It all ended happily with Tottenham winning the replay at The Lane 5-0, and going on to capture both the FA Cup and the League Championship.

THE BARKING BOYS ARE BACK *DON PRATT, Leicestershire*

As a schoolboy I was brought up on the Becontree estate and enjoyed many a kickabout in Parsloes Park with a very young but very skilful Jimmy Greaves. He and I, along with another friend, Brian Drain, made our first ever post-war trip to Wembley to see a football tournament involving Armed Services Cadet teams.

Later on after Jimmy's family moved away from Ivyhouse Road and the Fanshaw Football Club, we were thrilled when another of our parks team, Mortimer Costello, was picked for Barking Boys and we went to see him play at the old Vicarage Field alongside the future World Cup winning captain, Bobby Moore.

I was lucky enough to win the eleven plus in 1945 and was allocated to Leyton County High School which meant a daily commute from Becontree to Leyton High Road Station on the Barking to Kentish Town railway line. We schoolboys shared the train compartment with a number of Spurs players, who were travelling to training from Barking to South Tottenham.

I remember some intense, if not to say illicit, card games with the reserve team captain, Ron Henry and Sid McLlelland. One person who remained aloof from such activities, but was always polite and willing to engage in softly spoken conversation. This was Alf Ramsey, of course, who hailed from Church Elm in Dagenham, and made this England and Spurs fan very proud to watch two hometown boys celebrating at Wembley on that sunny summers day in 1966.

TRAINING WITH BILL NICHOLSON *ANDY GIRLING, Eltham*
In the late 60's when travelling back by train from Sheffield after the game, I saw the Tottenham team all get in the First Class compartments at Sheffield station. After some gentle persuasion from my mate I knocked on the carriage door where Mr. Nicholson was sitting, and politely asked him for his autograph. He gladly obliged and passed the programme around the compartment so that Eddie Baily signed it along with Ray Evans and Mike England. 'Sir Bill' then whispered in my ear and asked me to tell anyone else not to disturb them. I felt so proud and I still have the signed programme as a memento. Happy Days.

A TOUCH OF CLASS FROM SHERINGHAM *MARTIN KING, Poole, Dorset*
Born in Yeovil, Somerset, in 1955, I somehow found myself a Spurs supporter in 1961-62. Living so far away I got to see my team when my late, great Dad took me to Southampton to watch them in the 'old' First Division and at Ashton Gate against Bristol City in the League Cup in 1970-71 (the year Spurs lifted the trophy at Wembley). The thought of seeing my team, the Mighty Spurs, with my dad – a Wolverhampton Wanderers fan – was one of the great thrills of my young life. In the early 70s I even chose a college in London to attend so that I could see the Spurs every week.

From there I eventually moved to the USA to work for a while. I couldn't wait for Monday to come round to grab the mail at work. Dad would send me the Sunday Mirror, and even though it was eight days old I couldn't wait to read the report of a Spurs game (no internet then). My parents even rang me and held the phone to the TV so I could listen to the end of the UEFA cup final, what a day.

My proudest day however at the Lane, was taking my daughter Megan to the ground and see her as a mascot on the night we beat Chelsea 5-1 in the League Cup semi-final, running onto that pitch and having her picture taken. Teddy Sheringham was a true gent that day, even remembering her name after the game; now that's class.

I can't go too often now – expensive day out – but I have a great dad and daughter day once or twice a season, and hope that my daughter will remember days out at the Lane, as I did watching the Spurs with my dad.

A TIMELY MEMORY *COLIN ASHBY, formerly Haslemere, now in France*
I first started supporting Spurs as a 10 year old, living in Dartford Kent. I could not get to see them, but avidly read newspaper reports and listened when I could on the radio. I was finally able to see them live at The Lane the season we got into Europe. I was working in London by then, so instead of going home I went to the midweek game when we were playing Gornik. The hairs on the back of my neck still stand on end when I recall this fantastic night, the atmosphere, the crowd and of course the result. I did not get to see much of the game as I was standing in the Paxton road end, and because I am not very tall got glimpses of the game.

I was hooked, managed to go and watch a few games, before the crowd control, and the banter and crowd were always first class. At last I managed to get a season ticket in '82, and went to every game without fail. I travelled to watch us play Liverpool in the Cup in the January, a day that a friend hired a limousine to get us to Anfield. It was snowing heavily en route, and we listened to the radio half expecting to be told the game was off.

We had food and drink, but at Stoke on the M6 the limo broke down. The chauffeur had to walk to the nearest phone box and somehow managed to get a call through and arranged for a taxi to pick us up and continue our journey.

The cabbie took us to Anfield and we watched us getting beaten yet again (however we were there when Garth Crooks finally got the winner! MAGIC). We came out of the ground and immediately met the cabbie, how I don't know, and he drove us all the way back to London!

Later I would take my son and young grandson to the games, we had seats in the West Upper. Because of the little guy we would invariably have to run to the ground to be there before kick off. Very difficult for an overweight mid fifty! The game was against Watford , and we scored in the first half. Like everyone else I jumped up and applauded and cheered. A guy two rows in front turned round glaring, and I couldn't understand why. At half-time I noticed that I had lost my very expensive watch. It must have fallen off while running to the ground I thought and I resigned myself to its loss. We saw the whole of the game, because of the little grandson, we had occasionally left just before the final whistle. This time we stayed to cheer them off the pitch, and waited while people filed out. I suddenly had a thought and walked down the two rows in front of me to where the guy had been sitting who had turned around. To my astonishment the watch was under his seat. It must have flown off my wrist while I was clapping, hit the guy in front, who probably thought it was a missile thrown by someone and landed under him. It was undamaged, apart from needing a new strap.

BREATHING TOTTENHAM HOTSPUR *PETER CLEAK, Crouch End*

When I was a young boy I'd just have to go to The Lane on match day, even though I had no funds to buy a ticket. Just to be there and to buy a programme was enough. Wearing my Spurs shirt, I would walk around the outside of the ground at least twice, just to breathe Tottenham Hotspur! Sometimes, when the match was televised, I would sneak into a pub and watch on the big screen. It's amazing where a white shirt can get you. Now the sight of the Cockerel, the approach to the stadium, the first glimpse of the green. It's like the safest home in the world. There is nothing like it in life. When the whistle blows everything just vanishes and for 90 minutes everything is possible.

THE PITCH-INVADING STEWARD *MALCOLM CALLOW, Enfield*

In the early eighties I was short of money and couldn't afford to watch the Spurs, so I got a job as a steward in the north stand showing people to their seats. That season we reached the UEFA Cup final. As the game reached the end my manager asked me to go down to the pitch area and sit in front of the dugout and make sure nobody ran on the pitch.

We had to score to force extra-time and in the 75th minute Graham Roberts grabbed a goal and I jumped up and ran on to the pitch. leaping up and down like a mad man. My boss was shouting, "Sit down, sit down!" We then played 30 minutes extra-time with no added score, so it was down to penalties.

My boss then ordered me to go on the pitch and stand in the centre-circle and make sure no one ran on. Can you imagine? It was unbelievable. I was the first person to speak to Danny Thomas when he missed a penalty to win it, but then we all know what happened ... Tony Parks saved the next one and ran off like a nutcase and we had won the cup. Probably the best day of my life.

BLUE-TINGED MEMORIES *PETER HICKS, Brighton*

Although I was born in Brighton, my Dad had to move the family to Essex in January 1960 for his job (in Holborn, London). I was eight years old. Immediately he started going to the Lane and I at length persuaded him to take me. My first match was on

February 4 1961, against Leicester City. I had been to the Goldstone Ground a couple of years earlier, but nothing prepared me for White Hart Lane. The massive crowds outside the ground, the height of the East Stand, the noise.

It was a dull overcast day and in my memory everything has a blue tinge to it. We quickly bought a programme, got in just before kick-off, and Dad pushed me high up onto The Shelf. The view was extraordinary. The crowds below on the East terrace looked so far away, I felt I was in outer space! Of course, Spurs lost the game 3-2 , but I was hooked. I was Spurs.

The next time I went with Dad and one of his work colleagues, Harry Gilberg, who had played twice for the first team (and later went on to play for Brighton!). Obviously, I was in awe and he pointed out all the important features of the ground and game.

This time the lower terrace looked even further away, as we were in seats high up in the back of the East stand. Spurs beat Aston Villa 1-0.

However, greatest memories: 1963. By Easter of that year, Spurs were on a roll, although they came a real cropper at Anfield losing 5-2. However, on the Easter Monday (April 15th) at the Lane Spurs got sweet revenge. They totally demolished Liverpool 7-2! Jimmy Greaves scored four.

Sixteen days later on May 1, it was the second leg of the Cup Winners Cup semi-final against OFK Belgrade. Spurs were 2-1 up from the first leg but that night we were without Greavsie who had been sent off in Belgrade.

I remember seeing the 'Lilywhite Angels' in all their regalia parading in front of us. One of them carried a placard saying: "Repent OFK for thou hath Greaved"!

The atmosphere was electric. Five minutes before the kick-off it was obvious I wasn't going to see much. Suddenly a couple of blokes lifted me above everyone and said "Put him onto the track", so I was carried over the wall (with the iron hoops) and placed on the cinder track between the 'B' and 'C' of the half-time scores.

The view was fantastic – I couldn't believe my luck! Suddenly, Cecil Poynton, the Spurs trainer, came up, leaned over me, pointed his finger and said, "You can't sit there, son, you'll get hurt."

Just then the giant that was Maurice Norman trotted by and I saw what he meant. But the match started and everyone forgot I was there!

It was brilliant, and I didn't want the evening to end. My lasting impression of the Spurs team that night, and I suppose it's because I was so close to them, was the fact that in their all-white strip they looked invincible, especially Dave Mackay with his barrel chest pushed out. It never occurred to me that they would lose!

When we got home, we were in time for the end of the TV highlights. As the full-time whistle blew I saw this little chap in his Spurs bobble hat, leap up from between 'B' and 'C,' with his arms in the air in triumph!

AT FEVER PITCH DOWN UNDER *from MATT GRANT, Western Australia*

I've only been to the Lane once in my life, as I live in Australia, but as a foreigner in the UK, I will never forget it. It was a clear but cold day in North London, New Year's day in fact back in 2005, me and four mates had got tickets to watch Spurs play Everton months ago, and only because we wanted to see a Premier League game. I loved football but had never really supported any team until this day.

It all started with a very hung-over trip in the car, where to be honest, I had absolutely no idea where I was, keeping my stomach down was the main priority for the near future.

When we arrived at the Lane, I couldn't get over how many people were gathered around the gates, singing oh so loud. As we entered the stadium, I remember walking down a narrow walkway and coming out at the top of the stand on the far wing. We were seated right on the halfway line with Spurs kicking towards our left.

The game started at electric pace and Spurs where quickly away with goals from Dean Marney and Reto Ziegler in the first half hour before Tim Cahill cancelled it out just before half-time. The noise in the Lane was absolutely amazing, like nothing I had ever heard before. I remember eating a cold pie at half-time and just taking everything in as I sat in my royal blue seat.

As the game entered the second-half, Pedro Mendes stretched our lead with a powerful shot and there looked to be only one winner. This turned out to be the case when Robbie Keane slotted Spurs' fourth. But more was to come and I will never forget Dean Marney's 25 yard curler that put Tottenham 5-1 in front, and is still one of the greatest goals I've ever seen, not only at The Lane, but in the Premier League. Everton scored a late consolation goal but it was a happy New Year to Spurs and for us.

That was my first game as a Tottenham supporter, and ever since then I've had that special Spurs fever pulsing through me.

TRIBUTE TO A LEGEND *LORRETTA FONTAINE, Tottenham*

When you hear the name of Bill Nicholson, any Spurs fan will tell you that he was the greatest Manager to ever grace White Hart Lane. A double winner and the man who put the Glory Glory into Tottenham Hotspur. A man so great that he even had the road leading to the Lane named after him. A man who was a true Gentleman in every sense of the word.

I am too young to have been around when Bill was conducting his managerial greatness, but as a loyal Spurs fan I know my history and know how much of an important figure Bill Nicholson was to Spurs.

Bill Nicholson was and always will be Mr. Tottenham!

Therefore I have chosen to write about a rather sad occasion at the Lane as my memory, when we chose to remember 'Sir' Bill Nicholson. Sunday November 7th 2004 was the date of the Bill Nicholson Memorial Service.

It was a sad day but a fitting tribute to a man who was simply the best. Many a Spurs legend came to pay tribute to Bill, such as the great Steve Perryman, Glenn Hoddle and Gary Mabbutt.

There was one thing that still sticks in my mind to this day and that was when Bill's daughter, Linda, took to the stage to speak about her father. Her words: "My Dad loved the fans and in return the fans loved him."

Never a truer word has been said and was greeted by a deafening round of applause. A sad day but I was proud to have been a part of remembering and paying tribute to such a great man, who was and always will be a great part of Tottenham Hotspur Football Club.

'Sir Bill' will always have a place in the heart of the Spurs faithful. I know I speak on behalf of all the Spurs supporters when I say, "We love you Bill."

TONY PARKS AND SO MANY MEMORIES *RAY HENNESSEY, Biggleswade*
I started going to The Lane in the late fifties. I stood on the north terrace behind the goal and often felt like the filling in a sandwich as the ground got packed.

Into the sixties I moved to the standing enclosure in front of the main stand, and that later became season ticket only. When the main stand was demolished we were moved up onto The Shelf, and that was a great place from which to watch a game.

When The Shelf became seated I stuck it for about four seasons, but the price and the fact that the rain and sun was often a problem prompted me to move to my current seat in the north stand upper.

I have seen all the memorable moments and players at The Lane over the years and Jimmy Greaves is my all time favourite Spur followed by Ossie Ardiles.

There have been great matches in snow and rain and fog and on a pitch like a bog. I have seen Mackay and Mullery and Roberts lifting the team and driving them on by example.

I have seen Greaves and Smith, Chivers and Gilzean, Crooks and Archibald, Duncan, Allen, Sheringham, Ferdinand and Klinsmann score the goals that have brought us so much glory over the years. It is just impossible to pick out one memory when there have been so many.

I am in my 70th year now and am lucky to have been to all our cup finals from 1967 to date. We have only lost three and they have been my worst memories. One of my best has to be the UEFA Cup final at The Lane against Anderlecht and the penalty shoot out at the end. Tony Parks was a true hero that day.

So many memories. Thank you Tottenham, and thank you White Hart Lane.

A GIFT FOR BILL *SHAUN BOYLE, ex-Midlands now in Mallorca*

My special memory of Bill Nicholson goes back to the mid-1970s. Dismissed and, at the time, quietly discarded from the club he had dedicated his life to with extrarodinary success, some friends and I, mostly based in the Midlands, decided to play a couple of games of football to raise some money and get him a 'thank you' gift.

The dates and details are fading with time, but we got our gift and made contact with Mr. Nicholson. We assembled in the shadow of the White Hart Lane stadium at the pub on the corner and waited.

As it wasn't a match day, that night seemed so different and somehow sad. To add to the dismal mood it was raining. Friends Tony and Irene, who were neighbours of the Nicholsons, went to tell Mr. Nicholson and his lovely wife, Darky, we had arrived. They were never pretentious and lived in a modest house close to the ground.

I anticipated a rather sad evening, but Mr. Nicholson – he insisted on us all calling him Bill – was having none of it. He arrived with his wife, both of them immaculately dressed, he in his trademark smart suit and she in a beautiful coat.

He escorted his wife to a seat and she chatted amongst us, while he held court.

"You are a lucky bunch of lads," he said "This is the first time I've been to a pub round here for 20 years!"

He looked at Tom, a towering member of our assembly. "You should get a trial. At six foot five, you've got the makings of a centre-half."

Mr. Nicholson, sorry, Bill, was in good spirits, thanking us one by one for coming all that way from the Midlands. I made a short presentation speech, choking on my words, and as he accepted an engraved silver plate he said: "Who's got the camera?"

In the frenzy nobody had remembered to bring one. But it didn't matter. The picture of the moment was frozen into our minds for ever. The only thing that mattered was that we were there and we did it.

The local newspaper reported that we had given Mr. Nicholson a bigger send-off than the club. I have been proud to be a Tottenham supporter for 48 years and that evening I met a great man.

HAPPY FAMILIES *ANDY CURRAN, Dorset*

One of my best memories (so far) would have to be in the winter of 1995 against Liverpool. I took my younger cousin, who was a Liverpool freak. She was really giving me stick when we went 1-3 down (I believe a certain Jamie Redknapp had scored a couple for Liverpool!). But the comeback was fantastic, and when Darren Caskey scored the equaliser it was unbelievable! I have still yet in twenty plus years of visits to WHL to see them win a League match. I've seen cup victories and lots of away victories!

My other undying memory will have to be at the Families day last December, when

I took my youngest daughter to The Lane for the first time. Her face was an absolute picture when we walked out into the ground. She had her picture taken with Martin Chivers, and collected the autographs of Ralph Coates, Cliff Jones, John Pratt and Pat Jennings. The whole day was amazing and just to see her having so much fun was worth the effort of getting up there from Dorset.

DOGGED BILL NICK TO THE RESCUE *BARRY MIDDLETON Naezing, Essex*
My father and I were season ticket holders in 1981 and in those days Cup Final tickets were automatically sent out to ST holders in the post.

Unfortunately, my puppy retriever tore the tickets to shreds when they dropped through the letter-box.

Obviously mortified, I went straight to the old ticket office in what is now called Bill Nicholson Way. This was pre-computerisation of the match ticket process and the guy in the ticket office was saying that they couldn't produce duplicates and was generally unsympathetic. I could see my long awaited day at Wembley was looking difficult and began to protest at the attitude to my problem.

At that moment the great man himself - Bill Nicholson - happened to walk into the ticket office. Noticing that our discussion was becoming a little heated he came over and said: "What's the problem?" I explained that I was very sorry but the puppy had got into the hallway during the day and chewed up the tickets.

"Wait a minute," said Bill and went behind the counter and into the office. He re-appeared a few minutes later with TWO new tickets and said: "Hope you enjoy the game," and presented me with the tickets!

When we got to Wembley the seats were fantastic – close to the Royal Box – and although Spurs had to wait for a few more days before winning the replay against Manchester City my late father and I had a great day due to Bill's generosity.

The puppy's name by the way was Greaves.

A 50 YEAR ROMANCE *JOHN BAKER Johannesburg, South Africa*
My love affair with Tottenham and The Lane started when I was a schoolboy still in short trousers. My father took me to see his team, Burnley, playing there in 1959 (the year the Turf Moor club won the championship). But instead of falling in love with Dad's team I found myself admiring the style and panache of Spurs at a time when Danny Boy was just starting to put his stamp on the side.

From that day on I followed Tottenham avidly, and over the next few years they gave me more thrills, pleasure and excitement than can be imagined. I saw them lift the FA Cup at Wembley to complete the Double, and I was back at Wembley in 1967 to see Dave Mackay lead Spurs to victory over Chelsea.

These days I only get to The Lane once a year on visits home, but all the way down here in Jo'burg I don't miss a heartbeat of the club thanks to the internet and Sky TV.

Thank you spurs for nearly 50 years of a wonderful romance, and I'm still as in love with you as from the first day our eyes met across a crowded terrace at The Lane.

SMILING IN DEFEAT *PAUL DEFREITAS, Wembley*

My favourite memory of The Lane was the 5-4 defeat by Arsenal in Martin Jol's first match in charge in 2004 – one of the greatest games I've ever seen.

Spurs were 3-1 down and the game seemed over. Unbowed, the crowd started to sing 'I Can't Smile Without You'. Minutes later Defoe scored and the game was back on. We finally ran out of time in the nine-goal thriller.

It was the most amazing feeling leaving at the end and looking at the faces of the fans. They were all still smiling even though we had lost. It all summed up the Spirit of the Spurs.

DIARY OF A JUNIOR YID aged 13 YEARS, 5 MONTHS and 24 DAYS
DAZZA (Darren Burgess, West London)

It was a snowy cold morning in West London. While most of my friends were playing with yesterday's presents and my mum was out walking the hounds. I was running around trying to find the warmest clothes I could fit under my Parker. The anticipation had been building up for a couple of weeks, it had even over-shadowed the usual Christmas Day morning feeling. It was finally here! It was Boxing Day and I was going to my first ever game at White Hart Lane.

I'd been a fan of Tottenham longer than I could remember. I had shadowy memories of a Saturday afternoon in the late 70's when my Granddad, a QPR season ticket holder, had taken me to my first real match at a real ground. QPR v Spurs at Loftus Road. He bought me a nice blue and white striped scarf and bobble hat and let me take my uncle's big heavy wooden rattle. I'd have been about seven or eight. I think he was trying to make me a QPR fan but for some reason it backfired. I'll never know why.

So I'd followed Spurs on TV all through Junior School in the late 70's and then I went to "big school" in '82. I was in the same form as the twins, Samantha and Melanie, who me and my mate Dave used to walk home with after school. The discussion eventually came round to football and I found out they were Paxton Road season tickets holders along with their younger brother and their Grandfather. (Grandfathers have a lot to be thanked for!). Well this year, 1984, just as we were breaking for the Christmas holidays, Sam had asked me if I had plans for Boxing Day.

"Just the usual," I replied, "Why? You fancy meeting up?"

"My brother's down in Australia with my other Grandparents so his seat's available if you fancy coming."

Well you didn't have to ask me twice!

So the days had dragged until today. And I couldn't find my other Moon boot! Eventually I found it wedged behind the horse saddle in the porch and, now running late, had to scamper over the field rather than round the roads to get to the twins' house on time. Grr – two feet of snow! Wet jeans!! Frozen legs!

They met me on the main road and we walked down to catch the Central Line to Liverpool Street. This was to become my routine journey several years on, but for now it was all new and exciting and the heaters under the seats were slowly drying my jeans, too.

Liverpool Street station was HUGE compared to all the tube stations I'd been in before, and the noise of the other Spurs fans boarding the train to White Hart Lane will forever be etched in my memory. That was my first REAL memory of the chants of supporters. All the way to White Hart Lane station, down the stairs and along the High Road and there it was! My first glimpse of the stadium that was to become almost my second home so many years later. Entering the turnstiles and climbing the stairs to the Paxton Upper the noise was steadily increasing. That got louder and louder, then there was an almighty roar and the hairs on the back of my neck stood up like the hackles of an angry dog. I stood up to see the teams had just emerged from the tunnels. The roar had almost deafened me and by the time I got the ringing out of my ears the game was kicking off.

To be honest I had to check what the score was; we drew 2-2 with West Ham. Gary Mabbutt and Garth Crooks scoring. To me it mattered at the time but what has stuck in my memory nearly 25 years later was the anticipation of the day and that initial feeling of the prickles on the back of your neck when the White Hart Lane crowd roars!

I'm a season ticket holder on The Shelf now and I've been to away grounds in the League, the cups and Europe as well as working at the Old Wembley for a while, but no matter where I've been I've never felt the same electric feeling down the back of my neck as I do at The Lane. There is something about the place that is just magical to a true Spurs fan.

LORDING IT WITH DAVE MACKAY *JIM LOGAN, Enfield*

Starting on a personal note, as a young autograph hunter in the early '60s, I was a familiar figure during the school holidays waiting outside White Hart Lane for the players to emerge after morning training. On one occasion, I was walking to the ground from my home in Tottenham, carrying my scrapbooks, when Dave Mackay spotted me and stopped his car near Lordship Lane to check whether I had any photographs that I wanted him to sign. On another occasion, as a 12-year-old, he sat next to me at a reserve match to enquire about my broken arm. He was a true gentleman in addition to one of the greatest players of all time.

I've watched Spurs continually since 1962. My boyhood hero was Cliff Jones. Cliff would regularly collect the ball in his own penalty area, run the length of the field with it, and still be in possession when reaching the opposition's penalty area. I can also vividly remember him purposely colliding with a goalpost to score with a diving header in a 7-0 win over Burnley in 1968. My favourite defender was Cyril Knowles. Very skilful and a great crosser of the ball. The goals he laid on for Peters and Gilzean in the 2-2 draw with Manchester United in 1970 stand out.

One of my first great memories is of a 7-2 win over Liverpool on Easter Monday 1963. The scorers were Greaves (4), Jones (2), and Saul. Another memory is of my first ever trip abroad in 1972 to see Spurs draw 1-1 with Milan and progress to the Uefa Cup final. The outward flight left Luton at 9.00am on the morning of the match with the return flight leaving Milan at 5.00am the following morning. In Milan Airport, as we waited for our flight home, a seriously inebriated supporter somehow gained access to the Public Address System and serenaded the whole airport with 'Glory Glory Hallelujah and the Spurs go marching on'.

IT ALL STARTED WITH DITCHBURN *TONY BISHOP, Silkstone, Yorkshire*
I first visited WHL in 1957 at the age of 10 after I had picked up the morning paper to see that Ted Ditchburn was making his comeback against Arsenal following an injury. I told my mum I was going with my chum's dad and he did the same and we found our way from Enfield Town to The Lane by following the crowd from the railway station. Spurs naturally won as they often did against Arsenal in the 'good old days'. Spurs were struggling to survive in the old First Division in the late fifties but after Bill Nick's promotion to manager and subsequent 10-4 win against Everton we survived relegation by 6 points and began to fashion a team that would live in the memory of all those that were lucky enough to watch them perform in those glorious three seasons in the early sixties. I remember vividly the start of the double season when they won the first 11 league games and the win against Sheffield Wednesday when they clinched the title with a 2-1 win and I made my one and only appearance on the hallowed turf when the crowd swarmed on the pitch for the presentation of the First Division trophy - I never imagined that nearly 50 years later I'd still be awaiting another title.

A truly memorable night came when Spurs beat Gornik 8-1 in their European debut having trailed 4-0 at half-time in the first leg. The semi-final against Benfica was awesome with the 'Angels' doing their bit to create a tremendous atmosphere amongst the 65,000 crowd . Despite the 2-1 win with Danny's penalty deciding the match on the night it could have been so different had Dave Mackay's effort not smacked against the bar in the closing minutes.

The following season saw a 5-2 win against Glasgow Rangers (flying bottles as well) which led to the first European trophy by a British team. I remember the Easter weekend of 1960 when Cliff Jones took a penalty against Manchester City. The great

Bert Trautmann saved the initial kick and the referee blew for half-time – disallowing the 'goal' as the rebound was bundled into the net. That decision contributed to Spurs losing the match, the following game and subsequently the league title by a mere two points.

In 1963 Spurs lost to Liverpool (promoted the previous season) on Good Friday 5-2 at Anfield and then stuffed Liverpool on the following Monday 7-2 with Greavesie getting four goals. Those Easter fixtures with a 'return' game a few days later often created exciting matches with a hint of 'revenge' in the air. Another wonderful game at The Lane was in 1965 in a cup match against Burnley when Spurs fell two goals behind in the opening minutes only for Alan Gilzean to play his finest game and score a hat-trick in a 4-3 victory; unfortunately that took me to Preston on a ramshackle coach where Spurs had an off-day and lost 2-1.

I'm now relocated to Yorkshire and get to see Spurs' games in the north and the passion is still with me after all these years - I just hope 'Harry Hotspur' can inspire the club to get back into a challenging Premier League position in the next year or two and give us Champions League football in the new stadium.

HOW WE WERE NICELY SPOILED *BARRY HATCHER, West Byfleet, Surrey*
My memories of White Hart Lane started in 1946 when I was nine years old. My dad had supported the Spurs since seeing them win the Cup in 1921 – the strange thing was he was born and bred in South London but supported a North London team (at least it wasn't the Arsenal!)

Although my Dad first took me to White Hart Lane for the 1946/47 season, my first serious recollection of the joys of following the Spurs was the push and run team of 1950-51 managed by Arthur Rowe, which won the then First Division. The style of play was so simple and effective yet the team basically went into decline as the 50's went towards the 60's.

Then came the Glory Years with Bill Nick at the helm. He assembled a squad that gave all fans (except those from Highbury) such pleasure. I clearly remember the arrival of Dave Mackay in March 1959, and when he first played I wondered what all the fuss was about as he looked rather ordinary. It transpired he was injured at Hearts (his previous club), and he promised the following season would be better when fully fit – how right he was! Around the same time John White joined and I started to get the feeling the club was progressing towards being a pretty good side with the likes of Blanchflower, Bobby Smith, and Cliff Jones etc.

In August 1960 (I was married on the 13th – a week before the season started so missed the early games due to being on honeymoon) – the team won the initial 11 games and played a style of football that was out of this world.

All the home games were memorable for one reason or another but if I had to choose a particular game it would be the match against Burnley on December 3rd in front of 58000-plus fans. At half time Spurs were 4-0 up and coasting it. In the second half Burnley produced the most amazing fight back I can ever remember – they scored four times to make the final score 4-4 with Spurs hanging on for dear life.

The following season, having already won the double, they signed Jimmy Greaves and I remember his first game was against Blackpool, and he scored a hat-trick, with his first goal being a scissor kick following a corner. This season - 1961/2 - Spurs finished 3rd in the League as well as winning the FA Cup for the second year running. The following season they finished 2nd and were the last club ever to score over 100 goals (111 in the First Division). The Spurs also became the first English club to win a major European trophy by winning the European Cup Winners Cup 5-1 in Rotterdam. However, the outstanding game I remember was on October 31st 1962 against Glasgow Rangers which was billed at the Championship of Great Britain and Spurs won 5-2. I have never experienced such an atmosphere at any football before or after this wonderful and unique day. It was a privilege to be in the crowd.

I have to be honest and say having seen both the push and run and championship winning sides we were spoilt. We should have realised these halcyon days would never return, and thereafter everything seemed an anti-climax. In later years my dad and I would discuss the Glory Days and agree how lucky we were to have been there. This was without doubt the greatest club side I ever saw and it was such a privilege. Thanks Nick, Danny, Jimmy, Dave, Cliff and all the other players for producing a style of football that at club level I have yet to see equalled.

FIRST VISIT TO THE LANE *MARTIN CLOAKE, Forest Hill, London*
(Respected journalist Martin is author, with Adam Powley, of the excellent The
Boys from White Hart Lane, published byVision Sports Publishing)
Until 1978 I'd had to follow Spurs through the reports of Ken Jones and Frank McGhee in the *Daily Mirror*, Sport on 2's radio commentary and the occasional glimpse on Match of the Day or The Big Match. Although I grew up in Haringey, a W3 bus ride from the ground, the violence regularly reported at White Hart Lane meant my family weren't keen on me going.

But by the time I was 13 I could make my own decisions and, driven by the need to play my part in helping Spurs back up into the top flight, I found myself in the West Stand enclosure on April 8 1978 for the top-of-the-table clash with Bolton Wanderers. I'd made sure I arrived early and was one of the first in the ground. I vividly remember emerging onto the terrace and gasping as the expanse of green revealed itself before me. I stood by the halfway line and watched as the ground filled up, almost immediately fascinated with the noise generated from the fans in The Shelf section of Archibald Leitch's famous old East Stand structure which loomed opposite me.

The crowd that day was 50,097, our biggest for 13 years, and that number was jammed in a whole hour before kick-off. The chanting and the movement of the fans fascinated me, prompting a love affair with The Shelf that lasted until Irving Scholar's ill-advised destruction of the heart of the home support many years later.

It was an exciting game, with Spurs already showing signs of the footballing prowess that would make that great team of the early 1980s so entertaining. One goal settled it, a diving header from Don McAllister, and as the ball kissed the back of the net I was caught in that great bouncing, surging wave of joy I'd only witnessed before on TV.

But it is the occasion itself, rather than the details of the match, that remain vivid in the memory. I'd never been in a crowd that big before, and that day started my education in how to be a fan, what the chants were, the movements, the rhythm of the crowd that is a defining part of the English game.

What I also got was a passion for live football. Despite the wall-to-wall TV coverage today, despite the many changes to football grounds and to White Hart Lane in particular, you still can't beat being there. It's said that inside every man there is the heart of a small boy, and even at 43 years old I still have a touch of the wonder I felt as a 13-year-old every time I go to White Hart Lane.

MAKING A CASE FOR TRUANCY *ANDREW THEXTON, Darlington*
Being a Spurs fan of only 24 years old, I often, probably quite rightly, feel harshly done by in terms of the success, or lack of it thereof, that Spurs have served up to me over the years. Nonetheless I do still have lots of good memories of The Lane from more recent times.

My first trip to The Lane was 16th November 1996. Because I was brought up in the North, until this time I had been restricted to Northern away games. I was hugely excited, hardly slept a wink in the week leading up to the game and came down by train with my father from the Lake District. The game was against Sunderland, and we won 2-0 with goals from Sinton and Sheringham. I seem to recall Teddy missing a penalty although I may be wrong. The game was marred by ex-Spur Paul Stewart being sent off but my first trip to The Lane was still deemed a huge success; I was hungry for more and by 2002 I had a season ticket, making a 500 mile round trip every other week. It's funny what you remember; I recall that I sat in the old Paxton Road end and the floor was wooden.

My worst memory of The Lane was the 3-5 defeat by Man United in 2001. What I mostly remember is having a shocking trip down to London from the Lakes with the train delayed by three hours, then getting into the ground just in time for kick-off. Frustration quickly turned to elation, and then to sheer despair during the second-half. All I could think about was how much stick I was going to get at school from the Man United hordes on the Monday. It was never easy being a young Spur in a sea of Manchester United and Liverpool supporters, but I wouldn't have it any other way.

Let's finish on a positive, then - my *best* trip to The Lane. This would have to be the 5-1 win over Chelsea in the Worthington Cup semi-final, 2002. I was in the sixth form by this point, and had cunningly (or so I thought) managed to slip away from school at 12.30pm in order to get down to London for the evening kick-off. My father was waiting outside the school with the engine running and was fully compliant in my truancy, but it was a big game after all. I remember that my father cheered so hard when the first goal went in that he was unable to say anything for the rest of the game. What a night. Unfortunately I was frog marched into the head of sixth-form's office the next morning (having got back from London about three hours earlier) and was severely reprimanded for my devious absence. It was worth it though. Great memories, and many more to come.

THE ARRIVAL OF THE GREAT MACKAY *TIM DAVIS, Notting Hill*
I now have a season ticket at the Lane but fifty years ago I attended my first game there, along with my father, and watched Spurs lose 3-2 to Blackpool, for whom one Stanley Matthews was playing on the wing. He must have been well into his 40's by then but he gave Mel Hopkins a torrid time.

It's funny but the 1958/59 season bore a remarkable similarity to the one that we went through in 2008/09. The team flirted with relegation for most of the season, despite already having a number of the players on board who went on to win the Double with the team two years later. Probably the most significant event that year was the signing of Dave Mackay, just before the March transfer deadline. I saw his first game against, I think, Manchester City which we won 3-1. He immediately stood out, not just for the crunch of his tackling but also for the delicacy of his touch on the ball and he made a massive difference to the performance of the team. The following season Spurs finished third, having challenged for the First Division title for most of the season and we all know what followed that in 1960/61.

Let's hope that the parallels with what has happened this season continue into next year. Wilson Palacios could indeed be a latter day Dave Mackay, and there is also more than a passing resemblance to the late John White in the way that Luca Modric plays his football. As loyal but long-suffering Spurs fans, we have all more than earned another day in the sun and I have a sneaky feeling that next year will be the season in which we will finally see it all start to come together in the League.

ACCOUNTING FOR MY TASTE *BALRAJ RAMANATHA, Malaysia*
I have been supporting Spurs since 1967, from the days of outdated "Shoot" and "Match" magazines to listening to grainy BBC World Service transmissions at the ungodly hour of 4am ... to now in these modern times not missing a single match on satellite TV.

I qualified as a Chartered Accountant in the UK in 1980, stood on the terraces in the 'seventies when Spurs were in the Second Division, and watched them gain promotion,

These days I make sure to stopover in London to catch a match at The Lane whenever I am on a business trip in Europe. Nothing beats that! I'm 55 now and been a diehard fan since I was around 13. All in all, its been one hell of a ride!

SIXTY-PLUS YEARS A LILYWHITE *LEON RUSKIN, South Tottenham*

I have followed the Spurs since the midst of WW2 when my Uncles went off to fight with the last farewell of, "Always remember to hate two things...Hitler and Arsenal ....BUT not necessarily in that order." When they returned they revisited upon me the credo of Tottenham Hotspur, telling me the wonderful stories of pre-War Spurs. One Uncle purchased for me my first pair of soccer boots from the Sports Shop of the legendary Spurs goalkeeper, Ted Ditchburn, which was in Northumberland Avenue. It came with a poem in Ted's unmistakeable handwriting (as I later confirmed) which ended, "Always remember to regularly rub in - Lots and lots of good old Dubbin - You wont get cracks or other holes – and you will score some smashing goals!"

Christmas Day 1947 was that happy, happy day when I was first taken by my family to WHL. A Spurs team of Ditchburn, Tickridge, Buckingham, Nicholson, Woodward, Burgess, Cox, Baily, Duquemin, Bennett, Stevens entertained Chesterfield under the unhappy management of ex-Arsenal winger Joe Hulme. There were about 45,000 there that day to witness our inside trio of Baily, Duquemin and Baily secure a 3-0 win.

This was the beginning of the real romance. My visits to WHL were regular, and in those days there was no fear of my catching a bus from St Ignatius at South Tottenham to the ground by myself. In my pocket my money was tied in the corner of a handkerchief. The esprit on the ground in those days was wonderful. Supporter and visitors would share in extolling good play by either side. There was no aggravation.

We pay due homage to Billy Nicholson today, but let us remember that without Arthur Rowe nothing would have been possible. He transformed the team when he took over from Hulme.

Ramsey and Clarke were new faces but the main body of the side were existing squad members. However, what he gave us was a revolutionary philosophy "Make it simple, make it sweet." "Push and Run."

From the giant hands of Ditchburn the ball was kept in play with short accurate passing, players then running into vacant spots. No team could contain us and never has soccer looked more beautiful. Integral to the team was Nicholson who learned how sweet science could produce beautiful and very effective soccer. No hoofing the ball downfield but speedy, simple build up. As I see the type of soccer now dished up, not just by Spurs, but all teams, and the behaviour of many fans, I mourn for the Glorious Years that introduced me to the sport.

THE LANE OF LOVE AND MARRIAGE *PAUL COGGIN, Broxbourne*

I went to my first match at White Hart lane at the age of 11 in August 1971 when we beat Huddersfield 4-1, with two goals each from Gilzean and Chivers. I've been going ever since and a season ticket holder since 1982.

Among the many highlights: Beating Wolves in the Uefa Cup final in May 1972 after drawing 1-1 in the second leg. I got on to the pitch that night and the joy of dancing on the sacred turf will stay with me forever. Beating Leeds 4–2 in the last match of the 1974-75 season which resulted in us staying up, one of the best atmospheres ever. I recall the relief at the final whistle, and going to school the next day wearing a Spurs scarf with ALFIE CONN IS THE NEW MESSIAH written on it in ink.

Various matches in 1977-78 when were in the Second Division, starting off winning games comfortably, but as the season progressed the nerves kicked in for both players and supporters. We finally pipped Brighton on goal difference. Phew!

Ossie and Ricky's first match at Spurs, with smart people selling cups of ripped up paper at 50p a go. We created a South American carnival atmosphere to welcome the Argentines ... and, being Spurs, managed to lose 4-1 to Villa.

Queueing up for the 1981 Cup final replay tickets on a wet Saturday night after going to the first game, thousands of people outside the ground singing, talking about the match and being part of a great party family atmosphere.

Beating Arsenal 5–0 in April 1983 with probably the best Spurs performance against our rivals that I had seen. The two Mark Falco goals were brilliant, and dancing in The Shelf at half-time with anyone and everyone!

The 1984 Uefa Cup final against Anderlecht – I am sure the ground shook when Graham Roberts equalised that night.

The 2008 League Cup second leg victory against Arsenal. I didn't know I could feel like that about a game of football again, one of the great nights at The Lane.

On a personal note, when I proposed to my wife, Sarah, I had it announced on the jumbo screen in April 1994. We had our wedding reception at the Bill Nicholson Suite that summer. My daughter, Abigail, had a birthday greeting at the ground on her eighth birthday when we played Arsenal in February 2009. The look on her face when she saw her name on the big screen will stay with me forever.

THIS TIME NEXT YEAR, RODNEY *GARRY BACON, Basingstoke*

Ah, the memories. Not all good, in fact some of them are downright obscene (The scum winning at our gaff anyone? The culmination of God Hoddle's reign ending spectacularly badly in that defeat to Southampton?), but the good outweigh the bad when I think of that decrepit, crumbling, smelly, cramped church of football that is White Hart Lane.

How did I end up a Spurs fan, when my entire family are Chelsea? Well, when I was a mere five year's old, my earliest foray into watching football was Italia 90, and with Gazza and Lineker being my two favourite players, I innocently asked my Dad: "Dad, who do those two play for?" Oh I wish he'd lied to me, but from that moment on, that was it. I was Spurs. Spurs were me. I begged and begged him to take me, so it was with great reluctance on his part that we pitched up in Tottenham to see us take on Everton, a place that, even with me coming from a council estate in South West London, I could see was run down. It was alien to me. All these different cultures, people, smells. I sheepishly laugh when I remember – aged six – that I asked my Dad: "Why are all these people wearing bowls on their heads?"

I think nostalgia and romanticism has changed how the game panned out. I remember it was 3-3. But I also recall that Spurs were three up, and a Peter Beardsley inspired Everton turning things around. This was it, I thought. What I was looking for. Brief elation at winning the Cup, soon turned into realisation, that for all my wide eyed innocence and enthusiasm, we were not very good at all. But we've had some fun along the way.

I'll never forget my early trips to Highfield Road to see us spank Coventry 4-0 on a New Year's Eve (Jurgen in full effect). Seeing 20,000 Forest fans doing their Dambusters' impressions at The City Ground, and having it explained to me why. The trips to Wembley for the Man in the Raincoats Blue and White Army victory and the doomed Cardiff trip to see us beaten by an awful Rovers team.

In recent years it's been a bit better, even with the nomads down the road's success with the flirtation with that fourth spot, the majesty of seeing Carrick, knowing that with Berba, we had the best player in England, the ache of being at the Getafe game when Big Martin got the sack, the tears in his eyes and every other face on the South Lower that night a testament to the love we had for each other, the two successive trips to Wembley.

With a full preseason under Harry's belt, and a team that he builds, then maybe just maybe next year, Rodney….We say this every year. "Next year". I don't mind. I like being miserable. That's why I listen to The Smiths and why I'm a Spurs fan. It's that optimism that I love. It's like trying to pull the prettiest girl in the club. We love the chase, the not knowing what will happen next, the thrill of the thought, but what happens if we pull that girl? We'd probably moan that she was boring, and not be happy until we're back in the throng with the ten-pinter that's always left at the end.

I'll end this by saying that with me being a die-hard, Gazza-inspired, Shelf Side-raised, "We're The Park Lane"-singing Spurs fan, me and my Gooner-loving missus are expecting our first child this winter. I hope that in the first World Cup he or she watches, any Spurs players don't turn out to be his or hers inspiration. I couldn't let a child of my own go through the highs and lows, joys and miseries that I have. But this time next year, Rodney ...

YOU CAN'T WIN THEM ALL *MARTIN DELANEY, Margate*

The first time I went to White Hart Lane was in 1976 at the age of eight. Spurs were playing Manchester United and I was seated in the upper Paxton Road stand. It was in the days when the away fans stood in the Paxton, so all we heard for most of the match was United fans chanting. We lost 1-3 and I remember as I was walking out a United fan ruffing my hair and saying, 'Don't worry, sunshine, you can't win them all'. He was right you know, as any Spurs fan will testify.

We got relegated that season and my hero, Pat Jennings, was packed off to that lot up the road. I was lucky enough to go to every home match the next season because some fella who drank in my dad's pub had two season tickets. I remember particularly the debut of Colin Lee against Bristol Rovers. The final score was 9-0 and he got four goals. Again our seats were in the Paxton and I was in the toilet as the final goal went in. The fella standing beside me wasn't happy as he'd missed all nine! It was before the days of tv cameras at every game so he couldn't even watch it on the Big Match.

One memory away from The Lane: I was taken to a charity match at the Met Poilce sports ground in Chigwell. Jimmy Greaves was playing and I must have spent five minutes chasing him round the pitch during the warm up trying to get his autograph. I finally got it after much huffing and puffing and had it stuck on my bedroom wall for years after.

THE BLUES BROTHER *JOHN BROWN, Wokingham, Berks*

I have been visiting White Hart Lane for the best part of 40 years now and in that time have had the privilege to witness many of the "greats" in action, sadly just missing Greavsie, but lucky enough to have seen the likes of Jennings, Chivers, Gilzean, Perryman, Hoddle, Archibald, Crooks, Ardiles, Lineker, Gazza and Klinsmann to name but a few.

In that time there have been very memorable highs, and - let's be honest, it's never straight forward following Spurs - quite a few lows. Unfortunately one of my first memories falls into the "extremely low, I don't think I can cope with this" category. It was the 1971 end of season clash with our interloping neighbours!

My older brother Des (a die hard Chelsea fan, but always looking for an opportunity to gloat) said he would treat the pair of us, and promised not to laugh!

Obviously we knew a big crowd would be expected so we set off from Reading early enough (this of course was in the days before all-seater stadiums and you could turn up on match day's without a ticket and queue up). We arrived at the Lane around 1.30pm, but even at the time the place was already heaving, leaving us little option but to join the vast queue and hope and pray we would get in for the 7.30pm kick-off. Eventually we shuffled, pushed and crammed our way in.

With later estimates of 40-50,000 fans locked outside, and being only 4ft nothing, my view and recollection of the game are vague (probably just as well). All I recall is the sickening groans around us as Ray Kennedy headed in the only goal of the match to bring the title to Highbury and set up the Double-equalling feat in the FA Cup final against Liverpool six days later.

Still, even before the match, I was hooked and regardless of the results and performances over the years I have had no alternative but to keep coming back for more. It's a drug you just don't want to kick. But even now, well into my fifties, the excitement, enthusiasm and anticipation as I go through the turnstiles with my son Nick (also completely hooked!) is as strong as ever.

And as for our latest triumph in March 2009 over Chelsea (sorry big bruv Des) even with no Victoria Line and a delayed kick-off, well blimey, it doesn't get any sweeter than that.

SILENT CELEBRATIONS *ANDREW HODGSON, Keighley, W. Yorks*

I have been a long-distance Spurs supporter since 1960, following them through thick and thin, quite a lot of thin recently. Through all the years, I've had to take a lot of stick from various teams' supporters: Burnley in the early sixties, Leeds mid-sixties until now, Liverpool in the eighties and Man United seem to be today's favourites.

Several times I have watched them play "oop North", and even got in a Wembley trip (QPR), but mainly I've been a radio and television devotee, until I had an invitation to go with friends to White Hart Lane to see the mighty Spurs against Leeds United in the FA Cup in the early eighties.

Imagine my excitement on the way down when – on the North Circular – my pal said that we were nearly there. I asked how he knew, and he pointed to a burned-out car parked on a roundabout. I laughed and then we turned a couple of corners and there she was: White Hart Lane Stadium.

Once inside I realised quite an oversight – I was in the away end, surrounded by 5000 Leeds fans. I convinced myself that I had to be quiet, but when Garth Crooks scored what turned out to be the winner I forgot myself and jumped up ready to shout and suddenly realised where I was. All the Leeds fans were looking at me, so with self preservation in mind I suddenly sat down and blended in and cheered inwardly.

It was still a magical trip, and I am still there for every match in spirit – and not with the away supporters!

MEMORIES FROM ACROSS THE POND *BRIAN HUSSEY, Florida*

My dad started taking me to The Lane when I was about 10, unfortunately he also took me to Highbury and the first game I can remember was a match between the scum and Blackpool. I liked the colours of the shirts, red white and tangerine also the legendary Stan Matthews was playing. But sense prevailed and I plumped to go regularly to WHL.

I remember Bill Nicks first game a 10 4 win against Everton, but before that players like Tommy Harmer, George Robb, Ted Ditchburn to name a few. I used to go to the main gates to try and get their autographs. Also recall as a boy being passed down to the front over the heads of the men down to the white wall with the half ring top, because there were crowds of 60,000 plus, and later standing in the boys section. We beat Sheffield Wednesday to win the league with about 10 games to go. What memories!

Watching Dave Mackay hit the cross bar with minutes to go in the semi-final second-leg European cup against Benfica having lost first leg 3 1, We won the second 2 1 Mackay's goal that wasn't would have taken it into extra-time; a sad night but happy again next season when we won Cup Winners' Cup.

I moved to Florida about 12 years ago but was a season ticket holder at Spurs for years. I would take my son to games and give the guy on the gate a ten bob note to get him in. He is now a season ticket holder and when I can get over he takes me in for £45. How times change. I still have programmes from my era when they cost sixpence!

Obviously having been going to WHL for as long as I have been lucky enough to see great Spurs sides, none better than the 60-61 team. I saw all games that season at The Lane and all Cup games. I also had to suffer through the relegation in the 70s, but still went every week. Now, with Harry in charge, I think good times could be coming back. But regardless, they will continue to get my support.

BETTER THAN A LOO BRUSH *VIC POWER, Saffron Walden, Essex*
Football memories differ from most others. I'm not sure why but they touch a part of us that is unique. I mean why should we care about the fate of people we don't know? why do we share their joys and miseries? That's what football does to us so when we tap into the memory bank and withdraw a football memory, it is different, it evokes an almost mystical feeling which stays with us for life.

It's fairly universally true that we support the same team as our dads although with more women watching football these days it may well be our mum. So it was with me, my dad was a Spurs fan and there could be no other team for me.

Before I was deemed old enough to visit the shrine at White Hart Lane I would hear of names like Tommy Harmer, Len Duquemin, George Robb and the like. I ached to see them in person but it wasn't my time yet. There was to be another arrival at the Lane before I was to make my first visit.

It was Saturday October 11th 1958 and it was an eventful day. Firstly because my dad was to be taken shopping rather than be allowed to 'go down the Spurs' and secondly, Bill Nicholson was appointed manager for his first game against Everton.

As an eight year old, I was excused shopping and was dropped off at my grandparents Hackney council flat whilst the shopping torture took place with firm instructions to make sure I heard the results, or rather the result as Spurs was the only game that mattered. I duly obliged and sat in front of the telly to watch another debut. October 11th 1958 was not only the debut of my dad going shopping and Billy Nick managing Spurs, it was the first airing of *Grandstand*.

The clipped tones of Peter Dimmock waffled on about the sports action of the day but there was one match that stood out from the rest. The results were read:

"Tottenham Hotspur ten" (upward inflection followed by slight pause) ... "Everton four" (downward inflection). What? Ten-four? Ten bloody four? Broderick Crawford eat your heart out!

Minutes later a breathless dad rat-tat-tatted on the door and nan let dad in followed by a bag-laden mum. Years later I may have teased him a little but as an eight year old I lacked the finesse for a wind-up, so I excitedly blurted the score. "Stop messing about what was the score?" It took four or five attempts to get him to believe me. Then the realisation dawned. He had spent the last four hours traipsing round Ridley Road market and up and down Mare Street and had missed this earth shattering event. The look he gave mum will stay with me even though she was so pleased with the new loo brush.

If I didn't know before, I knew now that Spurs would be the only team for me and I'd never put a loo brush before the white shirt and cockerel.

A BUM GOAL FROM GREAVSIE *STEVE DRUCE, Croxley Green, Herts*

My late Dad, having been born and brought up a mile from the ground, was Tottenham through and through. As a boy he used to sneak in under the legs of older fans. If the game was dull he would leave at half-time, collecting a re-entry pass which he sold on. He would then use that cash to purchase chocolate from a wholesaler to re-sell outside the ground as the crowd left at full time.

My father introduced me to the two temples of his life, Shul (synagogue) and Spurs, and nowadays I can't go to either without thinking of him. There were many great moments, like the 13-2 demolition of Crewe when I bent down to pick up my rosette twice and each time Les Allen scored. Jimmy Greaves inexplicably bending down in the penalty area, then getting hit by a Mullery shot that he inadvertently deflected into the net off his bum! The time Chivers beat Gordon Banks from the left touchline a full 45 yards out. That fanatical Spurs fan Morris Keston bringing Bobby Smith, Terry Medwin and Mel Hopkins to my barmitzvah.

Dad and I were actually part of a trio of mad Spurs supporters that included my Uncle Nat, and during the season the mood of our weekends was always determined by the Tottenham result. If we lost we hardly spoke but when we won the whole world seemed a brighter place.

I guess the most poignant moment was the '81 Cup final replay, which was the last match the three of us attended together. It was apt that we should be together to witness the goal that somehow epitomised what our great love of Spurs was all about.

LOOKING FOR THE LANE *ANTHONY ROBERTS, Wessington, Derbyshire*

I live in rural Derbyshire, so it is quite a trek to The Lane! I don't get down as much as I'd like, but I guess being 33 with a wife, daughter, animals and career don't aid my cause! Anyway, my first trip to The Lane was with one of my best mates, who is also a Lilywhite, back in 1996. We were 19 at the time.

We caught the train from Chesterfield down to St Pancras; I remember the tickets costing us £50 a piece, yet they were never checked (gutted!). We then got the tube to Seven Sisters. I recall walking into a pub, it was half Spurs and half our rival Man City fans and the atmosphere was great. Good friendly banter.

After a couple of southern jars (how can you call that ale!!), we got a kebab. We asked the foreign national who served us (and took our cash) for directions to The Lane, as we had never been before. 'Lane?' he said. 'Me not know any Lane.' My response – ' You know mate, White Hart Lane, the home of Spurs'. 'No idea' was his reply.

'Can you tell us where the football stadium is please?' I pleaded. As straight and dull as you like. He looked blank. 'Don't know of a football stadium'.

We were dumbstruck and a little worried and wondering if we had got our bearings wrong. However, we walked just 100 yards down the road, eating our kebab, and suddenly there she was. The famous Lane. What a great sight! Now, whether the guy was winding us up or not, I will never know. He certainly seemed genuinely unaware that the ground was just a stroll away.

I will never forget that first trip to The Lane! We won 2-1. Went a goal down, Howells equalized, and The Man, Klinsmann, scored the winner with four minutes to go. Fantastic!

A CHILDHOOD MEMORY *HAYLEY TANNER, Brighton*

My first memory of Spurs (the first clearest memory of my life) was in 1982 when I was not quite four years old. Spurs were playing QPR in the FA Cup final, and it had gone to a replay. My Dad and my Granddad, being from Willesden, were QPR supporters, and they took my brother to the game, while my mum (she and her family are from Tottenham) had taken me into town to buy the Chas 'n' Dave single 'Spurs are on their way to Wembley' (which I still have).

When Dad, Granddad and my brother arrived home after Tottenham's 1-0 win we made sure we had it at the ready on the record player to greet them as they came through the door!

I've loved Spurs ever since, and while other young girls had posters of pop stars on their bedroom wall mine was decorated with heroes such as Steve Perryman and Glenn Hoddle. My first match at The Lane was also against QPR and I'm sure you can guess why.

I have been to see many more games over the years, and have been lucky enough to be entertained in the vice-presidents' lounge and the Pat Jennings lounge, and that feeling I still get in my stomach as I am walking to the ground from the Seven Sisters is like no other. When you are in the ground by the North Stand the atmosphere is amazing, and I think it has to be said Spurs fans are some of the loudest singers in football! Even at away games. I absolutely love it!

THE CHIVERS LIGHTHOUSE *JEREMY SIMMONDS, London*

Though my first game was a Saturday fixture (a relegation dogfight with Luton, which we narrowly won), I have to agree that the special times at the Lane were those '70s European nights. The team were generally in the all-white strip for such games, and I remember thinking Martin Chivers resembled a lighthouse as he stood, illuminated by the floodlights, awaiting a Mike England through-ball. The best of these games, for me, was a 2-1 semi-final home-leg win over AC Milan in 1972, the year we won the inaugural Uefa Cup. The Lilywhites were majestic, especially the young Steve Perryman, who scored twice - and the Lane was awash with sound. I'm sadly (?) too young to recall the 'sixties Glory-Glory nights, but we had some great times at WHL in the 'eighties as well. None were better than the second Uefa Cup triumph over Anderlecht in 1984, the heroism of Roberts, Ardiles, Thomas and, of course, Tony Parks. (And we knocked out Feyenoord and Bayern Munich on the way, too...). For those of my generation, they were *our* Glory-Glory nights.

JUST LIKE CHRISTMAS *DARREN 'DAZZA' VERNON, Epping*

We've had many stars that have graced the beloved turf over the years since I've been supporting Spurs – from the skills of Hoddle, Ardiles, Gazza, Ginola, Sheringham … the guts and drive of the likes of Mabbutt, Perryman, Roberts, Gough … the light-hearted humour and banter with Freund, Zokora, willing them to score, always giving their all.

I have to rely on DVDs to see the stars of the '60s and '70s, but have huge admiration and respect for Legends like Blanchflower, Greavsie, Peters, Chivers, Mullery, etc. I dont get to go to the lane as often as I would like, but when I do, it reminds me of Christmas Day morning seeing a new bike. I get all excited and have goosebumps, even though I'm now in my 30s. Hopefully the new stadium will not change those feelings, and it will always be like Christmas Day.

GREAVSIE AND THE GOLDEN GOAL *MICK McLAUGHLIN,* Leicestershire

I have been a Spurs fan since I was 10 years old and my family lived in Stamford Hill. My older brother, who was 17, became an Arsenal supporter so I did the only thing a younger brother could do – I decided to support Spurs. Those were the days of Johnny Hollowbread in goal, but I didn't get to see them much. A couple of years later I was big enough to go and see the team that Billy Nick put together and I was totally hooked.

Later I went to boarding school, which limited my chances of going to the Lane. I remember one night borrowing a mate's transistor radio (Yep, we really did call them that) with an earphone and went to bed (lights out at 9.30pm) and intended to listen to the European match against Gornik. Unfortunately, I fell asleep and only managed to catch one Bobby Smith goal. I couldn't believe the score was 8-1 and I missed it all.

A long time later I went to our opening match of the season against West Ham. Jimmy Greaves had signed for them, and – not unexpected – he equalized for them with a shot from the edge of the box. That got him and Billy Nick some abuse from me and others – 1-1, a bit disappointing.

I was still complaining that we should never have let him go half way down the High Street when I looked at my Golden Goal ticket (I think it was 51 minutes), and I went charging back to the office to claim my £25 quid. Caught up with my mates later saying: "Well it was not a bad bit of business."

Thanks for the dosh and the memories Jim.

OIL'S WELL THAT ENDS WELL *STEPHEN SMITH, Kazakhstan*

One of my best memories of being a fan is actually far away from The Lane, here in Kazakhstan. I am employed in the oil industry and work here on rotation, which means when I'm on leave somebody else does my job and sleeps in my room, so the job is covered 365 days a year. Back about seven years ago I had a "back to back" – Rod Downey – who was a staunch Newcastle fan. We were always winding each other up, then one day when I was on leave I received a birthday card from Newcastle Football Club, signed by Kevin Keegan. The little Geordie barsteward had registered me as a Newcastle Junior.

The following weekend I was at a Spurs game and decided to buy a few bits from the Spurs Store. At the end of my following rotation I left my back-to-back a few gifts. When he arrived at our camp reception to pick up his room key, I had attached a 'White Hart Lane' key ring to the bedroom key fob. When he opened the bedroom door, he saw a full-size Tottenham team photo on one wall, and a large Spurs flag on another. When he opened the wardrobe door to unpack his clothes, dozens of Tottenham balloons floated out.

At the office next morning, the office key had an additional Spurs key ring, his Newcastle coffee mug had been replaced by a Spurs mug. Our two national assistants arrived for work, wearing Spurs shirts. All around the office walls were photos of me and my girls in Spurs shirts. Finally, at the end of the day when he went to the bar for a well deserved beer, on the wall behind the bar was a Spurs shirt with 'Rod Downey Spurs No 1 fan' written on the back. And six months later on a site walkabout he discovered I had left a Spurs lapel badge on his winter coat.

"I have a cunning plan ..." Greavsie and Jimmy Robertson plot at a corner kick.

CHALKHEAD AND THE GHOST *MICHAEL BICKLEY, Bermuda*

My mother's family all come from Wood Green. Infact my grandmother's name was Wood. When I was a boy, my uncle told me that I could not walk down Wood Green High Street without passing a relative. I used to go to White Hart Lane every two weeks to see Spurs play. I remember different players. I know there were several "Ronnies" in the side. Ronnie Dix had a very bald head and when he headed the ball badly, we would all yell, "Get some billiard chalk Dix."

There was also the future captain and Welsh international Ronnie Burgess. I remember the captain was "Butcher" Ward. He was a very tough individual. Mackay reminded me of him.

When I first watched the team in 1946 at the age of 12, there were several players by the name of Hughes playing. The one in goal was a little erratic. We would groan when he let the ball in, but my uncle and father assured me that better days were coming and that a player who had the ability to fly through the air like superman and stop every attempt on goal was returning from war service. So it was that my first soccer hero appeared at The Lane: Ted Ditchburn.

He was a very good goalkeeper. He was not quite the best in the country (Swift was better), but he certainly was the most theatrical and the most exciting to watch. He would dive in all directions and push balls over the bar. I became a goalkeeper at school because of him.

My familly left England in 1950 and I have returned on occasions to see the later heroes. I was very impressed by John White who, although he was not as colourful a player as J.G., truly lived up to his name as "The Ghost" of White Hart Lane. I saw him twice on my infrequent returns to England. I am happy to report that my son and grandson, who saw us win the Cup, are all Spurs fans, as are my many cousins.

LOCKED OUT FROM THE LANE *NIGEL BAINBRIDGE, Grantham*

My visits to White Lane began in the 1977-78 season when Spurs were in the old Division 2. My outstanding memory of that season is arriving too late for the top of the table clash with Bolton and being locked out of the ground as over 50,000 fans were already inside. I can still remember dancing in the street when the loud roar told us Spurs (McAllister) had scored the winner.

Favourite memories come from introducing my eldest two children to White Hart Lane. In August 1999 as a birthday treat for my son Freddie (age 9) I took him and his sister Felicity to see the Everton game. Despite Ian Walker bringing down Francis Jeffers for two penalties, Spurs managed to win 3-2 with a late Steffen Iversen goal. The kids were hooked!

I decided to treat the children for Christmas by taking them to the Highlight Suite for the Boxing Day game versus Watford. At the time of booking I didn't realise it was a lunchtime kick off and that we would have to be there at 9am for the guided tour etc. A 5am start on Boxing Day is not ideal but David Ginola was brilliant and inspired Spurs to a 4-0 victory. I can remember the kids being totally unimpressed when I insisted they have their picture taken with an Irish guy in a suit – they had no idea who Pat Jennings was.

The next game (Jan 2000) was home to Liverpool – a brilliant 1-0 win thanks to a goal by the much maligned Chris Armstrong. The kids were really into collecting autographs at this time and Felicity chased Armstrong in his old Porsche down the street until he had to stop at the traffic lights. His face was an absolute picture as my daughter shouted, "Oi Armstrong, can I have your autograph please?" To his credit he stopped and signed their books.

Eventually Felicity and Freddie went to boarding school and due to sports fixtures we couldn't go to games very often. I had a brainwave I would take my youngest son William (now aged 9) to see the Sunderland match. It was a good game and Spurs won 4-1. On the drive home I said to William that tickets for the Liverpool game go on sale on Monday, would he like to go? His whispered answer was an emphatic "No". Being totally wrapped up in the game I hadn't realised he had hated the whole experience. Just shows you can't win them all, but at least he isn't a Gooner!

THE LONG WALK TO GLORY *MARTIN HAMILTON, Bishops Stortford*
When I was four we moved from one side of Tottenham to 55 Great Cambridge Road N17, which is about 100 yards from the A10 and White Hart Lane road crossing. Every other Saturday the police would be on that corner controlling the traffic lights, but at such a young age I never really understood what was going on. Then my Dad took me to my first game.

We walked all the way down White Hart Lane (which felt like miles and miles to a five year old) and then on to the High Road. I remember half jogging and half running to keep up with him, but as soon as the Stadium was in sight I just stopped and stared. I'd never seen anything like it.

The game was a reserve match and my Dad kept going on about some bloke called Ralph Coates! From that day a love affair was born. My Dad stopped coming to the games about four years ago – he's 79 now – but I will never forget that first match with him. My son is three and I hope he will be telling a similar story in 30 years time.

AN ESCORT FROM THE OLD BILL *NOEL HOLLOWAY, Hoddesdon, Herts*
I was working on the turnstiles on the Shelf side in the 86-87 season. I was 19 and getting paid to watch the team I've supported all my life. We used to shut up 15 minutes after kick-off and take the stubs back to the ticket office. In those days you had to walk around the outside of the pitch and then through the away support. Me and a colleague

had just reached the goal at the Park Lane end when we scored against the Scummers. The place went wild and the bloke I was with was waving and jumping around in front of the away end. Lucky for us the fencing was still in place in those days, as we were the only two standing there at the time! Once the celebrations had calmed he looked at me then realized we had to walk through Scummers to take back the stubs. As we approached the gate the Old Bill clocked what had happened then decided to escort us back to The Shelf side. Only down side to that day was they beat us 2-1, but we finished third at the end of the season, and them, where they belong, below us.

COME ON THE WHITE SHIRTS *ASHLEY GOLBY, Finchley*
I started 'dating' Tottenham Hotspur back in 1961 as a young boy aged five when, on instructions from my late father (a West Ham supporter), I sat down to watch the FA Cup final on television. As the game was starting I told my father I wanted the team in white shirts to win. He said that he also wanted the Spurs to win because they were the London club. My white shirts – or I should say my Spurs – duly won the game. Afterwards I went into the back garden to kick a ball around somewhat naively unaware of the significance of having witnessed the first Double of the 20th century being clinched; and how this first date would ultimately result in a lifelong relationship.

Although my association with Tottenham was born in 1961 my love affair was not consummated until October 16 1965 when I made my first visit to White Hart Lane. I had a seat in the South Stand and can instantly recall with total clarity when I first saw the inside of the stadium as I went to take my seat. The beautiful expansive green grass, the goal posts, the pitch markings, the enormous stands, the people and the noise. I think for the first time in my life I was truly overcome with awe, and the intensity of the moment at the magnificent sight before me. Incidentally that afternoon Spurs demolished Manchester United 5-1 with a certain James P. Greaves scoring a truly magnificent goal that was featured in the opening Match of the Day credits for many seasons until colour TV arrived.

Three years later I acquired my first season ticket (cost 17 or 19 guineas in Block G of the Old West Stand), I have been a season ticket holder ever since.

JUST THE TICKET *NIGEL CROPP, Hertford, Herts*
I have very fond memories of White Hart Lane, one of which was getting my 1981 FA Cup final replay ticket. I'd just turned 11 years old and couldn't get hold of a final ticket for the Saturday. I had to make do with watching the game on the box, Ricky Villa's tears and the outcome, a draw and a midweek replay!

That night I was suddenly awoken by my older brother. "C'mon, Nige, wake up," he said. "We're going to The Lane to get replay tickets!" I was up and dressed like a shot!

Me, my brother and his mate bundled into his old Hillman Hunter and off we went. A few hours kip in the back of the Hillman at Northumberland Park, then off to queue. There was already a sea of people down Park Lane. I thought I would never get a ticket. Eventually the turnstiles opened and there was a lot of pushing but I made it. I paid my money and couldn't believe it – I had a ticket for the replay!

I remember we had to walk through the ground once we had bought our tickets. It was a sunny morning, the new West Stand was still under construction. I stood there clutching my ticket, it was a very emotional feeling and I thought to myself this is the place where dreams come true. Yes, The Lane of Dreams.

We all know the outcome of the game and being behind the goal when Ricky Villa scored the best goal ever seen at the old Wembley and Stevie P lifting the Cup was a feeling I will never forget. It was just the ticket.

HAPPY BIRTHDAY TO US *RICHARD LUNDIE, Mitcham*

The day we turned 125 years old we played Aston Villa, and I took my friend Charlie – a Villa supporter – to The Lane on the proviso that we got seats as near to the away fans as possible. The girl on the ticket line was very suspicious and asked if I was a Villa fan. I told her my friend was, and she said I couldn't buy the tickets. After changing my story, she reluctantly sold me two.

When we arrived at the ground, we were all given the 125 years blue & white flags. Charlie didn't want his, so I got two. The pre-match parade was full of pride, with all the great players on view. But Charlie was bored stiff. Then the game kicked off and Berbatov scored with a header, which got all the flags waving. Charlie feared the worst. Two minutes later and we conceded at the other end following a bungling Chimbonda clearance that gifted a goal to Laursen. I put my flag down.

Then Laursen and Agbonglahor made it 3-1 down at half-time and Charlie was on the brink of exposing himself as an infiltrator amongst the ranks. The Villa fans were singing "Happy Birthday to you, Happy Birthday to you," and the home fans all laughed out loud. It was the funniest chant I'd ever heard. Charlie was wetting himself.

Second-half we went 4 -1 behind almost immediately and I thought I was never going to live this down.

Then, somehow as only Spurs can, we lifted ourselves when Defoe and Bent came on and Chimbonda and Keane got us back to 4-3, and I felt relieved that at least it was going to be a bearable defeat.

Then up steps Younes Kaboul with one of the sweetest goals I've ever seen at The Lane, from our centre-back! Charlie was devastated and inconsolable all the way home. This pretty much sums up supporting Spurs for me. It's not all about the winning. It's about being entertained and expecting the unexpected. You're guaranteed not to be bored! COYS.

THE GENIUS OF GLENDA AND GAZZA *ALEX MEARES, London W1*

I was first hooked on the Spurs when I saw Hoddle score that fantastic volley against Man United in 1979 on TV. My first trip to the Lane was in 1984 as my 10th birthday treat. We sat in the Paxton End (where I have remained to this day). An unremarkable win over Forest but I was once again mesmerised by Hoddle and his ball juggling skills in the pre-match warm up. I swear he received the ball on the floor and it appeared to just roll up his leg and body before rolling across his shoulders and down the other side.

I was lucky enough to see Glenda's last home match at The Lane and the genius that was his goal – ghosting past three Oxford defenders before the crowning glory, sitting the goalie on his arse with a dummy and rolling the ball in the net.

The only comparable moment was witnessing Gazza score in his home debut against the scum in just his stockinged foot before planting it on the advertising hoardings in front of the Paxton End. The fact we lost that game did not seem to matter, as we left the ground on a high, singing the praises of our new idol.

LAUNDERING MY MEMORIES *COLIN WEBB, St Merryn, Cornwall*

As my mum worked at Spurs for 28 years as the 'laundry lady' I was in a rather privileged position as in the school holidays I was allowed in the laundry, standing by the door as the players walked to the dressing rooms. In those 1970s they often trained at WHL. After a while I was allowed to help lovely kit man Johnny Wallis clean the boots and pack the kit, and the veteran trainer Cecil Poynton used to tell me tales of the 'good old days'. The players found him grumpy, but I thought he was a proper gentleman.

Some other priceless memories include: Bill Nicholson passing me a ball and it going through my legs … Steve Perryman having a kick around with me in the car park before he started training … Pat Jennings, Martin Peters and Terry 'Tiger' Lee taking penalties against me at Cheshunt training ground … Collecting pieces of turf from the boots when I helped clean them, and taking them home for my dad to replant in our lawn … Laying out the kit for the Uefa Cup final against Wolves and knowing that Alan Mullery was playing and sworn to secrecy. I didn't even let on to my Dad until just before the teams were announced minutes before the kick-off.

THE BEAUTIFUL GAME *GARETH KERSHAW, Chesham, Bucks*

I have a sort of endless, surround-sound, technicolor montage of countless memories – Hazard's cheek, Roberts and Mabb's steel, Ossie's tricks, Galvin's socks, Allen's 49-goal season, Klinsmann's guile, Ginola's panache ... and as for Hoddle... all glued together with incredible atmosphere, laughter, tears, and, above all, fantastic football. Never was the beautiful game so apt a description as at The Lane at 3 o'Clock on a Saturday. I just wish I could be a Dr Who Time Traveller, so that I could pop back to watch the likes of Jimmy Greaves playing. Now wouldn't that be something.

WHITE HEART LANE *MARIE-CLAIRE WALTON, Leighton Buzzard*

I had no choice but to be a Spurs fan – my brother Nick was a supporter for as long as I can remember, and since he was my hero, I followed suit.

Nick became a ball boy, and every Saturday my Dad, my other hero, drove us up to White Hart Lane to see the game, and watch Nick on the pitch giving the ball back to Ray Clemence and Tony Parks.

Sitting in the stand with my late, beloved father James, watching my brother so close to his team, was truly special. We parked in the ground, and my Dad spoke to players in the car park on our way to watch the game, with a flask of tea and sandwiches my Mum had prepared ahead of the game.

My memory is not of a specific goal or a game or a chant, but of a special time with my father and brother in the sanctuary of The Lane. I can close my eyes and I'm there. I think of it as White Heart Lane, because it is where the heart is.

JOINING THE MULLERY LAP OF HONOUR *EDDIE ELSLEY, Peterborough*

My first taste of Spurs glory came in May 1972: the return leg of the inaugural Uefa Cup final against a very good Wolves side. Spurs were leading 2-1 through two goals at Molineux from Chivers (one an absolute cracker that epitomised his lazy looking yet consummate skill).

The whole evening of going to The Lane for the return was a surreal haze from start to finish: making my way across North London, up to and into the Lane, watching from the East Stand as skipper Alan Mullery gave us the lead, and nervously waiting for the final whistle to ensure Wolves' goal wasn't enough to stop us claiming our second European trophy.

I confess to invading the pitch with hundreds of other delirious fans for my one and only time, revelling in the singing and general pandemonium that ensued. Little did I know that our captain and goalscorer's days at Spurs were numbered, but he'd helped give me my best Spurs day, and Alan fittingly made a one-man victory parade of the pitch, clutching the trophy and surrounded by all us fans.

Many have come and gone and many more will do so, but fans like me and countless others will always follow the Spurs. This is what appeals to me about your book: the input of true fans. If only all clubs would always put their fans' interest and love of the club at the forefront of their thinking.

UNDER THE SPURS SPELL *DEREK SCANNELL, Mill Hill*

My Dad first took me to see Spurs play Man Utd in the European Cup Winners' Cup in 1963, expecting me to follow the family tradition of being a United fan. Wrong! I fell under the Tottenham spell and I'm Spurs 'til the day I die.

I have lots of WHL memories, and amongst my best has to be the Jimmy Greaves goal against Leicester in 1968. It remains the best individual goal I have ever seen, and that includes efforts by the likes of Maradona and Messi.

He beat what seemed like seven or eight players with a run from the halfway line before walking the ball around Peter Shilton.

Then there was the night Steve Perryman scored two goals against AC Milan in the Cup Winners' Cup semi-final in 1972, and I recall Steve getting himself booked for a tigerish tackle against Barcelona in 1982. So many wonderful memories.

Note from Norman Giller: I was reporting the 1968 match against Leicester City for the *Daily Express*. On the way to the ground I had a minor motoring accident, and had to stop and swap insurance details with the other driver. As I came up the stairs to the Press Box, the ground was alive with wild applause and Greavsie was trotting back to the centre-circle with his right hand raised almost modestly and the wreckage of Leicester players behind him. I had missed one of Jimmy's greatest goals by seconds. And there were no TV cameras there! My article was headlined: "The Greatest Goal I Never Saw..." and I had quotes from everybody who mattered. Peter Shilts and Bill Nick both agreed it was Jimmy's best goal. All I got from Jimmy was: "That will teach you to drive more carefully, you silly git." Guilty, as charged.

GLORY GLORY AT LOVE LANE PATSY BUZEC, Norfolk
My entire family come from in and around White Hart Lane. In 1961 in the *Tottenham Weekly Herald* there's a picture and article showing my uncles outside their house decorated brightly in blue and white and wearing home made-hats and waving flags before they headed off to the 1961 FA Cup final when we clinched the historic Double.

In the article it states that the Buzec family initially started the Glory Glory anthem which has now become so synonymous with the mention of Tottenham Hotspur.

My sister's first home was a flat in Charles House in Love Lane. We loved the atmosphere on a match day, and used to stand on her balcony and breathe in the excitement and anticipation before the match, and you could almost reach out and feel the exhilaration and energy in the air when Spurs won.

My late father, George, was a historian on all things Tottenham. What a pity he is no longer with us because he had so many stories to tell.

A MINT OF MEMORIES *ANDY NICHOLSON, Somerset*
From 1968 through to 1990 when I went to Africa to work, I was a regular on The Shelf. My main memories include the amazing Jimmy Greaves goal against Leicester City (which sadly was not captured on film), the epic replay against Man Utd (Best, Charlton and all) in the third round of the FA Cup in 1968, WHL packed to the rafters

and the ever present aromas of tobacco and Percy Daltons as we craned our necks for a view. Later on, the development of WHL, the two great FA Cup runs to Wembley in the early eighties, Parksie's penalty saves in the Uefa Cup final and the integrity of Billy Nick and Keith Burkinshaw.

I live in Somerset now and can only watch on TV. I yearn for players to proudly wear the shirt, as both Greavsie and Perryman did with honour amongst many others, but this seems to be an exception these days across the board.

Finally, there's the enduring memory of the group of people I used to stand with on The Shelf, the sharing of cigarettes, mints and banter, and the group of people from the Spurs Supporters Club who used to hang the navy blue flag with "Come On You Spurs" above the tunnel leading out onto the pitch left of centre of the main stand; that to me meant game on.

THE PRIDE OF THE MABBUTTS *JESSICA MABBUTT, California*
I was born in London, and moved here to the United States when I was one with my father, Kevin. His brother is my Uncle Gary Mabbutt. I am now eighteen, and Uncle Gary had retired from the game by the time I was old enough to understand just what he meant to Tottenham. I have had many people telling me that he is a White Hart Lane legend, and the entire Mabbutt family is proud of all that he achieved. I have not yet been to The Lane to watch a match, but we were given a tour when we visited Uncle Gary. We were very impressed by the stadium, the pitch and the locker rooms. It was amazing, and my sister Isabel and I cannot wait to see a game played there when we next visit Uncle Gary, probably this Christmas.

WHAT IT MEANS TO SUPPORT SPURS *PAUL BEESON, Ilford*
It was 1973 the first time I went through those famous old turnstiles. I can still remember the excitement. The ground has gone through some changes, the team has had its ups (not enough but I remain hopeful that'll change) and the personnel and the kit, even the League has changed, but it's still *my* Tottenham Hotspur and it's *still* White Hart Lane, and yes I *still* get that same rush 30-odd years down the line.

Something my son said to me evoked a memory of my response in the '80s to a chap who ribbed me after a Tottenham defeat. This is what I said to him about what it means to support Spurs: "I go and watch my team regardless of the weather, cheering them on win, lose or draw. They are *my* Tottenham and nothing will ever change that – the smell,the noise, the friendships forged and the feeling that my one voice, my mere presence at the match could and does make that difference. So keep your Liverpools your Man U's, your mob down the road and give me my Tottenham Hotspur any day!"

It was not original. My father had said it to somebody ribbing him back in the 1950s! And it is true to this day.

THIS IS WHERE WE BELONG *KEVIN ACOTT, Woking*

Here is a quick run through my memory bank from back in the days of growing up in Enfield: Going with my mate's Dad when I was eleven and him saying, about every player who turned out for us, 'He's not as good as Jim The One' ... going to Greavsie's testimonial and spilling Bovril all over my (Charlton-supporting) Dad's suit (he'd come straight from work) ... my wife nearly starting a riot at an Everton FA Cup game when a mounted policeman was pushing us around outside the Paxton and she started shouting at him ... falling over on the stairs coming out of The Shelf and thinking 'this is it'... watching Graham Roberts chasing Norman Whiteside after Whiteside had fouled him ... taking my German exchange partner to our 9-0 thrashing of Bristol Rovers and pretending it was like this every week ... taking my daughter to the Bill Nick memorial day and standing there with tears in my eyes as an Annie Lennox song played ... a friend's 80-year-old grandfather switching off his hearing-aid so he couldn't hear the abuse as he pushed us through the queues to the turnstiles .. marvelling at the magic of Hoddle, at the cool and class of Klinsmann, at the cheek and imagination of Gascoigne, the intelligence of Sheringham ... feeling the simultaneous fear and strange rush of camaraderie as a bunch of Man United fans got into our bit of The Shelf ... the pride when my youngest first walked up the steps at the top of the Paxton and looked out onto the pitch for the first time, heard the crowd and went 'Wow' ... the feeling that this is where we belong.

THE PARKING GAME *ANN RECORD, Sheernesss*

I was born and bred in White Hart Lane and despite it having a reputation of being a slum area we were happy. Saturday home match days was the highlight of the week in the late 1950s when were were growing up.

We would put our furniture outside our house to save parking space for drivers going to watch the footie, and then we would go and play hide and seek under – yes, under – the Spurs pitch inside the ground until the final whistle went. Then we would run home to get our money for looking after the cars.

Now, all these years later, it remains Spurs 'til I die and God help anybody who runs the club down in my hearing.

BACK UP IN STYLE *SCOTT COOKIE, Edmonton*

My first season coincided with Spurs coming straight back up from the Second Division. I was just nine, and did not miss a home game that season. The crowds were fantastic, and showed just how loyal true Tottenham fans are in good times or bad. The hairs on the back of my neck continually stood up in that promotion season as I watched Spurs come back up in style. Highlight, of course, was the 9-0 hammering of Bristol Rovers. That was a match never to be forgotten. I am proud to be a Yid. Tottenham forever.

NEVER A DULL MOMENT *DARREN ATTWOOD, Evesham*

There is never a dull moment being a Spurs fan. We have massive, loyal *true* support that never waivers. I was at Old Trafford for the 2-5 defeat, and came away so proud to be supporting a club like ours with great history, fan base and tradition ... much more satisfying than following a club like United, Chelsea or Arsenal attracting so many glory fans. Spurs, winning, losing or drawing, will always be magical to me.

NAN FLYING THE FLAG FOR SPURS *JOJO EVANS, North Wales*

I grew up in Gooner territory of Barnet, and warmly remember happy days of bunting and flags hanging outside our house, FA Cup street parties, and – most of all – my lovely Nan, Babs Keogh, shouting for Spurs in the days of standing only. She continued to shout on Spurs when we all sat down. Once, she offered Teddy Sheringham a polo mint whilst he was on the sidelines warming up. Wonderful memories. The Lane – with her grandkids there with her – was Nan's life, God bless her. I am sure my Nan was steering the ball into the net as Tottenham started their climb up the table when Harry Redknapp arrived.

THE GOONER AND THE SISTER *ESPEN SJØTTEM, Norway*

I've been suporting Tottenham since I was 10 years old. I did not know any players by name back then, but instantly fell in love with the club. The funny thing is, it did not feel like I chose to support the club. The club chose me. Since then, Tottenham Hotspur have been in my blood. I grew up playing footy on the pitch imagining I was Greavsie, Perryman (although I have never seen these two play), Ricky Villa, Ossie Ardiles, Pat Jennings, and later it was Lineker, Gazza, Mabbutt, Ruddock, Thorstvedt, Hoddle, Klinsmann etc. I could go on and on.

Growing up in the Northern parts of Norway I did not care for any local clubs. It was just Spurs. There were always military exercises with NATO countries in the area where I grew up. And I recall discussing football with English soldiers. I remember arguing with a Gooner from the Royal Marines. I promised him a date with my older sister if he said Arsenal was a gang of wankers who belonged in Woolwich. He eventually did, but I did not have an older sister. He was quite grumpy to have been tricked by a 12 year old.

The funny thing is, I have never been to White Hart Lane. Now that I'm a father of two, I've decided it is about time to go, and I'm planning a trip to The Lane with my kids. Both of them are supporting Spurs, and are constantly hassling me about travelling over to the Lane. So, to me, The Lane has always been a dream. Soon I will wake up and see the historic ground for myself. I cannot wait.

THE *facts* of this book have been mine, but I want the *feelings* to be those of the true Tottenham fans who look on the White Hart Lane ground almost as their property, and the club as their family. Clawing my way into the modern world, I set up an 'If You Worship at White Hart Lane' group on the Facebook social network. I was astonished by the response, quickly gaining hundreds of members, many of whom I communicated with on a one-on-one friendly basis. Suddenly they made me feel part of the Tottenham family, and I experienced that Spirit of the Shelf that sets Spurs apart from most other clubs. I asked for a brief answer to a simple question: *What does White Hart Lane mean to you?* These – along with many memories inspired by helpful website masters – were among the scores of replies (have some Kleenex ready!):

Jacqueline Hayles, Northampton: "I remember as a little girl in the 1960s going with my father (David Watts) to the Paxton Road end where there was a gate you could peep through. We used to catch fleeting moments of the play and 'feel' the atmosphere that is unique to White Hart Lane. When Dad died in 2007 the funeral procession stopped for several moments outside his beloved ground, and I remembered those times when we stood there at the Paxton Road gate. That would have meant so much to him."

Donna Watts, Palmers Green: "I am Jacqueline's sister, and I would just like to add that as well as faithfully supporting Spurs, my Dad managed the Duke of Wellington pub team in Turnpike Lane for 20 years when they were in the Haringey and Enfield District League. He was always trying to get them to play Tottenham style! He was the best of all Dads and it is so fitting that he should be remembered in a book about the White Hart Lane ground that has been so special to him and our entire family,"

Chris Thomas, Cardiff: "I followed in the footsteps of three generations when I took my first long walk down Seven Sisters in 1984. Then, taking our place on the Shelf, all I could think was, "How green is that pitch!" ..."How big is this stadium!" And then the noise when we scored! From then on, it was Tottenham 'til I die."

Louise Kelly, London: "As a bouncy little two-year-old I watched the team bus glide down White Hart Lane in 1981 following our FA Cup win. It was as if a Tottenham angel had taken me under her wing and since that day Spurs have been in my heart."

Horace Patterson, London: "I have only good memories of The Lane, starting with begging my mum to let me go with some friends who were much older than me. I was about 11 and standing on a stool looking up at The Shelf – a sea of people singing football songs you don't hear anymore. It was the start of seeing a procession of legends playing for Spurs. Long live The Lane!"

Claire McDonald, Hertfordshire: "I was always destined to be a Spurs fan, from when my mum stood in the High Road, eight months pregnant with me as Spurs paraded the 1981 FA Cup ... then being born just a mile down the road. I remember being taken as a child to The Lane when there was standing in the ground. My dad had to take it in turns to put me or my little brother on his shoulders so that we could get a glimpse of our favourite players Hoddle, Gazza, Lineker and Co. I was there when all the greats came back to celebrate 125 of Spurs. Fantastic! Many happy memories, and many more to come."

Violet Cope, Wood Green: "Whenever we got into any cup final my Mum and Dad would take me and my three brothers to the ground, and we would line up with all the other fans to get tickets. It was like one big family, every one chanting the songs and never a fight broke out. This was in the 1960s. My sons have continued to go and now take my grandson. Supporting the best team is a family tradition."

Martin Weatherstone, Tottenham: "My first game was in the eighties and what I vividly remember is walking to the top of the steps and coming out at the Paxton Road end and seeing the pitch for the first time. And that was it! This proved what they say is true – Tottenham picks you to support them! After spending that first 90 minutes there I knew that I could never support anyone else."

Michael Charles Knott, London: "White Hart Lane makes the hairs stand up on the back of my neck just thinking about it. This is the place where I can forget everything in the world and feel like I'm part of the same family, ready to fight for the team and even the stranger next to me in the crowd because we are all as one."

Dino Gatt, Colchester: "I have been Tottenham since the year dot. I was raised Tottenham and grew up through the glory days of the early 80's. I would still support them if they went down to the Conference. Don't care! Come on you, Lilywhites!"

Terry Whitty, Brazil: "These days I live in Brazil, but I used to be a regular at The Lane and my heart is still there. My old man is Chelsea (poor bugger), but I have been a Yid since the first game that I ever saw on TV on my 10th birthday – the 1987 FA

Cup Final against Coventry. My younger brother and sister both became Yids. My kids are Yids and my wife is a Yid, too. I have converted many Brazilians in the town where I live to the joy that is Spurs, and we watch every match on the net. The Lane is (and will always be) a cauldron of sound, of passion and above all, the home of our Spurs. When we beat Chelsea in March 2009 I rang my Dad and congratulated him!"

Keith Hewitt, Leicester: "My first game at The Lane was many moons ago as a lad of 12. Me and my friend were sitting on the floor by the turnstile doors before 12.30. I had waited for this day for weeks. The doors opened, through the turnstile and then we both ran flat out up the the stairs to The Shelf. Then we caught our first glimpse of the pitch and stands; had never seen anything like it before, so big, so exciting. We were just in awe of it all. That was it. I was now a Spurs supporter."

Lee Carson, Havering: "One game I particularly recall was a League Cup tie against the mighty Southend in the 1989-90 season. It was no great game but stays in my memory because I caught Erik 'The Viking' Thorstvedt's glove at the Park Lane End at the final whistle. Still got it at home. Going back to earlier matches, it was a really special honour standing in The Shelf watching Spurs. The noise was just deafening. One Bank Holiday, I remember seeing Waddle and Hoddle arriving together for the match in their mate's Fiesta! Don't think you'd see that today!"

Lee Anderson, Chirk, North Wales: "Quite simply, The Lane is the home of football, where the game is played the way it should be played. From the likes of Bliss to Blanchflower, Mackay to Greaves and Hoddle to Gascoigne, some true legends have graced the hallowed turf that is OUR Lane. I look forward to continuing to enjoy the entertainment and pure genius that we once all saw at the place which is called, and will always be called White Hart Lane."

Louise Sharp, London: "I became a Spurs fan by accident. My brother made me pick a team at the age of five and I liked the name! Probably not the best choice seeing as my father, uncle and grandfather are/were all – ssssh – Arsenal fans. Growing up in Northern Ireland, I didn't get the chance to go to the Lane until I moved to London. I have since got to love The Lane. It has an atmosphere and sense of history and excitement that it's hard to find anywhere else. It will be a sad day when The Lane closes, but it's the fans that make a ground, and 60,000 Spurs fans will make one hell of a noise."

Richard Grant, Sydney: "I have been in Australia for many years, but on one return visit to The Lane, when The Shelf was still there, I homed in to my old standing position near one of the barriers. The only supporter I recognised from years before was a huge

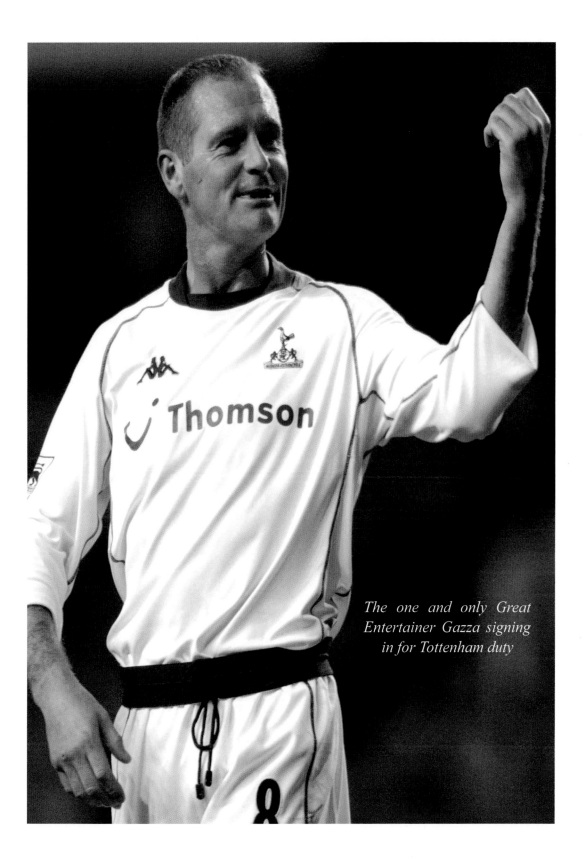

The one and only Great Entertainer Gazza signing in for Tottenham duty

On the run for Spurs, crisp finisher Gary Lineker

Robbie 'The Juggler' Keane, the striker who goes for the jugular

It was thumbs up for Tottenham when Harry Redknapp became manager

guy who always had as much room as he wanted. 'Haven't seen you for a week or two,' he said. It was seven years! The good news is my Grandson, Zach, in East Dulwich, is following the Spurs. I'm sending him this book so he knows the complete history."

Sarah Waters, Harlow: "I know I am, I'm sure I am, I'm Tottenham 'til I die."

Marc Fewell, Hastings: "The Lane means everything to me. It's my happiness and my pain, and it will always call me back. To me it means family; everybody there for the same reason no matter creed, race or belief. It as much a home to me as my house. It's my temple. God bless The Lane."

Paul Reynolds, Tunbridge Wells: "The first game I remember was the 1984 Uefa cup final, when Tony Parkes saved that penalty. What a fantastic moment. The whole ground erupted and the noise level was deafening. I will never forget that night at The Lane."

Simon Miller-Humphries, Devon: "Living in the west country, I find it difficult to make trips to The Lane. I saw us draw against Portsmouth in January 2009. Nothing can compare to the feeling I get as I walk through the narrow tunnel and out into the stand. To look up to the two big screens, the perfect pitch and knowing I am surrounded by 36,000 other Spurs-loving people fills me with a tribal pride. The players come on near to touching distance and I can't hide the butterflies! I know this sounds soppy but it's the best way to describe White Hart Lane."

Kevin Cottrell, Bristol: "To me The Lane is everything; can't ever wish to be anywhere else. I've been there through a lot of highs and just as many lows. It will be a shame to see it knocked down, but I guess we have to move with the times and get a bigger fortress to be able to compete with the other teams. But The Lane will never ever die."

Clinton Turner, London: "The Lane is an awesome place. My uncles used to take me there in the East stand when the seats were wooden. Next, I remember standing up in Park Lane. The Lane means everything to me. Pure football has always been played there. It's a shame that we have to move with the times and get a new, bigger stadium, but if we want to compete with the so-called big boys, it's in our interest."

Andy Mason, Hoddesdon, Herts: "My first game was in the late 70s v Man United. We lost 3-1. I then went to every home game for almost 20 years until rising ticket prices priced me out. The game that sticks in my memory is the Uefa Cup final v Anderlecht in 1984. Spurs had style, grace and flowing football and players like Hoddle, who wore the shirt with pride. I now work at The Lane as a steward and as far as I am concerned I am living my dream of working for the team I love. One of my most treasured memories was attending the memorial for Bill 'Mr Spurs' Nicholson and being with the family I call Tottenham Hotspur Football club."

Mark Brazier, Manningtree, Essex: "The Lane means just about everything. To be in a place where you can mix with people from all walks of life, any cultural background, rich or poor and unite and believe in one thing that produces passions from scaling the walls with ecstasy one minute to utter despair the next … and to keep coming back, rain, shine, good times, bad times. Well that can't be bad can it? Show me a political party that can provide half of this and I will gladly pop the 'x' in the box.."

Juno Sobers, Edmonton: "Live, breathe and die a Yid! White Hart Lane forever. That's what The Lane and the club means to me."

Karla Hannah, London: "I'm a Yid thanks to my Gramps, despite the best efforts of my mum and her side of the family trying to make me support that Arse lot. He's Spurs because someone once told him, 'If you want to see how to play football, son, then get yourself down The Lane!' My first game was watching us win 1-0 against Liverpool when I was nine. The atmosphere was electric and I sung all the way home.They've made me cheer and made me cry but whatever happens I'm Tottenham 'til I die."

Al Jennings, London: "I've been supporting Spurs from as early as I can recall. Growing up, WHL was like a place of worship for me. Even now on the train up from Liverpool Street station I still look across in awe at the stadium. The Lane to me is a place where I can be who I am for two hours and be with fellow fans and really feel at home. For those couple of hours it's as if the outside world is blocked out and all that matters is being there, In my opinion, it is the most beautiful place in the world, and to lose WHL will be hard to take. To imagine never standing in the Park Lane again hurts, but I suppose as a club we have to move forward. The Lane will always be in our hearts."

Peter Beckford: "I've been supporting Spurs since the season they were relegated from the top flight back in 1977. I went to my first game in February 1986, and I've been a member since 1993. Tottenham has been part of my DNA for thirty-three years of my near forty years on this planet. I simply can't imagine life without them!"

Rich Williams, Surrey: "White Hart Lane is a place where I'm always smiling. I love seeing us score, especially when I get the view from behind the goal. To me, The Lane is a place where I keep the company of legends."

Peter Brotherston: "Spurs beat Chelsea in the FA Cup final, April 1967, the month and year I was born. It's in the blood. Love the Lane, special place, great atmosphere."

Christopher Bracher, Watford: "Tottenham are my religion. It's in my blood. The Lane has an atmosphere all its own, so much better than the Emirates that has as much atmosphere as a library. Tottenham 'til I die!"

Joann Parker, London: "I first went to The Lane when I was just three in 1975. What a memory and that was it. I was hooked."

Alan Lithins, South Africa: "May 1967, I am five years old and Spurs win the FA Cup. My grandma knits me a scarf based on a photo published on the back page of the Sunday Times in South Africa … and 41 years on I still have the scarf! First live match I saw at The Lane must have been the worst game ever ... Spurs 0 Palace 0 without a shot on target from either side. I thought to myself, "If this is the Spurs I love OMG!" If ever there was a team that could keep you on the edge of your seat season in and season out then its got to be Spurs. Never a dull moment in any season at The Lane. If it weren't for the cost I'd be there every week. Both my boys are now supporters as well."

Nick Hamper, Milton Keynes: "I love The Lane. Saw my first game at five years old, and 48 years on I still can't kick the habit. What a great drug! Great times, sad times, proud times. So pleased my son and daughter have got the addiction as well. I can't wait to take the grandkids there. Spurs For Life."

James Day, Plaistow: "Every home game on parade, love The Lane, love the club! I cried the day the great Martin Jol left, but Harry has put a smile back on my face."

Steve Johnston, Leicester: "I started to go down The Lane when I was about 16, always going in The Shelf. No messing with tickets, you just paid to get in. Oh I miss those days, but the spirit of The Shelf lives on."

Dave Eaves, Windsor: "Nothing can take away the memories of standing on the terraces of The Shelf in the late 70s and throughout the 80s, surging forward in unison, screaming at the hordes of away fans in the Park Lane. There was no fuss, no mess, just pure impact. We were the chosen few and going to The Lane was part of life. Still going to The Lane week in week out now, but with the seats it's different. The atmosphere is still amazing, but we will never get those far off days of a terraced Lane back. I consider myself lucky to have stood on the cold concrete slabs of The Lane for many years, and it will be a sad, sad day when she finally disappears to memory."

Tom Edwards: "I must have been about six years old when going to my first game at The Lane with my dad. We parked near the factories by Northumberland Park station. We then strolled up Park Lane and when I first saw the stadium it was like, 'Wow!' I had no idea it would be that big. We then walked around the whole stadium and went in the Spurs shop. When I walked into the stadium and heard the singing it was special, but the best bit was walking through the gangway to the seats and it put the biggest grin on my face ever. And it still does now."

Lucas Constanti, Lexington, USA: "White Hart Lane was the first stadium I went to. I remember walking around the corner to see the beauty sitting there. It was an amazing thing for me, couldn't help but keep looking up as I walked closer and closer. I compare every stadium to the Lane. It is a perfect place for a kid and parent to share a day together, to watch the best game on earth in one of the greatest stadiums. Tottenham won that first game, and I will never forget the sounds, and what it looked like. As I walked away after the game, I couldn't help but look back as if saying farewell to somebody I had fallen in love with. That was the last time I saw her (moved to the US of A two weeks later). Believe me, there is nothing like the Lane, anywhere on this planet."

John Hanning, Spain: "The early sixties, and I remember queuing at 11am at the boys turnstiles, getting in and going straight to the wall around the pitch … 50-odd thousand people with just a few crash barriers ...then when the crush got too much I was pulled onto the pitch and sat around the running track to watch the game ...Brown, Blanch-flower, Mackay, Norman, Jones, Medwin … and later Jennings, Gilzean, Greaves, Chivers, Peters, Mullery, Naylor, Perryman, Pratt, Taylor, and the list goes on and on and on. My memories of the Lane will stay with me for ever. I love the Spurs and always have, always will. Getting a bit tearful just thinking about it now. Just hope all the youngsters follow them like I and thousands of others used to. Don't forget, once you're a a Yid it's for life."

Aaron Jones, London: "My first game was in '93 against Oldham with my Dad. I've still got the scarf I bought that Day. We smashed them 4-1 and I'll never forget that first time I walked up the stairs of the East Upper and overlooked the pitch. It was like a carpet and made such an impression on me that I remember the magical moment as if it was yesterday."

Cormac McGreevey, Northern Ireland: "My first trip to the Lane was home to Liverpool under the man in the raincoat and we played great and won 2-1. I couldn't get over the amount of Norwegians who were there to watch Iversen! Have since been a further seven times and we have won every time. The club really should pay me to go! Last trip was home to Pompey when we were under Jol and they were under 'Arry; great second-half which was all I saw due to train issues!"

Max Devere, London: "My Lane debut was '94 aged 12. I was desperate to see Klinsmann to find out what the fuss was about, and he didn't disappoint. Sheffield Wednesday took an early lead but Klinsmann unleashed a piledriver past Pressman and wheeled off to be mobbed by the team. I was sold forever. Anderton also tried a lob from his own half which went higher than the East stand, and there was such an atmosphere that to this day, when you feel it, you never want the match to end. If only the Scum 5-1 could have gone on for a month, I would still be there with my scarf from my debut game and so would everyone else I bet. When Euro nights came back we finally got to see what the old boys were on about – that's where our club should be, proud of its home and history."

Ann-Marie Court-Wood, London: "White Hart Lane has seen it all! Happiness, sadness, tears and laughter! Footballing stars come and go and some even come back again! I have many happy memories and some not so happy ones but White Hart Lane will always hold a special place in my heart!

Paul Russell, Abingdon, Oxfordshire: "Wherever I go, wherever I end up The Lane will always be my home. I clearly remember in the early '80s going to the ground and heading for the cafe which was next to Rudolph's pub. It was about 10.30 and we ordered breakfast. We had just sat down when some members of the Spurs squad walked in and had tea and breakfast before going off to play. They included Steve Perryman, Micky Hazard and Tony Galvin. I later met and told the story to Steve Perryman at a dinner. He said he could remember the cafe because they used it all the time. You would not see that today."

Lal Hardy, internationally renowned tattooist from Muswell Hill: "My grandfather and father were both ardent fans of Tottenham Hotspur, and I carried on the family tradition. They had the joy of seeing the Glory-Glory side of the early 'sixties. The first match I attended at The Lane was against Arsenal in 1968. Sadly we lost, but the atmosphere and passion of the Spurs supporters at White Hart Lane ensured that I am Tottenham 'til I die."

Gavin Nielsen, London: "The 77-78 season – I was 9 and it was our first game in the old Second Division and my first game ever. We won 4-2 against Sheffield United and I was hooked. Didn't miss a home game that season and my mum still has the crate I stood on – Courage, of course – in her loft."

Dave Williams, Manchester: "As far as I'm concerned White Hart Lane is my church. I have worshipped Spurs since I was about five when we lived in London and I am now thirty-five. I cannot remember a time when I did not support them."

Robert Holdaway, Braintree: "I am reliably informed that I was taken to White Hart Lane for my first match when I was just eighteen months old. It is a place where we experience joy and tears. What makes The Lane so special is the fans, singing and supporting and creating a great mood. White Hart Lane is the home of Tottenham. I think that's enough said!"

Martin Bradly, Enfield: "Spurs from the cradle to the grave. I have started taking my young son regularly, also introduced my two daughters to The Lane. It is the true home of football to me and to mine, as it will be to my grandchildren one day. I've been to games all over but The Lane has the best atmosphere by far. It is in my heart and soul."

Brian Hussey, Orlando, Florida: "My outstanding memories of The Lane are going there in the early 50s and being passed down to the front over the heads of the spectators, and later being in the boys' section watching Spurs win the Double. So many memories, with uppermost in my mind Dave Mackay's overhead kick in the last minute against Benfica in the semi-final of the European Cup; one of the best games I ever saw."

Andy Wright, Andover: "May 1986 and my first game at the Lane was against Villa. I will always remember it … 1-0 down after two minutes and 1-1 after four minutes! Eventually we won 4-2, with two goals each from Clive Allen and Mark Falco. I remember approaching the ground for the first time and couldn't wait to get inside. I will never forget that whole day of my first home game. Only a small crowd there but that didn't make a difference to me. Loved every bit of it and caught the bug for Spurs and the Lane which will stay forever."

Tom Ward, Angmering, West Sussex: "White Hart Lane! What a place, what an amazing set of supporters – and I mean *true* supporters who really get behind the lads when times are tough. I was eight years old when I saw The Lane for the first time. It made the hairs on the back my neck stand up then and it still does now, 15 years on. I've seen some great games at The Lane and I've seen some shockers. Regardless, I love The Lane and I love The Club!"

Jacquie Wood, Portsmouth: "Simply put, The Lane is the home of the faithful and the believers."

Mark Morris: "I fell in love with Spurs as a (nearly) eight year old boy watching the TV on the night that Ricky Villa waltzed through the Man City defence in that Cup Final replay in May '81, but it was another six years until all my nagging finally paid off and my Dad took me and my little brother to a Boxing Day derby vs West Ham at The Lane. The gasp of breath that I felt rush out of me as we reached the top of the stairs in the East Stand is a feeling that I still get every time I go to The Lane. I'm hoping that I get a chance to take my daughter (she's only three) to experience a game there before time catches up with the old place. I know that our new big shiny stadium is my quickest way of moving through the waiting list for a season ticket, but it'll be a sad day when those bulldozers start tearing into those old historic walls."

Toby Benjamin, Brighton and Hove: "I first visited the Lane in 1978. I was in the West Stand, and remember the stand opposite being louder and wanting to go over there! I switched to The Shelf from the '80s and it was like being part of a huge living being. When we scored we tumbled forward in a crazy surge. The singing was passionate and most songs had 5000 people joining in. When the whole ground sang, White Hart Lane was an incredible place to be. Halcyon Days!"

Nicola Anne Rayner: "I remember first going to White Hart Lane in 1990 with my friend Tracey. We were 17 and it was the first time our parents had let us travel over from South London on our own. Walking up the stairs and pushing our way to the front of the West Stand looking around at the floodlit ground took our breath away. The atmosphere and the friendliness of the other fans was amazing. Singing the old Spurs tunes and jeering at the away supporters, shouting at our players and the cheers when we've scored gives a buzz that stays with you long after you come away."

Norman Osland, Cheshunt: "One of my favourite memories of The Lane was hearing my brother-in-law say, on his first visit to the ground: 'WOW, what a view – I support Spurs now.' – not a bad comment from a Chelsea fan of 15 years."

Julian Shuter, London: "What The Lane means to me is happy times, sad times, great times – but above all it means simply Tottenham Hotspur. I have spent the best days of my life there, met many good friends there, and it will be such a sad day when they knock down my second home."

Katie Billings, Kent: "I remember going to The Lane with my Dad when I was only a young girl. It seemed so big to me at the time. I've got a little boy now and am hoping to take him to The Lane before it gets demolished. Tottenham is a permanent part of my history."

Marc Fry, Wales: "I have been a fan of the Mighty Lilywhites since 1994. My early years of life were made up of rugby, so therefore I was a late bloomer into the ways of football. But the first time I ever saw Spurs on Match Of The Day I fell in love! I have not been to White Hart Lane as of yet, but it is a mission of mine to see the ground and my beloved Spurs before the bulldozers move in. It will be the greatest day of my life when it happens. I can't wait!"

Steve Prescod, London: "I'm a Tottenham boy born and bred and would never support any other team, even though they do drive me near to death at times. I will always remember being able to smuggle a way on to the hallowed pitch with schoolmates back in the early '80s after school, and getting chased away by the groundsman as we climbed on the goal posts. Looking back, no wonder the groundsman was so upset!"

Lisa Court, London: "From the days of Steve Perryman and the genius Glenn Hoddle to the great players we have today, The Lane will always be in my heart."

Katie Mead, London: "The first time I walked up the steps of White Hart Lane I was just amazed. I couldn't get over the atmosphere there and how much ear-shattering noise all the fans could make. I have supported Spurs all my life, but only started going to live games a few years ago, Spurs against Pompey being my first, and sitting right next to the away fans. I soon picked up the songs everyone was singing … some not to the taste of my Dad who was with me and didn't particularly like the language we we're shouting back! Going to The Lane is a bit of an addiction, what with the support and the feeling of being safe and knowing all us Yids are looking out for each other, and even better, when we score a goal and celebrate together. Nothing can top the buzz I get being there."

Dean Wigzell, London: "White Hart Lane is the only place you can go and forget everything going on outside of its four walls. Spurs are all that matters for an hour and a half every other weekend. From the tingle down your spine that comes with pre-season friendlies, to the hoarse throat that follows the North London derby it all sums up what White Hart Lane is. A store for history, tradition and glory. The provider of joy and sorrow. A generator of excitement and deflation. The home of Tottenham Hotspur, White Hart Lane!"

Mark Smith, London: "Standing in The Shelf for the 1984 Uefa Cup final second leg. Crammed like sardines, the stench of beer, body odour, and pee ...not being able to watch the penalty shoot out...and getting bundled and knocked all over the place when Tony Parks saved the penalty to win it for us. Pure unforgettable quality moments."

John Joseph Murphy, London: "I will never forget my first game at The Lane. I was only five and I remember sitting on my Dad's shoulders as it was the only way you could see the game. From that day on Tottenham and White Hart Lane became part of my life. The long walk from Seven Sisters tube is one of the best walks you can do because of what waits at the end of it … The Lane."

Simon Denman, London: "I worship at White Hart Lane. It's holy ground."

Jason Moser, London: "There's no better place on earth than The Lane, home of the Yid Army."

Carol Bowtell, London: "Going to The Lane is just like coming home."

Liam Boyle, London: "Going to White Hart Lane gives me a very special buzz."

Darren Webb: "White Hart Lane is truly a place of highs and lows. It's the home where my team have brought me so many good times and also times of true sadness. I remember when me and my best mate at the time fell out over a girl as friends do from time to time, but we still had our love for football and for Tottenham Hotspur. Nothing could break that."

Craig Goodson, London: "I was lucky to have had a season ticket for two years but couldn't afford to keep it up. I particularly remember us beating the likes of Arsenal 2-1, and I was there when Stephen Carr smashed that wonder goal in the win against Man U. It's sad that after all these years we're losing The Lane. If you haven't been yet I suggest you get there before the turnstiles close for good."

Kayla Hume, Massapequa, USA: "My Dad moved from London to the United States in 1985. My sister and I were born and raised in America, but we'd always wanted to go to White Hart Lane (being raised Spurs fans). Finally, in November 2008, my family and I went to two games at The Lane, where we met Martin Chivers, John Pratt, Alan Mullery, and other legends, as well as Woodgate and Gomes. Being in the stands was unreal, and to hear everyone singing like I'd been hearing on television for so many years was amazing."

John Gill, Swindon: "There is a large band of spurs fans down here in Wiltshire. For me there is something really special when you arrive at The Lane, even just walking towards the ground. You can feel the hairs on the back of your neck stand up as you get nearer, and when you get to your seat the atmosphere is quite wonderfully unique."

Paul Smith, Sheffield: "What does The Lane mean to me? Well, there's The Shelf - a unique structure in British Football. Part of the old East Stand upon which stood a magnificent golden cockerel. The upper structures of that stand which were always a bit of a mystery to me. Just who did use it? Then there was the enclosure. A chance for ordinary fans to stand inches away from stars such as Peter Cook and Warren Mitchell in the lower part of the 'posh seats.' Best of all were the players that graced the Lilywhite and Blue. Heroes such as the Double Team and my personal hero James P. Greaves. I'll never forget October 5th 1968 and that goal that left five or six Leicester defenders in various stages of collapse or frustration at the sheer wizardry of little Jimmy Greaves. The last man beaten was a very young Peter Shilton. Finally there was and remains the legend that was and is Bill Nicholson, who embraced Tottenham Hotspur and its fans, and who fittingly was known as Mister Tottenham."

Simon Pepper, Mansfield: "My everlasting memory is of Gary Mabbutt playing. It's still a great thrill just to think of him in the Spurs shirt. What a man, what a player."

Steve Hall, Newcastle: "White Hart Lane - even the name is different to any other ground in the country – and as such is special anyway. My first game there was over 40 years ago, when 55000 was the regular attendance. I got goose bumps then and still get them now."

Paul 'Yido' Freeman, London: "My contribution … 'We are Park Lane … we're Park Lane… we're Park Lane.' That says it all."

Kirsty Poppy, London: "I sit in Paxton Upper with my Dad, just like he did with his Dad. Unfortunately I won't get the chance to with my own children. Hopefully I am proved wrong, but I feel that watching Spurs just won't be the same in a new stadium."

Jenna Lucy Bennett, Scarborough: "I remember the first time I walked to The Lane on a match day. From the moment I got there I couldn't stop smiling. The atmosphere was mesmerising. It still has that affect on me now. I had to ask my Dad what everyone was chanting because I couldn't understand the accent! I grew up in Yorkshire, but I've always loved the Spurs. There are two reasons why Paul Robinson made an impression as my favourite player. My dad caught me one of his gloves once, and in the last game he played for us he threw his boots in the crowd and one hit me in the face! Then my dad pushed me to grab it, competing with Paul's own daughter! I got it in the end though. I also got my photo taken with Robbo at The Lane, a truly amazing place! My great great Uncle Les Bennett played for the famous Spurs push-and-run team, so the club means something to me on a family level, and has a special place in my heart."

June Egalton, Liverpool: "I have some really wonderful memories of the games I've seen at The Lane, from the days of Gary Mabbutt and the great Glenn Hoddle among a few of the great modern players. The Lane will always be in my heart, and I just hope I'm around to see the Glory-Glory days return. We need another 'Sir' Bill Nicholson. He always knew how to raise the morale of the players and is very sadly missed."

Simon Wightman, Woking: "White Hart Lane is the home of great football, the way the game is meant to be played. Since my first game in 1987 (a 4-0 trouncing of Man United) to my last in 2004 (the 4-5 reverse to Arsenal), it has been about entertainment and great memories far outweighing the bad. And all those great players. In my brief time, I have seen Waddle, Gazza, Stewart, the Allens, Lineker, Klinsmann, and Ginola, to name but a few, and count myself lucky. Long live the Lane, which I now watch from afar for economic reasons."

Jason Quinney, Wales: "I haven't been yet and doubt I will get the chance before the ground is knocked down. But even without having got to the ground I love The Lane, and all that it means in the glorious history of Tottenham Hotspur."

Brian Folgate, London: "I love the walk from Seven Sisters! I used to enjoy standing in The Shelf before they put the fences up, and you could walk around the ground. They used to have the disabled bit below the Park Lane and you were able to leave the ground via the big blue doors between the Park Lane and the Shelf next to the floodlights. Took me a while to get to used to all seater and I've still not sat in the West Stand. I remember the first game I went to and hearing the roar as you climbed the steps. I used to love watching Hoddle, he was amazing even in the warm up. Last games of the season were always a great atmosphere. I almost caught Ossie's shirt, Paul Robinson's glove and Roberts' shin pad! Still the best pitch and the loudest singing in the League."

Yidette Kels, London: "I've sat in virtually every stand in The Lane (including the away end, free tickets!), and I can honestly say the Park Lane is the tops. Going to The Lane is not just about the football for me, it's also my social life. I've met some wonderful people there and made friends for life. When I enter The Lane and I hear the familiar theme music I get goosebumps and can't wait to cheer the Spurs on."

Sarah Williams Giller, Ringwood, Hants: "I support Spurs because my wonderful Grandpa Ray Beadman did, so I wanted to be just like him. He loved Spurs but told me a story about how he was disappointed after the war, when he wrote asking if they could send him (a veteran and a hero) a ticket. They refused! That hurt him, but he never lost his allegiance to his beloved Spurs through most of his 95 years."

Douglas Papworth, London: "Without a doubt the atmosphere at The Lane on big match occasions such as cup games or playing that lot down the road can not be equalled anywhere. Having had the privilege of seeing the likes of Mackay, Greaves, Peters, Hoddle, grace the sacred turf, I feel truly blessed."

Alan Papworth, London: "To me, the evening matches were and are that little bit special – seeing the ground lit up from afar and the anticipation of knowing that you were going to see a good match, and once inside the atmosphere is always that much more special then any other ground I have ever been to. Just looking around the ground you are reminded about past great players and matches and old friends you used to go to the matches with...yes White Hart Lane is a very special place and not just with Spurs supporters; other fans also are aware of its uniqueness and place in English football."

Tim Armes, Swiss Cottage: "As a lifelong supporter, – I'm 55 now –I'm sure you can appreciate what a rollercoaster ride supporting Tottenham has been. However, I wouldn't have missed a moment of it as I can remember the giants from the double winning side, followed by the likes of Greaves, England, Gilzean, Jennings, Peters, Chivers, Coates, Perryman, Kinnear, 'Nice One Cyril' Knowles through to Villa, Ardiles, Hoddle and up to today. I think Dawson, Huddlestone, Lennon, Modric, Palacio, Woodgate, King and Keane, plus one or two others, should form the nucleus of a very good side."

James Yid Carolan, Coventry: "White Hart Lane. Our Theatre of dreams. The feeling you get on match days is indescribable, not only in the ground but the journey to the stadium and the walk along the High Road, every fan together! Sadly, I'm too young to have experienced the Glory-Glory days, but I have seen some great entertaining games at The Lane! Always in my heart."

Peter Devlin: "My first experience of The Lane is etched into my memory – April 19 1975, versus Chelsea in front of a 50,000-plus crowd. It was 'going off' all over the place, with the losers almost certain to go down. You could reach out and feel the tension. We won 2-0, and it was Chelsea who got relegated. What a day!"

Barry O'Connor: "As a kid growing up in Kilburn going to The Lane was the most important thing in my life. It sounds ridiculous but it really was. We were fairly poor and the trip to The Lane gave me an identity; it made me feel like part of something great. It still does."

Nolan Johnson: "To do is to dare sums up the spirit of Spurs and of The Lane. I've got my new season ticket. Roll on next season …!"

'Nice One Cyril' Knowles, a much-mourned Legend at The Lane

Nick Georgiou, Brighton: "What can I say about The Lane except it is a love affair for the rest of my life. I grew up in White Hart Lane, first at number 29 then 178. My first game was against Millwall in the old Second Division and will always be remembered for my Dad throwing me in his arms and running home with me as fans started to riot all over the place. I can actually remember watching the fighting from our flat window and asking my Dad, 'Why are Spurs fans fighting each other? (both sets of warring fans had blue and white scarves).

The most beautiful thing about the place for me though is belonging to a big gang, where race, age, religious beliefs don't matter, as long as you follow the Spurs. That's what binds us together."

Darrell Hill, London: "My first game at The Lane was in January 1991, a goalless draw with the Arse, but a few weeks later I went to Wembley to witness us beating the Scum 3-1 in the FA Cup semi-final thanks to a magical free-kick from Gazza and two goals by Gary Lineker. The Lane means everything to me."

Graeme Bowie, Horsham: "Just thinking about The Lane sends shivers down my spine, because it is quite simply a PROPER football stadium. I must admit, my first visit in 1970, to see Spurs draw 0–0 with Crystal Palace in the FA Cup was pretty uninspiring. However since then, so many great memories of a packed stadium – playing Liverpool in the Uefa Cup semi-final in 1974, or welcoming Ossie and Ricky in 1978 (remember the ticker tape?), and 1984 in the Uefa Cup final, when there was not a dry eye in the house. My Son Matt has now been coming with me to Spurs for the last nine or so years, and he is very proud, too, of The Lane and its history. Even for a young man of seventeen, he feels passionately that the new stadium should retain the world famous name of WHITE HART LANE. I think that says it all really….those three magic words."

Trevor Dunkin, Sturminster Newton: "I am a third generation Spurs supporter, and still get to watch them despite moving from St Albans to Dorset. Greavsie was my all-time favourite player, followed by Glenn Hoddle who I saw score a goal against Ipswich with a shot that I swear flew into net like a guided missile. I was standing on The Shelf with my cousin, David, an Ipswich fan, and he was gobsmacked. Now my son, Chris, is following in the family tradition. Once a Lilywhite, always a Lilywhite."

Harvey Bloom, Redbridge, Essex: "White Hart Lane is where my late Dad took me when I was four years old, where I took my sons when they were eight and where I will take my grandsons in the near future … where I had the honour of seeing the legends: Nicholson, Blanchflower, Smith, Mackay, White, Jones, Greaves, Gilzean, Waddle, Hoddle, Ardiles, Jennings and the rest."

Mike Drain, Great Baddow, Essex: "My first memory of White Hart Lane is sitting in the very back row of the Paxton Upper against Manchester City in the early 1990s. Great times. Have been an avid fan all my life, going to as many games as I can each season with the old man and mates. The Lane is one of my favourite places on earth, the highlight so far seeing at first hand our 5-1 drubbing of Arsenal in the Carling Cup semi-final."

Nick Brown, Oxford: "My greatest night at The Lane was, no doubt like for many others, the Uefa Cup final in 1984. I was only 13 and we didn't even have tickets. But my dad knew one of the policewomen on duty that night and she snuck us in. We were up in the rafters at the Park Lane End and I've never felt the ground shake like that before or since. After Parks saved the second penalty I was crying my eyes out, hugging a complete stranger who was also in tears. It's the memory of me my Dad said he'd take to his grave. Another moment to cherish was Hoddle's final game at The Lane when he ran through three players from inside his own half, sent the 'keeper to the floor with a dummy and slid the ball home against poor Oxford United. Or how about Gazza's first goal for the club after losing his boot against the Gunners? I could go on and on …"

Gerald Schneider, Woodford Green: "I have been going to The Lane since the late '50s and one match that sticks in my mind above all others is the 1962 European Cup semi-final against Benfica, who somehow survived 90 minutes of football hell that would have destroyed almost any other team on earth. They went through to the final 4-3 on aggregate, and to this day Jimmy Greaves insists his 'goal' should not have been flagged off-side. That would have taken the match into extra-time."

Jim Munson, Cheshunt: "A sunny day in August 1980, nine years old, Glenn Hoddle coming over to take a corner and giving me a wink. Staying in touch with my Dad, despite not growing up with him. Learning how to play the game by watching a team who knew how to play it and ending up being rated by my Sunday club as their own Stevie P. Arriving in hope but not in expectation, never taking anything for granted but always enjoying the ride. That first glimpse of the pitch when you climb the steps into the stadium. Hoddle, Waddle, Gascoigne, Lineker, Ginola. The sound of the crowd. Simply magic!"

Paul Morris, Czech Republic: "I am a Spurs fan living in the Czech Republic, but I remember visiting the Lane when I was a boy from about 1987 to 1995. I lived in Gillingham, but I followed Spurs and visited regularly thanks to my Dad who was a lifelong fan, as was my Granddad who used to talk about the Dimmock generation. I remember White Hart Lane as the place where I got my first footballing experiences and where I could feel really close to my Dad and Granddad's memory."

David Dodge, Jersey: "It will be sad to lose the old WHL stadium and the incredible atmosphere it creates, but we need the seats and the new design seems to acknowledge the atmosphere issues. My father was a Londoner, albeit I should be a Millwall fan! I grew up on Bill Nick's glory, glory days. Len 'The Duke' Duquemin, main marksman of the Push and Run, remains a Channel Island legend, a title we Jerseymen only accord to the very finest Guernseymen. Perhaps we could do with a confident rock solid number 9 in the squad today, but that's another thing!"

Kymberley Bradshaw-Howard, Broxbourne, Herts: "I was born in the late 70s, and Dad wasted no time ensuring I grew up as a Spurs fanatic. I've got two brothers, Steve and Glenn - both named after Dad's favourite Spurs players, so I guess I never stood a chance. I went to many matches at the Lane in the 80's, when my Spurs obsession went full-blown, and have many, many fond memories (as well as heartbreaking ones) – including getting trampled by a police horse at a North London derby. My maternal Granddad was an Arsenal fan, who moved to Love Lane in Tottenham when he got married. He learned to love Spurs as well, and used to get so excited watching the matches at The Lane that he often had two cigarettes alight at the same time. My boyfriend Robert is in the British Transport Police and is a Spurs fan who is often on duty at matches … sadly for him, at Millwall!"

Keith Preston, Romford: "My first trip to The Lane was back in 1964 when Jimmy Greaves (the main reason I became a Spurs supporter) scored the only goal of the game. I can remember my feelings as I entered the ground for the first time and staring in awe at the East Stand; as an eight year old it looked massive. I stood on the Shelf from that day on until it became an all-seater stand. My season Ticket now is as close to the spot as I could get to where I used to stand."

Paul Kramer, Winchmore Hill: "I have many memories, good and bad having supported Spurs through thin and thin going back to 1964. The recent passing of Jimmy Neighbour brought back a memory of when he once went to take a corner and missed the ball, kicking the flag instead by mistake! I have made many friends through the years as a result of supporting the best team in North London. I even took on a temporary job working the corporate lounges for three seasons when the price of my season ticket in the West Upper became too much for my budget. I now sit with my two boys (Daniel 12 and Joseph 15), who I have had to drag to games when the team have been under-performing. But I'm pleased to say they are now acclimatised to a life of suffering!"

Fiona Meredith, Tasmania: "I dragged my Spurs-mad husband Nic away from England to Tassie back in 1987! Since then I've been on the sidelines 'enjoying' the ride of Tottenham's fortunes, and sleepless nights. Watching Nic shouting at the screen in the early hours is quite a sight. Tottenham remains an important part of his life."

Paul Szysz, Slough, Berks: "My memories of Spurs go back to the late seventies/early eighties, and great players like Hoddle, Ardiles, Perryman and Archibald. As a small kid I remember watching us play the Scum and I said to my uncle, a fanatical Spurs supporter: 'Why are we cheering their goalie?' He explained: 'That's Pat, the world's best goalkeeper, and we let him go.' I'm older and wiser now and know Big Pat is a Tottenham Legend, but, oh well, I was only about five or six then!"

Judy Masters, Queensland: "My husband, Peter, has been addicted to Tottenham since the Double team. He turned 13 in 1961, when Spurs were the glamour club. He was hooked from that day. The internet and pay TV have enhanced his ability to get information on Spurs and to watch games. He's been to White Hart Lane in 1975, 1980 and again in 2006, managing to get a ticket for Spurs v Man City by paying £145 to a reseller. It was the only way, and I considered it unthinkable we would travel 12,000 miles and him not see his beloved Spurs. We plan to be in England again in 2011 and the first item on the travel agenda will be tickets to a game."

Stuart Onslow, Shoreditch: "White Hart Lane means to me just sheer excitement, total nervous excitement from the time I get into the N17 postcode until the time I see the green of the pitch. I was too young to see Stevie or Glenn Hoddle play but my first memories are of being taken to the stadium by my Dad and standing in the old wooden top part of Paxton Road and watching Chris Waddle play. I even had the spikey on top, mullet at the back hair style for a while. Happy times!"

Geoff Taylor, Islington: "As I grew up in Dorset, my first Spurs game was at Southampton, sitting at the home end (the only way I could get tickets!). So when we scored first, it took all the will in the world to dampen my celebrations. I thought this was the safest thing to do, but now my only regret in life is not representing the mighty Spurs at any cost! Having lived in London for the past six years, I've had a typical rollercoaster life, but the friendships I've formed with fellow Yids, and the passionate arguments with Gooners will remain the most loved and vivid in my memory."

Espen Engdal, Norway: "The first time walking into The Lane both my father Ståle and I thought, "What an amazing atmosphere." We lost but the rush we got has made me come back for more glory at the Lane and in Europe. It is always worth the long journey from my home in Trondheim. Let me say to my five-year-old niece Julie: 'Lage mitt er Tottenham!' It is never too early to get her supporting Spurs!"

Steven Wensley, Denmark: "My father was English, and we shared our passion for Spurs until he passed away in 2006. I have already been to White Hart Lane with my oldest daughter, who is six. I had the great fortune to be shown around the Lane in 1993. We were there to watch the game against Norwich (5-1), and asked if we could get a tour. Unfortunately you had to book in advance; however, a family invited us to come along on their tour and the staff kindly obliged. We got the grand tour, meeting a couple of the players (Vinny Samways and Justin Edinburgh), and culminating with us down on the turf, on our knees kissing the grass. It was very emotional and something I will never forget. The atmosphere alone is something of the other world."

Stuart Posthuma, Northants: "My father took my brother and I to evening games, where we would stand in the Paxton Road End. The atmosphere was always electric. The silky play of Ardiles and Hoddle in the midfield, and Perryman was a true leader. I'll always cherish the memories of, 'We'll take good care of you, Ar-chi-bald, Ar-chi-bald!' ringing round the stadium, in addition to the Chas and Dave anthem, 'Spurs are on their way to Wembley!' Our voices were inevitably hoarse after every game, and the nights would end with a trip to one of the chippy's to give us sustenance on the long walk back to the car, win, lose or draw! My Dad grew up watching Jimmy Greaves, and a young Steve Perryman, so this book can only be a joy to him."

Stuart Porter, Florida: "I was born in Brighton 34 years ago and have been a Spurs supporter since almost before I could walk. As my family moved to the States when I was seven I have only had the opportunity to visit the Lane once (in '92, a loss to Liverpool), but I was also at the '82 Charity Shield at Wembley (also a Liverpool victory). I witnessed both defeats with my Dad, who is a Liverpool supporter, so maybe he was bringing us bad luck. To me The Lane is a cathedral, and whenever I watch a game on television or internet or listen on the internet radio I still get chills when I hear "Come On You Spurs." And I can still vividly remember the scene of my one and only trip to the Lane with my Dad. Unforgettable."

Baljit Atwal, Leicester: "I have been a Spurs fan for 30 years. Living in the Midlands, I go to all away games even if it means sitting with the away fans! I have some great memories of going to WHL during the early '80s onwards. My wife blames me for ruining my kids lives as they are also Spurs fans, and being a Spurs supporter you have to realise the weekend is usually going to be ruined! It is all part of the wonderful experience of following Tottenham."

Robert Rockett, Maidenhead: "The Lane is almost my first home, the place where I met good mates Steve Price and Milan Hampson and where I have great times watching the always exciting ups and downs of *our* team."

Brett Stapleton, Cambridgeshire: "My Granddad Clifford Stapleton was a North London policeman and used to patrol around the Spurs ground in the early 'sixties. He used to get my Dad, Graham, in for free, and Dad sat near the touchline and saw the great European games, etc. Sadly, Dad was seduced by Best, Charlton and Law, but I managed to follow in Granddad's footsteps as a Spurs fan. My first game was in the late 'eighties v Coventry. I was a member for 10 years and now a season ticket holder for the past three years. Thanks, Granddad."

Steve Grubb, Dunfermline: "I live in Scotland, and have only seen Spurs previously when they played pre-season games at Hearts or Celtic, etc. But in the 2008-09 season I decided to make a pilgrimage to The Lane; not because it was going to be knocked down and rebuilt, but because how can I call myself a fan without every going to a home game? I got the Caledonian Sleeper down for the Hull game, and although a) it was chucking it down, and b) we were awful and lost, I was probably the only person in the West Stand Upper Tier to be smiling for the whole three hours. I was in the ground. I felt fulfilled, and 'genuine' at the end of it all. I belonged. Officially."

Tony Fletcher, Bournemouth: "I've been a Spurs fan since birth and come from a Spurs family. My memories of The Lane are of going along with my late grandfather between about 1973 and 1984 and sitting in the West Stands, both old and new. The smell of the timber seats, the cigar smoke and the noise of fans stamping on the floor still remains with me. I'm 41 now and as soon as I smell a cigar I'm back at The Lane as a boy watching Chivers, Hoddle, Perryman and Jennings. Our last game as season ticket holders was the 1984 Uefa Cup Final 2nd Leg. What a night! My maths O-level the next day was a less exciting experience."

Stuart Allison, Worcester: "White Hart Lane has always meant anticipation, excitement and exhilaration, mixed at times inevitably with despair, of course. My first game was in September 1961 against Gornik of Poland – the first of the great European nights. I remember the white shirts, the flowing football, the goals and the noise. Not many games reach that standard of course, but fabulous nights such as the 1983-84 Bayern Munich and Anderlecht games, and the more recent 5-1 London derby victories have continued the magic.

Throughout the years, however, regardless of the outcome of the match, White Hart Lane has meant humour, friendship and a great feeling of belonging."

Tim Tudor, Hastings: "My best memory of The Lane has to be seeing Maradona grace our famous turf in the Ossie Ardiles testimonial, and to hear the crowd singing, 'Sign him up, sign him up.' Only trouble was, the board thought we were joking! Second best memory was meeting and chatting to Bobby Smith and his wife after the 125th anniversary game against Aston Villa, which ended in a thrilling 4-4 draw. Bobby is our second highest all-time goal scorer and an absolute gentleman. He was a player who I believe would fetch £30 million-plus if he were playing today."

Michael Mackman, Tiptree, Essex: "I am one of the grandsons of Bobby Buckle, who was the first Captain of Spurs and instrumental in the acquisition of WHL after he had become a Director of the club. We are very proud of his input to our great history and the allegiance to Tottenham continues with our family to this day."

Geoff Gosbee, Eltham: "I have been in the Paxton Road end since 1988. I was seven when I first went to The Lane. I walked up the steps to the terrace and was overcome with goosebumps as I saw Chris Waddle and Co warming up. I still get the same feeling every time I walk up the steps and see the hallowed turf. It will always be like that."

Rob Suart, Lewes: "The Lane means to me the camaraderie shared by the fans – so many characters with their own opinions and memories means that every day you learn something new about our beloved club. The ups and downs all serve to keep us on the edge of our seats and the future is looking very bright indeed!"

Pete Dennis, Devon: "I was first taken to watch Spurs play by my Dad in 1962 and was hooked straight away. I remember seeing Jimmy Greaves score a wonder goal against Man United in 1965 when he ghosted through a defence including the likes of Pat Crerand and Nobby Stiles. I also recall taking three days to get home after a Uefa Cup victory over Anderlecht. So many great memories. Yids for ever!"

Drew Bower, Wensley, Derbyshire: "Sadly, I've only ever had one trip to The Lane when I was around seven. My mum was determined that I would see Jurgen Klinsmann play, so thanks to a friend of a friend who lived in London, she organised a trip for us. What a great time to be a Spurs fan watching Teddy and Jurgen in full flow! As good as it gets. I am always at The Lane in spirit."

Chris Burling, Epping Green, Essex: "I have been going to The Lane for 25 years since I was seven. For all the wonderful things I have seen, the best memory I have was taking my daughter, Tegan, to her first game against Reading in 2007. Keano tucked the penalty home, we cheered and I turned and said, 'This is what it's all about.' I said it with a tear in my eye, such a proud father who had waited for that day for many years. She now loves Tottenham as much as her old man."

Sammi Hamper, Milton Keynes: "My dad is Spurs mad so we had no choice with our team, but I'm so glad that he chose Tottenham. From supporting Spurs you never take a win for granted, and you learn never to get complacent. This way, when three points come they are so much sweeter. I'm a Yid through and through, and have even had the THFC symbol tattooed on my ankle to prove that it's for life."

Sam Bearman, Chatham: "My greatest memory – the first time I saw us beat Chelsea in the Worthington Cup semi final. In the morning I was debating whether to go because I had a paper round back then at the age of 13, which consequently meant a 5am wake up. However, I went, and the 5-1 victory made it all worthwhile, even if it did cost me sleep and the gloating at school the next day was a great bonus."

Lawrence Issacharoff, Whetstone: "My second game as a nine year old was in 1968 (v Leicester) when JG scored probably the best goal he ever scored – that amazing slalom dribble in the opening moments around five players that ended in him tucking the ball past Peter Shilton and receiving a five minute standing ovation."

Steve Parish, Kings Lynn: "The Lane to me makes worthwhile all the mickey taking from the non-believers I willingly endured growing up in Norfolk surrounded by Leeds, Man U and Liverpool supporters. The first time I went to The Lane I had goosebumps for hours, especially when I got to see the awesome Glenn Hoddle majestically stroll around, pinging balls all over the park. This place really is The Lane of Dreams."

Kevin Newall, Detroit: "I am an exiled Tottenham fan currently living in the US. My son Paul, coming up 21, is also a lifelong Spurs fan, who started coming to the Lane with me when he was four. He won a junior Spurs competition by drawing a picture of Steve Perryman, which won him a place in the Team Photo the season we signed Jurgen Klinsmann and also had Teddy Sheringham in what was his dream team."

Martyn Byrne, High Wycombe: "The year we were relegated I went to every home game. We were an aging side, not up to much but the support remained strong. The best thing Gooner Terry Neill did was bring in Keith Burkinshaw. The rest is history,"

Ben Christie, East Lower Block 25: "I cannot say what The Lane means to me because everytime I try to type I get too emotional. So I guess that sums up what the ground means to me and so many other blue-and-white blooded Spurs supporters."

Bill Nicholson, a perfectionist in everything he did – even posing for a photograph

THE following list of 50 post-war Tottenham heroes has been compiled from selections in the dream teams submitted by visitors to our Lane of Dreams website, with additions by Norman Giller, who has seen each of the players in action. The one rule was that the players had to be retired. The likes of modern icons such as Ledley King, Robbie Keane, Aaron Lennon and Jermain Defoe must wait their turn to go into the White Hart Lane Hall of Kings. The 50 Heroes are paraded in order of year of birth:

RON BURGESS 1939-54. Born Cwm Villa, Wales, April 9 1917, died February 14 2005. A former miner, Ron proved himself a powerhouse of a wing-half for Tottenham and Wales (32 caps). He was the driving force of the great Push and Run Spurs side, mixing industry with creativity. Robbed of his peak years by the War, he was an exceptional captain and he later managed Swansea Town and then Watford (where he discovered Pat Jennings). He came through Tottenham's Gravesend and Northfleet nursery. Spurs stats: League games 297 (15 goals), 27 cup matches (1).

LES BENNETT 1939-54. Born Wood Green, January 10 1918, died April 29 1999. He joined Tottenham just as war broke out and served with distinction in Burma and Egypt before shooting with deadly accuracy for the Push and Run Spurs. He and Len Duquemin went together like bacon and eggs, and few defences were ever comfortable against their twin-engined thrust. Les had loads of energy and was a no-nonsense finisher in the biff-bang style of the days when the game was about physical contact. Spurs stats: 272 League games (104 goals).

BILL NICHOLSON 1938-55. Born January 26 1919, died October 23, 2004. 'Mr. Tottenham' earned his place in this Heroes table with his performances on the pitch and long before he established himself as the club's greatest of all managers. He was a perfectionist of a right-half, supporting the slowing Alf Ramsey behind him and prompting his forwards with neat passes in the Push and Run era. Nick was in Billy Wright's shadow at international level, and scored with his first kick in his one and only international. His greatest days came after he had hung up his boots, creating history in 1960-61 by steering Spurs to the first League Championship and FA Cup Double of the 20th Century. Spurs stats: 314 League games (6 goals), 27 cup matches.

ALF RAMSEY 1949-54. Born Dagenham January 22 1920, died April 28 1999. Best remembered as a master manager, Alf was a studious and solid right-back who joined Spurs from Southampton at the age of 29 and became a key man in the Push and Run side. Nicknamed The General, he was capped 32 times before starting his new career as a manager. First he performed miracles by turning Ipswich Town, a team of veterans, discards and misfits, into League champions. Four years later he was knighted for steering England to the 1966 World Cup (after leaving Spurs idol Jimmy Greaves out of the team for the final!). Spurs stats: 226 League games (24 goals), 24 cup matches.

TED DITCHBURN 1939-54. Born Gillingham October 24 1921, died December 26 2005. Until the arrival of Pat Jennings there was no doubting that Ted Ditchburn was the greatest goalkeeper that ever stood between the posts for Tottenham. He came up through the Gravesend and Northfleet nursery teams, and became the reliable last line of defence for the magnificent Push and Run team. He would have won many more than his six England caps but for the overshadowing presence of the fabled Frank Swift. Spurs stats: 418 League games, 34 cup matches.

LEN DUQUEMIN 1946-56. Born Guernsey July 17 1924, died April 20 2003. This Channel Islander was known as 'The Duke' and was worshipped by Spurs fans during the Push and Run era. Surrounded by more skilful players, Len was a no-frills, no-nonsense centre-forward from the old school, who worked hard, attacked ferociously and always let the goalkeeper know he was around with solid shoulder charges. Spurs stats: 274 League games (114 goals), 33 cup matches (20 goals).

EDDIE BAILY 1946-55. Born Clapton August 6 1925. 'Cheeky Chappie' Eddie was the player who put the polish into Push and Run. He patrolled majestically in midfield on trademark thick-thighed legs, picking out team-mates with beautifully delivered passes. The only surprise is that he did not collect many more than his nine England international caps. After skilled service with Port Vale, Nottingham Forest and Leyton Orient, he returned to The Lane as Bill Nicholson's right hand man. Spurs stats: 296 League games (64 goals), 29 cup matches (5 goals).

DANNY BLANCHFLOWER 1954-64. Born Belfast February 10 1926, died December 9 1993. The brains of the Double side, controlling everything from midfield. An inspiring captain, he led Spurs through the Glory-Glory years. He formed a midfield monopoly with John White and Dave Mackay, and also had a potent partnership with Jimmy McIlroy for Northern Ireland, wining 56 caps. He was a great journalist who wrote a biting column for the *Sunday Express*. Managed Chelsea and Northern Ireland with little success. Spurs stats: 337 League games (15 goals), 45 cup matches (6 goals).

TOMMY HARMER 1948-59. Born Hackney February 2 1928, died December 25, 2007. 'Harmer the Charmer' was the archetypal ball-juggling inside-forward in the Wilf Mannion/Len Shackleton mould. He would have made as big an impact as these legends had he been a few inches taller. At 5ft 2in, the Tom Thumb of football was considered too small for internationals. He could bamboozle any defence with dribbling and feinting, and starred in Bill Nicholson's debut match, the 10-4 victory over Everton. Spurs stats: 205 League games (47 goals), 17 cup matches (4 goals).

BILL BROWN 1959-66. Born Arbroath October 8 1931, died December 1 2004. 'Safe Hands Bill' was goalkeeper in the Double team, giving confidence to the back line with his excellent shot stopping ability. He had a particularly good understanding with giant centre-half Maurice Norman, and together they gave Spurs great stability at the heart of the defence. Bill won 28 Scottish international caps, He played for Northampton and then finished his career in Canada, to where he emigrated. Spurs stats: 222 League games, 40 cup matches.

PETER BAKER 1953-65. Born Hampstead December 10, 1931. Stylish, upright right-back and a regular in the Spurs Double team; a perfect partner for Ron Henry. The only member of the side not to win international honours because of the presence of outstanding full backs like Jimmy Armfield, Don Howe and George Cohen. Emigrated to South Africa where he was player-manager of Durban. Spurs stats: 299 League games (3 goals), 43 cup matches.

TERRY MEDWIN 1956-63. Born Swansea September 25 1932. He won a championship medal in the Double season, although generally second choice to Terry Dyson. A quick and clever winger, he was a student of the game and would have made a bigger impact but for a succession of injuries. Capped 30 times by Wales, he was forced into early retirement by a broken leg in 1963 and switched to coaching, first with Fulham and then as assistant manager to John Toshack at his original club, Swansea. Spurs stats: 197 League games (65 goals), 18 cup matches (7 goals).

BOBBY SMITH 1955-64. Born Lingdale, Yorkshire, February 22 1933. Big, muscular and bulldozing, he took the eye with his physical presence but he also had subtle touches. Bobby was top marksman in the Double year with 33 goals. He had memorable partnerships with Les Allen and then Jimmy Greaves. The Smith-Greaves duo was also dynamic for England, Bobby banging in 13 goals in 15 games including two in the famous 9-3 slaughter of Scotland at Wembley in 1961, with Greavsie netting a hat-trick. The ex-Chelsea centre-forward wound down his League career with Brighton. Spurs stats 271 League games (176 goals), 46 cup matches (32 goals).

MAURICE NORMAN 1955-65. Born Mulbarton, Norfolk, May 8 1934. He was the towering man mountain in the middle of the Tottenham defence in the Glory-Glory days. 'Big Mo' played 23 times for England and was favourite to wear the No 5 shirt in the 1966 World Cup finals until a broken leg in a meaningless friendly in 1965 brought a premature end to his career. He was powerful in the air and would often get into the opposition penalty area to head useful goals from corner-kicks. Spurs stats: 357 League games (16 goals), 54 cup matches (1).

RON HENRY 1955-65. Born Shoreditch August 17 1934. Full-back partner to Peter Baker, he was a thoughtful and tidy defender who deserved more than the one England cap awarded to him in Sir Alf Ramsey's first match as England manager (5-2 defeat by France). Mel Hopkins had been No 1 choice at left-back until an injury let in Henry in 1958, and for the next four years he hardly put a foot wrong. He rarely took the eye, but his consistency made him a vital cog in the Spurs machine. Spurs stats: 247 League games (1 goal), 40 cup matches.

DAVE MACKAY 1959-68. Born Edinburgh November 14 1934. The heart and soul of the Double team, he terrorised opponents with his ferocious tackling. He could also be surprisingly subtle and delivered left foot passes on a plate. Brave beyond the call of duty, he twice overcame a broken leg to lead Spurs to the 1967 FA Cup and late in his career proved himself a great sweeper for Derby. Capped 22 times by Scotland, he won the League title with Derby as manager and coached with distinction in the Middle East. Spurs stats: 268 League games (42 goals), 50 cup matches (5).

TERRY DYSON 1955-65. Born Malton, Yorkshire, November 29 1934. Forever remembered for his two goals for Tottenham in the 1963 European Cup Winners' Cup final, Terry was a tiny tot of a player with a big heart. He was lightning fast down the wings, preferring to operate on the right. He scored some crucial goals for the Double-winning team and was always duelling with Terry Medwin for second wing selection after Cliff Jones. Wound down his League career with Fulham and Colchester. Spurs stats: 184 League games (41 goals), 25 cup matches (14 goals).

CLIFF JONES 1958-68. Born Swansea February 7 1935. From a family steeped in football (his Uncle Bryn was a pre-war star with Arsenal), Cliff was a flying left winger with a giant heart and excellent ball skills. A feature of his play with the Double side was his fearless diving headers. He was capped a then record 59 times by Wales, and had a wind-down season with Fulham before going into non-League football. There were few faster and more productive wingers in the world. Spurs stats: 318 League games (135 goals), 56 cup matches (24).

Cliff Jones, who specialised in flying headers and flying runs down the wing

JOHN WHITE 1959-64. Born Musselburgh April 28 1937, died July 21 1964. The legendary Ghost of White Hart Lane, who made the Double team tick with his precise passes and intelligent off-the-ball running. Defenders just did not know how to mark him because he was so clever and cunning with his positional play. Tragically cut down at his peak when struck by lightning while sheltering under a tree during a solo game of golf. He was just 27. Signed from Falkirk for £20,000 in 1959, he was capped 22 times by Scotland. Spurs stats: 182 League games (40 goals), 26 cup matches (7 goals).

LES ALLEN 1959-65. Born Dagenham September 4 1937. A quick, incisive striker (father of Clive), he had a natural instinct for where to be at the right time and scored 27 goals in the Double season and worked well in tandem with his former Chelsea side-kick Bobby Smith. He was an England Under-23 international, and unlucky to always be in the shadow of the great Greavsie. Later played for and then managed QPR and also Swindon. Allen, Smith and Greaves all started their careers at Stamford Bridge. Spurs stats: 119 League games (47 goals), 18 cup matches (14 goals).

ALAN GILZEAN 1964-73. Born Coupar Angus October 22 1938. An extraordinarily gifted forward who could thread a ball through the eye of a needle, and he specialised in glancing headers. He and Greavsie went together like fish and chips and they were the most dynamic duo in the League for three or four years. Gilly won 22 Scottish caps, and settled to another winning partnership with Martin Chivers when Jimmy moved on. He wound down his exciting and often eccentric career in South Africa. Spurs stats: 343 League games (93 goals), 96 cup matches (40 goals).

JIMMY GREAVES 1961-70. Born East Ham February 20 1940. The greatest finisher in the history of the game. He scored 357 'old' First Division goals to prove it, a record that will stand for all time. Greavsie was an Artful Dodger of the penalty area, stealing goals with the ease of a skilled pickpocket. His 44 goals for England came in just 57 games. He holds the Tottenham club record of 220 goals, held the Chelsea record (124) and later played for West Ham before becoming a TV personality. Spurs stats: 320 League games (220 goals), 60 cup matches (46 goals).

ALAN MULLERY 1964-72. Born Notting Hill, November 12 1941. He took over in midfield from Danny Blanchflower, an impossible act to follow. Once the fans appreciated him for his strengths – determination, high energy and driving power – he was accepted as a great player in his own right. Capped 35 times by England, and a huge favourite at the Fulham club where he began and ended his career. A motivational captain, and later manager of Brighton, Charlton, Crystal Palace, QPR and Barnet. Spurs stats: 312 League games (25 goals), 61 cup matches (5).

MIKE ENGLAND 1966-74. Born Holywell, Wales, December 2 1941. A Welsh mountain, he was one of the finest centre-halves of his generation. He arrived from Blackburn to take over from Maurice Norman and matched and often surpassed the standards set by his predecessor. Powerful in the tackle, he used his height to advantage in both penalty areas. He was capped 44 times by Wales, and later became team manager after playing and managing in Seattle and having a season with Cardiff. Spurs stats: 300 League games (14 goals), 97 cup matches (5 goals).

TERRY VENABLES 1966-69. Born Dagenham January 6 1943. Bought from Chelsea where he had been king of the Bridge, Terry struggled to settle at Spurs but did enough to prove himself a class act as a midfield conductor. His greatest moment was helping Spurs overcome his old Chelsea team in the 1967 FA Cup final. Capped twice by England, he later managed the national side after interesting experiences managing Barcelona and then, memorably, Tottenham! El Tel was never anything less than interesting. Spurs stats: 115 League games (5 goals), 26 cup matches (4).

MARTIN PETERS 1970-75. Born Plaistow November 8 1943. All style and guile, Martin was famously described by Alf Ramsey as being 'ten years ahead of his time.' He joined Spurs from West Ham in 1970, with Greavsie as makeweight in the record deal. Peters proved his weight in goals, and won over the fans with his intelligent and incisive running from midfield. He scored the second England goal in the 1966 World Cup final, and won 67 caps. Ended his career as player-manager of Sheffield United. Spurs stats: 189 League games (46 goals), 71 cup matches (30 goals).

CYRIL KNOWLES 1964-73. Born Fitzwilliam July 13 1944, died August 30 1991. The TV jingle 'Nice One, Cyril' helped to turn this engaging and entertaining player into something of a footballing folk hero. A former winger, he developed into a skilful and at time reckless left back who won four England caps. He thought nothing of dribbling the ball out of a packed penalty area, causing manager Bill Nicholson early grey hairs. He was a lovely, humorous man who was taken too early from us at the age of 47. Spurs stats: 403 League games (15 goals), 104 cup matches (2 goals).

PHIL BEAL 1963-75. Born Godstone January 8 1945. A utility defender who was comfortable in any position. Phil was an unsung hero in many Tottenham matches, when his team-mates appreciated that it was his effort and energy that had made the difference between winning and losing. He was an exceptionally disciplined man marker, always playing with tenacity and tact. Later played for Brighton and Crewe before a stint in the United States. An apprentice in the Double season, he served the club for 15 years. Spurs stats: 330 League games (1 goal), 87 cup matches.

PAT JENNINGS 1964-77. Born Newry, Northern Ireland, June 12 1945. Blessed with shovel-size hands, Pat used them to great effect while establishing himself as one of the finest goalkeepers ever. He was a bag of nerves when first joining Spurs from Watford, but once he had settled down he became a legend. It was with total disbelief that Spurs fans greeted the news that Tottenham had allowed him to join Arsenal for the last third of his glittering career. Capped 119 times, he returned to the Lane as a goalkeeping coach. Spurs stats: 472 League games, 118 cup matches (1 goal).

MARTIN CHIVERS 1968-76. Born Southampton April 27 1945. At his peak, big Chiv was as potent a centre-forward as Spurs ever had. After arriving from Southampton he took time to settle to playing with the G-Men – Greaves and Gilzean – but then established himself as a feared marksman. He had a deceptively casual looking style, and defenders were surprised by his changes of pace and ability to shrug off tackles. He scored 13 goals in 24 England games, and is third highest ever Spurs scorer. Spurs stats: 278 League games (118 goals), 89 cup matches (56 goals).

RALPH COATES 1971-77. Born Hetton-le-Hole April 26 1946. A bustling player with good acceleration, he was equally at home on the wing or in midfield. He had been outstanding with Burnley, but struggled to fit into the Tottenham jigsaw until a winning goal in the 1973 League Cup final boosted his confidence and earned him hero status with the fans. He won four England caps, and had a spell as player-coach at Orient and brief experience in the Australian league. Spurs stats: 173 League games (13 goals), 56 cup matches (10 goals).

JOHN PRATT 1965-79. Born Hackney 26 June 1948. There were a lot more skilful players than John, but few who could match him for endeavour and a natural footballer's tactical intelligence. He epitomised what the team player should be about, working his socks off to support colleagues either in possession or under pressure. During his long, loyal service to Spurs he played in virtually every outfield position without letting the team down. He wound down his career in the United States, and later coached the Tottenham juniors. Spurs stats: 331 League games (39 goals), 84 cup matches (10).

RAY CLEMENCE 1981-87. Born Skegness August 5 1948. A safe last line of defence for the all-conquering Liverpool team of the 1970s, he added to his reputation as one of the all-time great goalkeepers with his service to Spurs. He followed the legendary Pat Jennings on to the Tottenham goal line and always performed with agility and style. He was Peter Shilton's rival for the England No 1 jersey, and managed to win 61 caps despite being considered second to Shilts. Later served in England's back room team. Spurs stats: 240 League games, 90 cup matches.

STEVE PERRYMAN 1969-86. Born Ealing December 21 1951. Tottenham's 'Mr Loyalty' who played a record 655 League games. He was a team player, beavering in midfield to make opportunities and openings for others. Steve became an inspiring skipper, leading by example. He won 17 Under-23 caps and one full cap. Later moved to Oxford and Brentford before managing at Griffin Park and then briefly returning to the Lane as assistant manager. Managed with success in Japan, and became Exeter Director of Football. Spurs stats: 655 League games (31 goals), 199 cup matches (8).

OSSIE ARDILES 1978-88. Born Bell Ville, Argentina, August 3 1952. After his startling arrival from Argentina, Ossie (wanting to "win the Cup for Tottingham") settled more quickly than his compatriot Ricky Villa. He and Glenn Hoddle seemed made for each other as they forged a skilful midfield partnership that produced magical moments for Spurs fans. Capped 63 times, he has since had an eventful managerial career, including a brief spell in charge at The Lane. Spurs stats: 238 League games (16 goals), 73 cup matches (9 goals).

TONY GALVIN 1978-87. Born Huddersfield, July 12 1956. Discovered by Bill Nicholson when he switched to scouting for Keith Burkinshaw, Tony lived up to his early promise as a left winger with excellent ball control and good acceleration. He played more than 200 matches for Spurs before moving back to Yorkshire with Sheffield Wednesday; later playing for Swindon. An intelligent man who spoke fluent Russian, after retirement he taught at a London college. He collected 29 Republic of Ireland caps. Spurs stats: 201 League games (20 goals), 72 cup matches (11 goals).

RICKY VILLA 1978-83. Born Roque Perez, Argentina August 18 1956. He will always have legendary status because of his 'Wembley Goal of the Century' in the 1981 FA Cup final replay. That was the highlight of a chequered Tottenham career during which he struggled to hold down a regular place. He was capped 25 times before arriving at The Lane with his 1978 World Cup team-mate Ossie Ardiles. He returned home in 1983 to concentrate on politics before coming back into the game as a coach. Spurs stats: 133 League games (18 goals), 44 cup matches (7 goals).

STEVE ARCHIBALD 1980-84. Born Glasgow September 27 1956, He and Garth Crooks were one of the most devastating duos in the old First Division when they came together for Spurs. He had been a lethal striker for Aberdeen under the management of a young Alex Ferguson, and after four years with Spurs travelled the football roundabout with Barcelona, Blackburn, Hibernian, Espanyol, St Mirren, Reading, Ayr and Fulham. He scored four goals in 27 games for Scotland. Spurs stats: 131 League games (58 goals), 58 cup matches (19).

Tony Galvin, English-born Irishman, who was fluent in Russian and fluent when rushing on the wing for Spurs

GLENN HODDLE 1975-87. Born Hayes October 27 1957. One of the most naturally gifted footballers of modern times, Hoddle graced Tottenham's midfield with his precocious passing and wicked, swerving shots. He was capped 53 times by England, and it was his penetrative passes that made Spurs a power in the 1980s. He took his talent to Monaco before returning to play at Swindon and Chelsea. His managerial career included a controversial run in charge of England and a brief spell at The Lane. Spurs stats: 377 League games (88 goals), 113 cup matches (22 goals).

GARTH CROOKS 1980-84. Born Stoke March 10 1958. The Crooks-Archibald double act was one of the most exciting shows in town in the early 1980s when they merged perfectly with their positioning and precise finishing. Crooks, bought from Stoke City, was electric in the penalty area and could turn a half chance into a goal in the blinking of an eye. He won four Under-23 caps and deserved full honours. Intelligent and articulate, he was a natural for a TV career after hanging up his shooting boots. Spurs stats: 125 League games (48 goals), 57 cup matches (27 goals).

CHRIS HUGHTON 1977-90. Born West Ham December 11 1958. He came through Tottenham's youth system and established himself as an outstanding full-back. Stylish and industrious, he was a disciplined marker and had neat distribution. The first black player selected by the Republic of Ireland, he won 53 caps. He later played for West Ham and Brentford before becoming a Spurs coach under a procession of managers. Sacked at the same time as Martin Jol, he took his coaching talent to Newcastle. Spurs stats: 297 League games (12 goals), 101 cup matches (7 goals).

GRAHAM ROBERTS 1980-86. Born Southampton July 3 1959. He was one of the rocks of the successful Spurs side of the early '80s, defending with determination and an enthusiasm that lifted the players around him. Graham always tried to use the ball intelligently out of defence, and Spurs fans recall his stirring performance in the 1984 UEFA Cup final. He was later successful with Rangers and Chelsea before going into management in Scotland. At his peak, he was capped six times by England. Spurs stats: 209 League games (23 goals), 78 cup matches (12 goals).

GARY LINEKER 1989-92. Born Leicester November 30 1960, Typical of a born predator, Gary scored 80 goals in an all too brief stay at The Lane. Without question, the finest scorer of his generation, he is second on the England list to Bobby Charlton with 48 goals in 80 games. In his three seasons at Spurs, Gary was top scorer including two goals in the FA Cup semi-final victory over Arsenal in 1991. He took his shooting boots to Japan before returning home to start a broadcasting career. Spurs stats: 105 League games (67 goals), 33 cup matches (13 goals).

CHRIS WADDLE 1985-89. Born Tyne and Wear December 14 1960. An idol at Newcastle, Chris quickly won the hearts of Spurs fans with his weaving runs, clever ball skills and positive attitude. He and Glenn Hoddle struck up a telepathic understanding, and produced some magical moments together. He took his dribbling skills to Marseille and later Sheffield Wednesday and a cluster of other clubs. Scored six goals in 62 England games, and famously missed a world Cup penalty. Spurs stats: 138 League games (33 goals), 36 cup matches (9 goals).

CLIVE ALLEN 1984-88. Born Stepney May 20 1961. Son of Les, he was born in the month that his Dad helped Spurs complete the Double. He scored at an even faster rate than his Dad and, supported by a five-man midfield, he had an unforgettable season in 1986-87 when he netted an astonishing 49 goals. Capped five times by England. Clive moved to Bordeaux in March 1988 and went on to play for Manchester City, Chelsea and West Ham, and later coached at Tottenham. Spurs stats: 105 League games (60 goals), 30 cup matches (24 goals).

GARY MABBUTT 1982-98. Born Bristol August 23 1961. Signed from Bristol Rovers in 1982, Gary developed into the Miracle Man of Spurs while playing more than 600 games over a stretch of 16 years. He fought a constant battle against diabetes, overcame an awful facial injury and made a comeback after a leg break that was feared to have finished his career. Gary was a thoughtful and resilient central defender alongside Richard Gough, and he won 16 England caps. Lifted the FA Cup as captain in 1991. Spurs stats: 477 League games (27 goals), 134 cup matches (11).

JURGEN KLINSMANN 1994-95/1997-98. Born West Germany July 30 1964. In two short spells at The Lane, Klinsmann became a huge hero with his wholehearted performances. It was his explosive finishing that hauled Spurs out of the relegation rut in his second stint when he buried forever the reputation he had for being a persistent 'diver.' He was a have-boots-will-travel mercenary, who scored 47 goals in 108 matches for Germany. Later, as manager, he steered Germany to third place in the 2006 World Cup before returning to Bayern Munich. Spurs stats: 56 League games (29 goals), 12 cup matches (9 goals).

TEDDY SHERINGHAM 1992-97/2001-03. Born Highams Park April 2 1966. In two spells at Spurs Teddy was appreciated for his tactical awareness that put him a thought and a deed ahead of the opposition. He played for many clubs, but Spurs had a special place in his heart because he supported them as a boy. Teddy did not win his first England cap until he was 27, but made up for lost time by collecting 51 before his retirement. Spurs stats: 236 League games (97 goals), 54 cup matches (27 goals).

David Ginola, full of French flair and finesse but sometimes frustrating

DAVID GINOLA 1997-2000. Born January 25 1967 Gassin, France. Rarely has a player made himself so popular in such a short spell at any club. The Frenchman's flair and finesse won him an army of Tottenham fans, who will never forget a string of stunning goals that he scored before moving on to Everton and then Villa. Capped 13 times by France, he was often accused of decorating rather than deciding matches. He has cashed in on his good looks as an actor and a regular face in TV commercials. Spurs stats: 100 League games (13 goals), 39 cups matches (9 goals).

PAUL GASCOIGNE 1988-91. Born Gateshead May 27 1967. The Great Entertainer sparkled briefly but brilliantly at The Lane before taking his magic boots to Italy. He will always be part of Tottenham legend because of his spectacular free-kick goal against Arsenal in the 1991 FA Cup semi-final. On a sadder note, he will be remembered for the reckless tackle against Nottingham Forest that saw him stretchered off early in the final. He won 57 England caps, and later played for Everton, Middlesbrough and Burnley before an odd spell in China. Spurs stats: 92 League games (19 goals), 19 cup matches (14 goals).

WE invited visitors to our Lane of Dreams website to select a dream team from the 50 post-war Tottenham heroes, and a handful of modern ones. Norman Giller had the final say after considering all selections and taking on board the opinions of Jimmy Greaves and Steve Perryman. This was the winning line-up in the most popular formation (4-3-3):

PAT JENNINGS

ALF RAMSEY   MIKE ENGLAND   RON BURGESS   LEDLEY KING

DANNY BLANCHFLOWER   GLENN HODDLE   DAVE MACKAY

JIMMY GREAVES   BOBBY SMITH   CHRIS WADDLE

Goalkeeper Pat Jennings got the greatest support, included in 97% of the teams. Alf Ramsey beat off all modern challengers for the No 2 shirt, while New Millennium hero Ledley King got votes in several defensive positions and just edged out Cyril Knowles at left back. Mike England pipped Maurice Norman at centre-half, and Ron Burgess had many supporters in midfield and as a central defender. Gary Mabbutt narrowly lost out for a place in the back line.

Paul Gascoigne, Ossie Ardiles, John White, Martin Peters, Steve Perryman and Alan Mullery appeared in many teams, but the Blanchflower-Hoddle-Mackay combination had the most popular support.

Greavsie, appearing in 95% of the teams, had the biggest backing of any forward. It was tight for the No 9 shirt, with Bobby Smith just getting in ahead of Matin Chivers, Gary Lineker and Jürgen Klinsmann. Chris Waddle was the winger with most support, finishing just ahead of Cliff Jones, David Ginola, Tony Galvin and Aaron Lennon.

Terry Costello, a long-time Tottenham supporter from Whetstone in North London, was selected as the winner of the Jimmy Greaves/Steve Perryman autographed copy of the book with this sound reasoning for his choices:

‘I have based my memories on my dream team selection, and I have had the pleasure of seeing each of my chosen ones play: Pat Jennings; Alf Ramsey, Mike England, Gary Mabbutt, Ledley King; Danny Blanchflower (capt). Dave Mackay; John White,

Bobby Smith, Jimmy Greaves, Cliff Jones. Subs: Ron Burgess, Paul Gascoigne and Ted Ditchburn.

GOALKEEPER: Jennings was the best goalkeeper I saw just in front of Gordon Banks, Bert Trautmann and Jack Kelsey who to my mind kept Arsenal in the old First Division in the mid fifties.

RIGHT BACK: Alf Ramsey was the best passing full back we ever had (except of course the back pass intercepted by Mudie in the 1953/54 FA Cup semi-final against Blackpool; still it did provide the Mathews/Mortensen final).

LEFT BACK: It has to be Ledley King, he could swap with Gary Mabbutt as I had to have both in the team, Ledley for me is one of the best defenders in Europe and should have won many more caps than he has.

CENTRAL DEFENCE: Mike England, the best centre half we have ever had. Gary Mabutt, like running into a brick wall for the opposition. Mr Blood and Guts. To come back from the John Fashanu assault showed tremendous courage for the cause, even turned down the chance of playing for Liverpool (a true Spur).

MIDFIELD: Danny Blanchflower and Dave Mackay need no explanation; they were simply the best.

FORWARDS: John White I have chosen to play down the right, although he could play anywhere across the forward line as he probably covered more ground than any other player at Spurs (strong legs and lungs). Nearest I've seen to Peter Doherty. Bobby Smith was a great centre forward feared by most defences he played against. Jack Charlton said of him he was the only centre forward he played against who fully contested the ball, all the others looked as though they were. Jimmy Greaves? What can I say, fantastic skill and a goal start the minute he stepped on the pitch. The Rolls Royce of goal scorers. Cliff Jones, brave, fast and great header of the ball. As a left winger only challenged by David Ginola.

SUBS: Ronnie Burgess, I had the most difficulty in leaving out. Although mainly an attacking midfielder he did switch to defence later in his career at Spurs but was up against Blanchflower and Mackay. Paul Gascoigne, again a difficult decision but I felt John White would give more to the team as a whole. I have chosen Gazza as sub as opposed to Gary Lineker because Paul could make goals as well as score them.

Ted Ditchburn, I have chosen over Ray Clemence, although there isn't anything between them. Ted for his presence and longevity just gets the vote. I feel goalkeeper being such a specialist position had to be one of the subs. Every player mentioned brings back wonderful memories for me. **'**

Note from Norman Giller: Thank you all those who took part in the selection game, particularly younger fans, many of whom were knowledgable and realistic enough about Tottenham history to choose yesterday's heroes ahead of their modern favourites.

WHITE Hart Lane has not been exclusive to football. It's been home to baseball, and has staged several explosive boxing matches that, controversially and calamitously, included one of the most savage contests of modern times.

If the first Tottenham chairman, Charles Roberts, had got his way baseball would have been the No 1 sport, with "soccer" second on his list of priorities.

Roberts had spent much of his youth in the United States, and used to pitch for a Brooklyn baseball team. As the 20th Century dawned there was a huge effort to make baseball a challenger to cricket as the main summer sport, hence the specially designed Baseball Ground at Derby.

The Tottenham chairman was among the most enthusiastic backers of the idea, and he set up two Tottenham teams. The first- team played in the British League, along with several Football League clubs looking for extra revenue in the summer months, and the reserves played in a London League. Tottenham were first winners of the British Baseball Cup in 1906, and the sport briefly caught on with spectators, who paid five shillings (the equivalent of £13 today) for a baseball season ticket.

But groundsmen around the country complained that they were not being given sufficient time and access to prepare the pitches for football, and baseball's popularity quickly dwindled. King Football and Queen Cricket had seen off the invader.

Boxing was a huge draw at White Hart Lane in the 1940s. Freddie Mills famously defeated Len Harvey in two rounds for the British light-heavyweight title in front of a virtually all-khaki crowd in 1942. Another major contest at The Lane featured Bruce Woodcock taking the British heavyweght championship from Jack London in July 1945. Woodcock knocked out London – father of Brian London – in the sixth round.

More recently, Frank Bruno handed out a hiding to comeback man Joe Bugner when he hammered him to an eighth round defeat at The Lane of Pain on October 24 1987.

Sadly, the last fight staged at White Hart Lane ended in near-tragedy. Michael Watson collapsed at the end of his 12-round war with Chris Eubank, and was rushed to hospital fighting for his life.

Michael survived but is now confined to a wheelchair. Nobody has mentioned promoting boxing at The Lane again since that regretful incident. It is expected that the new stadium will be used to bring in money outside the corridors of football.

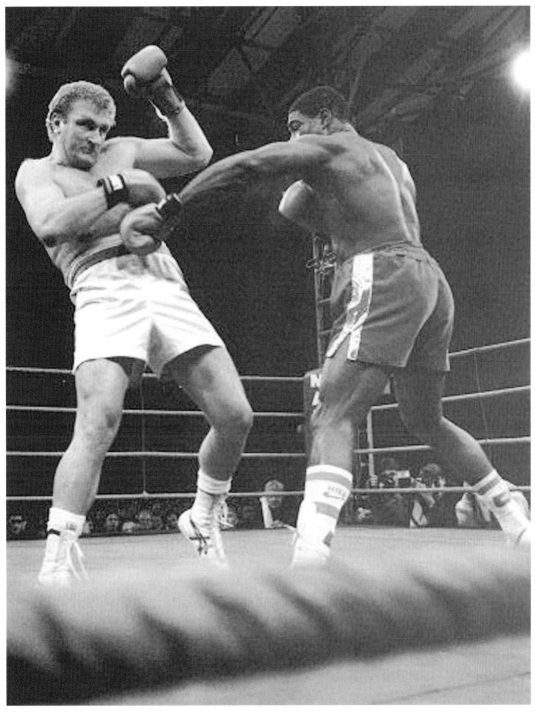

It's a nightmare at The Lane of Dreams for Joe Bugner as he is pummelled to an eighth round defeat by Frank Bruno at the Tottenham football ground in 1987.

WHO has done what, where and when for Tottenham? **MICHAEL GILLER**, a sport statistician for more than 20 years who used to sleep in Steve Perryman's shirt, digs into the record books,climaxing with every end-of-season finishing place since the first League match in 1908.

Attendance: 75,038 v Sunderland, FA Cup, March 5 1938
FA Cup Victory: 13-2 v Crewe, FA Cup, 4th round replay, February 3 1960. Team: Brown; Hills, Henry; Blanchflower, Norman, Mackay; White, Harmer (1), Smith (4), Allen (5), Jones (3).
European defeat: 0-8 v FC Köln, UEFA Intertoto Cup, July 22 1995
First Football League match: Won 3-0 at The Lane against Wolves in Division 2 on September 1 1908. Team: Hewitson; Conquet, Burton; Morris (1), D. Steel, Darnell; Walton, Woodward (2), Macfarlane, R. Steel, Middlemiss.
Football League Victory: 9-0 v Bristol Rovers, Division 2 October 22 1977. Team: Daines; Naylor, Holmes, Hoddle (1), McAllister, Perryman, Pratt, McNab, Moores (3), Lee (4), Taylor (1).
Football League Defeat: 0-7 v Liverpool, Division 1, September 2 1978
Most League Points (2 for a win): 70, Division 2, 1919-20
Most League Points (3 for a win): 77, Division 1, 1984-85
Most League Goals: 115, Division 1, 1960-61
Most League Goals: 220 Jimmy Greaves, 1961-70
Most Goals in a season: 49 Clive Allen, 1986-87
League Appearances: 655 Steve Perryman, 1969-1986
Most Appearances: 854 Steve Perryman, 1969-1986
Most capped player: Pat Jennings 74 (of 119) for Northern Ireland
Youngest first team player: John Bostock, 16 years, 295 days v. Dinamo Zagreb, November 06, 2008; before that Ally Dick, 16 years 301 days v. Man City February 20 1982.
Transfer Out: £30.75m from Man United for Dimitar Berbatov, September 2008.
Transfer In: £15m (clauses to £16.5m) to Charlton for Darren Bent, June 2007.

Greavsie Tops the Goals Table

The all-time top ten table of Tottenham marksmen below reveals the impact that Greavsie made in his nine years at White Hart Lane. His average score per First Division game was .691 and he was leading First Division goal scorer a record six times. His total goals in all matches before his retirement at 31: 491.

Player	Games	Goals	League	Cup	Euro
Jimmy Greaves	379	266	220	37	9
Bobby Smith	317	208	176	22	10
Martin Chivers	367	174	118	34	22
Cliff Jones	378	159	135	17	7
George Hunt	198	138	125	13	0
Len Duquemin	307	134	114	20	0
Alan Gilzean	439	133	93	27	13
Teddy Sheringham	277	124	97	27	0
Les Bennett	294	117	103	14	0
Jimmy Dimmock	438	112	100	12	0

National record breakers

First team to win the 'Double' of FA Cup and League Championship in the 20th Century (1960-1961)
Most consecutive League victories from the kick-off of a top table season: 11 wins (1960-61, the Double season)
Most wins in a League season – 31 out of 42 games (1960-1961, the historic League Championship and FA Cup Double season)
Most points in Division 2 (2 points for a win): 70 (1919-20
Only professional team to have won the FA Cup as a non-League club (1900-01, while in the Southern League)
First British team to win major European trophy – '63 European Cup Winners' Cup
First team to win a major trophy at the new Wembley – the League Cup (2007-08)
Fastest ever Premier League goal – after 9.7 seconds, scored by Ledley King at Bradford City on December 9 2000.
British record eight consecutive victories in major European competition

Bill Nicholson celebrates the 1971 League Cup win with Alan Mullery and Joe Kinnear

New manager Harry Redknapp welcomes home old Tottenham favourite Robbie Keane

Frank Brettell 1898-1899
John Cameron 1899-1907
Fred Kirkham 1907-1908 Caretaker: Arthur Turner and trainers 1908-1912
Peter McWilliam 1912-1927 Wartime caretaker: Arthur Turner 1914-1918
Billy Minter 1927-1929
Percy Smith 1930-1935
Wally Hardinge 1935
Jack Tresadern 1935-1938
Peter McWilliam 1938-1942
Arthur Turner 1942-1946
Joe Hulme 1946-1949   Caretaker: Jimmy Anderson 1949
Arthur Rowe 1949-1955
Jimmy Anderson 1955-1958
Bill Nicholson 1958-1974
Terry Neill 1974-1976
Keith Burkinshaw 1976-1984
Peter Shreeves 1984-1986
David Pleat 1986-1987 Caretakers: Trevor Hartley/Doug Livermore 1987
Terry Venables 1987-1991
Peter Shreeves 1991-1992   Caretaker: Doug Livermore 1992-93
Ossie Ardiles 1993-1994
Steve Perryman 1994-1994 (one game as manager)
Gerry Francis 1994-1997
Chris Hughton 1997
Christian Gross 1997-1998 Caretaker: David Pleat 1998
George Graham 1998-2001 Caretaker: David Pleat 2001
Glenn Hoddle 2001-2003
David Pleat 2003-2004
Jacques Santini 2004
Martin Jol 2004-2007
Jaunde Ramos 2007-2008

Harry Redknapp took over on October 26 2008.

Season	Division	P	W	D	L	F	A	Points	Position
1908-09	Division Two	38	20	11	7	67	32	51	2nd
1909-10	Division One	38	11	10	17	53	69	32	15th
1910-11	Division One	38	13	6	19	52	63	32	15th
1911-12	Division One	38	14	9	15	53	53	37	12th
1912-13	Division One	38	12	6	20	45	72	30	17th
1913-14	Division One	38	12	10	16	50	62	34	17th
1914-15	Division One	38	8	12	18	57	90	28	20th
1919-20	Division Two	42	32	6	4	102	32	70	1st
1920-21	Division One	42	19	9	14	70	48	47	6th
1921-22	Division One	42	21	9	12	65	39	51	2nd
1922-23	Division One	42	17	7	18	50	50	41	12th
1923-24	Division One	42	12	14	16	50	56	38	15th
1924-25	Division One	42	15	12	15	52	43	42	12th
1925-26	Division One	42	15	9	18	66	79	39	15th
1926-27	Division One	42	16	9	17	76	78	41	13th
1927-28	Division One	42	15	8	19	74	86	38	21st
1928-29	Division Two	42	17	9	16	75	81	43	10th
1929-30	Division Two	42	15	9	18	59	61	39	12th
1930-31	Division Two	42	22	7	13	88	55	51	3rd
1931-32	Division Two	42	16	11	15	87	78	43	8th
1932-33	Division Two	42	20	15	7	96	51	55	2nd
1933-34	Division One	42	21	7	14	79	56	49	3rd
1934-35	Division One	42	10	10	22	54	93	30	22nd
1935-36	Division Two	42	18	13	11	91	55	49	5th
1936-37	Division Two	42	17	9	16	88	66	43	10th
1937-38	Division Two	42	19	6	17	76	54	44	5th
1938-39	Division Two	42	19	9	14	67	62	47	8th

Season	Division	P	W	D	L	F	A	Points	Position
1946-47	Division Two	42	17	14	11	65	53	48	6th
1947-48	Division Two	42	15	14	13	56	43	44	8th
1948-49	Division Two	42	17	16	9	72	44	50	5th
1949-50	Division Two	42	27	7	8	81	35	61	1st
1950-51	Division One	42	25	10	7	82	44	60	1st
1951-52	Division One	42	22	9	11	76	51	53	2nd
1952-53	Division One	42	15	11	16	78	69	41	10th
1953-54	Division One	42	16	5	21	65	76	37	16th
1954-55	Division One	42	16	8	18	72	73	40	16th
1955-56	Division One	42	15	7	20	61	71	37	18th
1956-57	Division One	42	22	12	8	104	56	56	2nd
1957-58	Division One	42	21	9	12	93	77	51	3rd
1958-59	Division One	42	13	10	19	85	95	36	18th
1959-60	Division One	42	21	11	10	86	50	53	3rd
1960-61	Division One	42	31	4	7	115	55	66	1st
1961-62	Division One	42	21	10	11	88	69	52	3rd
1962-63	Division One	42	23	9	10	111	62	55	2nd
1963-64	Division One	42	22	7	13	97	81	51	4th
1964-65	Division One	42	19	7	16	87	71	45	6th
1965-66	Division One	42	16	12	14	75	66	44	8th
1966-67	Division One	42	24	8	10	71	48	56	3rd
1967-68	Division One	42	19	9	14	70	59	47	7th
1968-69	Division One	42	14	17	11	61	51	45	6th
1969-70	Division One	42	17	9	16	54	55	43	11th
1970-71	Division One	42	19	14	9	54	33	52	3rd
1971-72	Division One	42	19	13	10	63	42	51	6th
1972-73	Division One	42	16	13	13	58	48	45	8th

Season	Division	P	W	D	L	F	A	Points	Position
1973-74	Division One	42	14	14	14	45	50	42	11th
1974-75	Division One	42	13	8	21	52	63	34	19th
1975-76	Division One	42	14	15	13	63	63	43	9th
1976-77	Division One	42	12	9	21	48	72	33	22nd
1977-78	Division Two	42	20	16	6	83	49	56	3rd
1978-79	Division One	42	13	15	14	48	61	41	11th
1979-80	Division One	42	15	10	17	52	62	40	14th
1980-81	Division One	42	14	15	13	70	68	43	10th
1981-82	Division One	42	19	11	12	65	50	68	6th
1982-83	Division One	42	20	9	13	65	50	69	4th
1983-84	Division One	42	17	10	15	64	65	61	8th
1984-85	Division One	42	23	8	11	78	51	77	3rd
1985-86	Division One	42	19	8	15	74	52	65	10th
1986-87	Division One	42	21	8	13	68	43	71	3rd
1987-88	Division One	40	12	11	17	38	48	47	13th
1988-89	Division One	38	15	12	11	60	46	57	6th
1989-90	Division One	38	19	6	13	59	47	63	3rd
1990-91	Division One	38	11	16	11	51	50	59	10th
1991-92	Division One	42	15	7	20	58	63	52	15th
1992-93	Premier League	42	16	11	15	60	66	59	8th
1993-94	Premier League	42	11	12	19	54	59	45	15th
1994-95	Premier League	42	16	14	12	66	58	62	7th
1995-96	Premier League	38	16	13	9	50	38	61	8th
1996-97	Premier League	38	13	7	18	44	51	46	10th
1997-98	Premier League	38	11	11	16	44	56	44	14th
1998-99	Premier League	38	11	14	13	47	50	47	11th
1999-00	Premier League	38	15	8	15	57	49	53	10th

Season	Division	P	W	D	L	F	A	Points	Position
2000-01	Premier League	38	13	10	15	47	54	49	12th
2001-02	Premier League	38	14	8	16	49	53	50	9th
2002-03	Premier League	38	14	8	16	51	62	50	10th
2003-04	Premier League	38	13	6	19	47	57	45	14th
2004-05	Premier League	38	14	10	14	47	41	52	9th
2005-06	Premier League	38	18	11	9	53	38	65	5th
2006-07	Premier League	38	17	9	12	57	54	60	5th
2007-08	Premier League	38	11	13	14	66	61	46	11th

THE FINAL WHISTLE by NORMAN GILLER

When I started writing this book Tottenham were stranded at the bottom of the Premier League, with relegation a real risk. By the time I added these final words they were proudly in eighth place under Harry Redknapp's stimulating leadership. Somehow the roistering rollercoaster of a season has encapsulated just what Spurs are about – never predictable, always with a surprise up their sleeves, likely to cause coronaries and celebration in equal measure, up, down, aggravating, inspiring, frustrating, fabulous, exasperating, exciting and never ever boring. I know that the many Spurs supporters who have contacted me since I started compiling the book would not have it any other way. True Tottenham fans have, to quote Kipling (not the cakes man), learned to treat those two imposters triumph and disaster just the same.

Once the bulldozers and wrecking balls knock White Hart Lane into history I know the memories of the grand old ground will live on, and I hope this book goes some way to preserving the past.

We can hear the ghosts of football past seconding that thought ... we can hear you Bobby Buckle, Bertie Bliss, Jimmy Dimmock, Arthur Grimsdell, Willie Hall ... we can hear you Arthur Rowe, Ted Ditchburn, Les Bennett, The Duke, Alf Ramsey, Ronnie Burgess ... we can hear you Charmer Harmer, John White, Bill Brown, Danny Boy ... Cyril 'Nice One' Knowles, Jimmy Neighbour ... we can hear you. We can hear you dear Bill Nicholson. We can hear all of the voices shouting from The Shelf. Soon it will be the final whistle for The Lane. But ... Glory Glory Hallelujah, the spirit of Spurs will march on into the new ground.

Thank you for your company. If you like the book, please tell other Tottenham fans. If you don't like it, please tell me by emailing normangiller@thelaneofdreams.co.uk. But please bear in mind that I prefer praise to being pilloried. COYS.

PREVIOUS BOOKS BY NORMAN GILLER

Banks of England (with Gordon Banks) **Footballing Fifties**
The Glory and the Grief (with George Graham)   **Banks v Pelé** (with Terry Baker)
Football And All That (an irreverent history of the game)
The Seventies Revisited (with Kevin Keegan)
The Final Score (with Brian Moore)   **ABC of Soccer Sense** (Tommy Docherty)
Billy Wright, A Hero for All Seasons (official biography)
The Rat Race (with Tommy Docherty)   **Denis Compton** (The Untold Stories)
McFootball, the Scottish Heroes of the English Game
The Book of Rugby Lists (with Gareth Edwards)
The Book of Tennis Lists (with John Newcombe)
The Book of Golf Lists   **TV Quiz Trivia**   **Sports Quiz Trivia**
Know What I Mean (with Frank Bruno)   **Eye of the Tiger** (with Frank Bruno)
From Zero to Hero (with Frank Bruno)   **The Judge Book of Sports Answers**
Watt's My Name (with Jim Watt)   **My Most Memorable Fights** (with Henry Cooper)
How to Box (with Henry Cooper)   **Henry Cooper's 100 Greatest Boxers**
Mike Tyson Biography   **Mike Tyson, the Release of Power** (Reg Gutteridge)
Crown of Thorns, the World Heavyweight Championship (with Neil Duncanson)
Fighting for Peace (Barry McGuigan biography, with Peter Batt)
World's Greatest Cricket Matches World's Greatest Football Matches
Golden Heroes (with Dennis Signy)   **The Judge** (1,001 arguments settled)
The Great Football IQ Quiz Book (The Judge of *The Sun*)
The Marathon Kings   The Golden Milers (with Sir Roger Bannister)
Olympic Heroes (with Brendan Foster)
Olympics Handbook 1980   Olympics Handbook 1984
Book of Cricket Lists (Tom Graveney)   **Top Ten Cricket Book** (Tom Graveney)
Cricket Heroes (Eric Morecambe)   **Big Fight Quiz Book   TVIQ Puzzle Book**
Lucky the Fox (with Barbara Wright)   **Gloria Hunniford's TV Challenge**
Comedy novels: **Carry On Doctor   Carry On England   Carry On Loving**
Carry On Up the Khyber   Carry On Abroad   Carry On Henry
A Stolen Life (novel)   **Mike Baldwin: Mr Heartbreak** (novel)   **Hitler's Final Victim** (novel)
Affairs (novel)   **The Bung** (novel)

Books in collaboration with **RICKY TOMLINSON**
Football My Arse   Celebrities My Arse   Cheers My Arse
Reading My Arse (The Search for the Rock Island Line)

PLUS books in collaboration with **JIMMY GREAVES**:
This One's On Me   The Final (novel)   **The Ball Game** (novel)
The Boss (novel)   **The Second Half** (novel)
Let's Be Honest (with Reg Gutteridge)   **Greavsie's Heroes and Entertainers**
World Cup History   GOALS!   Stop the Game, I Want to Get On
The Book of Football Lists   Taking Sides   Funny Old Games (with The Saint)
Sports Quiz Challenge   Sports Quiz Challenge 2
It's A Funny Old Life   Saint & Greavsie's World Cup Special
The Sixties Revisited   Don't Shoot the Manager